THE PENTECOSTAL THEOLOGY OF EDWARD IRVING

C. GORDON STRACHAN, M.A., B.D., Ph.D.

HENDRICKSON
PUBLISHERS
PEABODY, MASSACHUSETTS 01961-3473

J. M. JACKSON

THE PENTECOSTAL THEOLOGY OF EDWARD IRVING

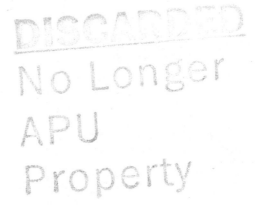

ACKNOWLEDGEMENTS

I WOULD like to thank the Rev. Bill Maclean for first introducing me to the teachings of the Pentecostal movement in 1961 and Mr. John Busby and Dr. Eric Stevenson for first telling me about the life and work of Edward Irving the following year. I am most grateful to Professor John McIntyre for his teaching when I was an undergraduate and to Professor Tom Torrance for his supervision of my postgraduate work. Canon Roland Walls was my tutor throughout the studies and I am greatly indebted to him for his direction, enthusiasm and good humour. I thank the Rev. James Torrance for his interest and friendship and the Rev. Brian Casebow for sharing many points and for reading through and correcting the proofs.

During my researches in London I was greatly helped by Mr. R. J. Watson and Mr. A. G. Esslemont, librarian and secretary of the United Reformed Church Historical Society and by Mrs. Olive Russell, manageress of the Tavistock Bookshop. In Dumfriesshire I enjoyed the assistance of Mr. Wyllie Irving of Lochrutton, Dumfries and Mr. George Gilchrist, registrar, and Mr. Alex Milton, museum curator, at Annan.

Many friends, especially in the Glasgow and Edinburgh areas, have given me continuous prayerful encouragement for which I am most thankful. I should like also to express my gratitude to my mother with whom I lived while writing this book. Her hospitality, companionship and support throughout turned the whole project into a joint venture and a shared joy.

Edinburgh   C.G.S.
Spring 1973.

PIETAS PARENTUM
J.H.L.   C.G.S.   A.P.S.

CONTENTS

INTRODUCTION

Edward Irving: Reformed Pentecostal Theologian

IN 1827, the Reverend Edward Irving, M.A., minister of the National Scotch Church, Regent Square, London, was first suspected of heresy for preaching that Christ assumed fallen humanity in order to redeem it. In 1828, he published a book of sermons on the Incarnation which confirmed him as a heretic in the eyes of many. In 1829 opposition to his views increased and in 1830 the Scots Presbytery of London took action against him on the allegation that he taught that Jesus Christ was a sinner. He refused to submit to its authority and withdrew himself from its jurisdiction. He was found guilty of the charge and of contumacy. The Kirk Session and Trustees of his church however stood firm in his support and by doing so effectively overruled the judgement of the higher court.

On Sunday, 28th March, 1830, Miss Mary Campbell spoke in tongues and some days later was miraculously healed of consumption at her home at Fernicarry on the Gareloch in the parish of Roseneath, Dunbartonshire. On 30th April, 1831 Mrs. Cardale spoke in tongues and prophesied at her home in London. On the morning of Sunday, 30th October, 1831, Miss Hall spoke in tongues in the vestry of Regent Square Church. Outbursts of tongues and prophecy interrupted the worship services on the following Sundays. The trustees met to plead with their minister to stop these unconstitutional occurrences but Irving, believing them to be the operation of the gifts of the Holy Spirit, refused. After three months of more manifestations in church and remonstrance in the vestry, the trustees resolved to take action themselves. On 17th March, 1832, they decided to ask Presbytery to receive their complaint against the minister in terms of the Trust Deed which stated that only those ordained or appointed by the Church of Scotland could lead public worship. Presbytery agreed to act, providing the trustees once more submitted to its authority and concurred in its previous condemnation of Irving. This they did. Irving's trial began on 26th April, 1832. On 2nd May, after three days' hearing, the court decided against him and he was ordered to be removed from his charge. On Friday 4th May, he found himself locked out of his church.

The General Assembly of the Church of Scotland of 1832 instructed the Presbytery of Annan to take action against Irving on the same grounds as his first arraignment before the London Presbytery. On 13th March, 1833 he was tried at Annan, found guilty and deposed from the ministry of the Church of Scotland.

The majority of the members of Regent Square who had left with Irving, were formed into an ecclesiastical body which became known as the Catholic Apostolic Church. The first of its twelve Apostles was called on 7th November, 1832 and Irving, who now had no ministerial status, was ordained Angel or Pastor of the new congregation on Friday, 5th April, 1833.[1] Soon his health began to fail and he died of consumption in Glasgow on 7th December, 1834. He was forty-two.[2]

Most religious revivals have claimed to some degree to have enjoyed the experience of Pentecost but very few have spoken in tongues. After Montanism there are only isolated cases recorded and it was not until the late seventeenth century that it was claimed to be a 'symptom of divine inspiration' on a large scale. Extensive outbreaks of tongues occurred 'among the Huguenots of the Cevennes and the appellant (but still nominally Catholic) Jansenists.' There are no further instances until those associated with the ministry of Edward Irving.[3]

When speaking with tongues did occur in earlier times and among the Huguenots and the Jansenists, it was always one of many phenomena generated by religious enthusiasm and intense evangelical feeling. Because of this it was scarcely distinguished from jumping and jerking, roaring and ranting. It has been thought by many from 1830 to the present day that this was also the case in the West of Scotland, at Regent Square, and among the members of the Catholic Apostolic Church. Nothing could be further from the truth, for unlike any previous manifestations of the Spirit, they were occasioned not by the overflow of powerful religious feeling but by faithful response to the systematic study and preaching of the Word of God. Theological understanding was central to all that happened and preceded all forms of experience of spiritual gifts. It is the centrality of a coherent theological system which makes the Pentecost of 1830–32 unique and quite distinct from all previous revivals.[4]

Irving says that it was during 1827 while preaching a series of sermons on the sacrament of Baptism that he first articulated to himself, and then to his congregation his belief that spiritual gifts should still be in operation in the Church. He could find no Scriptural text to justify the generally accepted belief that they had been irrevocably removed. He thought it quite illogical to believe in sanctification and not in the gifts of the Spirit for the former was as supernatural as were the latter. It could only have been lack of faith over the centuries that could have stopped the Church from asking for and receiving the gifts. In this belief he echoed John Wesley, but unlike Wesley he went on to argue that if this was the case, it should follow that God would still give the Holy Spirit to all who ask him.[5]

For the next three years he was so taken up with 'the full preaching of Christ's coming in our flesh and his coming again in glory' that his convictions regarding spiritual gifts received no further expression. His thinking on this subject had not developed at all 'when the tidings of the restoration of the gift of tongues in the West of Scotland burst upon us like the morning star heralding the approach of day.'[6] He was delighted to receive this news but his joy was mingled with caution because he realized that, if true, it would have far-reaching effects. He made extensive enquiries before he committed himself to the belief that these manifestations were definitely of God. He found that the people who had come into the experience of tongues and other spiritual gifts, had been influenced by John McLeod Campbell who was in the process of being deposed from his pulpit in Row (Rhu) on the Gareloch for teaching the love of God for all men. Campbell's preaching of universal atonement had led to the conversion of many in that area and to the assurance of salvation not then taught by the limited atonement of Confessional Calvinism, but it was his own assistant minister, A. J. Scott, who had planted the seeds of Pentecostal teaching on the ground prepared by John McLeod Campbell. Scott had often discussed the gifts of the Spirit with Irving but had, until that time, failed to convince him as to the possibility of their immediate reception by the Church. While on holiday at his father's manse at Greenock late in 1829, Scott had had a better response from many of these souls who included Mary Campbell of Fernicarry. He convinced her that Christ's work in baptizing with the Holy Spirit was distinct from His work in regeneration which she came to believe after re-reading St. John's gospel and the Acts of the Apostles. She then began to pray for the baptism with the Holy Spirit with a group of friends and on Sunday, 28th March, 1830 'the Holy Ghost came with mighty power upon her . . . and constrained her to speak at great length and with superhuman strength, in an unknown tongue. . . .'[7]

After finding out the details of the story, Irving concluded that these manifestations were of Divine origin. It was not long before he was testifying to the truth of these reports, urging his own congregation to seek the gifts of the Spirit and encouraging prayer meetings for the same. It was nearly a year later that Mrs. Cardale became the first person to speak in tongues in a house prayer meeting, and six months after that that Miss Hall became the first person to speak in tongues during Sunday worship in Regent Square Church.

The five points in the libel against Irving brought before the London Presbytery by the trustees of Regent Square Church on 17th March, 1832, were all concerned with the minister having allowed unauthorized persons to interrupt and to exercise 'the supposed gifts' during the public worship of God.[8] Under the terms of the Trust Deed they were quite within their rights for it had been specifically laid down that only the forms of worship of the Church of Scotland should be practised and that if the trustees had a complaint against the minister they were to lay it before Presbytery.[9] Irving's interpretation of the practice and procedure of the Kirk, his appeals to Scriptural authority and discussion as to whether 'the gifted' were gifted or not, were all considered to be beside the point.[10] The only question which the court would allow was whether or not he had departed from the constitution of the Church as laid down in the Trust Deed.

On the third day of Irving's trial a petition was handed in asking the Presbytery to stop the proceedings against him. It did not affect the course of events because the court decided that it had been presented too late to be considered as evidence. It was signed by an unknown number of Elders, Deacons, Members and seat holders of the National Scotch Church who expressed their support for Irving against the Presbytery as wholeheartedly as had the Kirk Session at the time of his previous condemnation. Their hostility was specifically directed against the trustees who they accused of plotting to get rid of their beloved pastor without their knowledge or consent. They even denied that the worship services had been disturbed for any length of time and affirmed:

> That although, at first, there were unseemly disturbances in the Church, arising, not from the people of the flock, but from strangers, it soon, by the divine blessing, passed away, and the worship of God has, for many months past, continued to proceed with the utmost regularity and order.[11]

This affirmation gives the lie to all the adverse criticism which, from that time to this, has branded this whole movement as wildly fanatical and hysterically emotional.[12] It vindicates Irving's handling of the manifestations and substantiates his assertion that in all things concerning spiritual gifts he followed the canon of the Apostle as he understood it.[13]

These petitioners spoke for ninety-five per cent of the congregation in their expressed opposition to the action of the trustees. This was demonstrated when Irving was found guilty and locked out of his church. The vast majority followed him to the new hall in Gray's Inn Road and left only a handful at Regent Square.[14]

Since that time, the majority of commentators on this aspect of Irving's ministry have been in agreement with the decision of the Presbytery. Irving himself has been represented as a great man who was by that time rapidly going out of his mind, the manifestations have been seen as delusions and those by whom they were manifested as hysterical. All these opinions have been based on psychological or psychiatric surmise and not on theological fact.[15] As such, they cannot claim serious Scriptural or theological attention. There have, however, been a minority of writers who have disagreed with the decision of the Presbytery and with the support which its action received from the whole religious world at that time. All of these writers who support Irving give Scriptural or theological reasons for doing so. Some of them do so with reluctance and misgivings but all feel bound to admit that if he is to be judged by the canons of Scriptural authority or theological consistency, then he must be exonerated and cleared of the charges for which he was condemned.[16] The reason why these supporters have not written on his behalf with more conviction is that until recent times there have been no parallel events or theological explanations with which to compare him and the startling occurrences associated with his ministry.

Historical judgements are based on analogies between similar sequences of events.[17] If no comparisons can be found for a certain series of occurrences, then historians have difficulty in making any adequate assessment of the events in question. Such has been the fate of Irving and the events surrounding him. In his day he was likened to John the Baptist,[18] Luther,[19] and Knox,[20] but only in a general way because of his pulpit power and commanding personality. There was no yard-stick by which to measure him exactly. This was why so many unjustified opinions circulated about him.

The centre of his ministry was the systematic, doctrinal exposition of the Word of God and, from his intellectual and spiritual application to Scripture, he developed the doctrine of the Baptism with Holy Spirit 'whose standing sign, if we err not, is the speaking with tongues.'[21] He also expounded a detailed teaching on the gifts of the Holy Spirit[22] and gave the whole of his theology an immediacy by his expectation of the immanent second coming of the Lord.[23] The extreme opinions that were formed either for or against him were occasioned as much by the novelty of his doctrine as by the power of his personal eloquence. People were aware that they had never heard anyone like him before and when the preaching was followed by the manifestations of the Spirit they were even more certain that they were witnessing events both unique and novel in the tradition of the Reformed Church. They were right. Speaking in tongues had never occured before on any large scale in British church history, and never since biblical times, except for Montanism, as a result of theological understanding. The only possible analogy by which to understand these things was by the parallel events of the biblical Pentecost. Irving explained and justified these things from Scripture and it was as a repetition of the biblical Pentecost that people either believed and understood or disbelieved and ridiculed.

The absence of any known parallel outside Scripture to the miraculous events of 1830 to 1832, explains why those writers on the subject who have supported Irving, have been unable to do so with the sustained conviction which alone could have led to the complete vindication of his position which they have felt he was justified in receiving.

This need now no longer be the case for in our own day there has arisen, on the ecclesiastical and theological scene, a parallel to the Pentecost in the West of Scotland and in the National Scotch Church which enables us to see Irving in a light that has so far been denied him.

The beliefs and experiences of the various branches of the contemporary Pentecostal Churches are so similar to those of Irving and his followers that one might suspect that they had been handed down by word of mouth or rediscovered like some Deuteronomy of the Spirit. The fact that there was absolutely no collusion between the two movements and that the last of the Catholic Apostolic apostles died a few months after the modern Pentecostal movement started, only emphasizes the power and validity of the comparison. For all their striking similarities these two movements were ignorant of each other's existence.[24]

The twentieth-century Pentecostal revival began when Agnes Ozman spoke in tongues as a result of a spiritual quest based on a re-examination of Scripture similar to that of Mary Campbell seventy years before.[25] This was on 31st December, 1900, at Bethel Bible College, Topeka, Kansas. She was followed by the rest of the college students and during the next few years the experience of tongues and other gifts of the Spirit were shared by thousands in various countries over the world. The self-conscious theological formulation of their belief was summed up in the doctrinal statement: 'Speaking in tongues is the initial evidence of the Baptism in the Holy Spirit'[26] – an almost exact parallel to Irving's 'standing sign'.

The new speakers in tongues found opposition in their churches as strong and stronger than the trustees of Regent Square and the London Presbytery. For many there was no trial, only summary excommunication. The result, as at the National Scotch Church, was the formation of a new sect. Unlike the followers of Irving, the Pentecostals found that their beliefs, apart from the basic agreement on the Baptism in the Spirit and their expectation of the immanent return of Christ, had certain differences. As the years passed these differences emerged as four main types of Pentecostalism: The Apostolic, who believed in the fourfold ministry of Ephesians Chapter 4 as well as the nine gifts of the Spirit of I Corinthians Chapter 12; the Assemblies of God, who believed only in the nine gifts and a congregational type of ministry; the Elim who were similar but with a type of Presbyterian

19

church government and the Independent whose only difference was their congregational autonomy.[27] Within these denominations there was reproduced on a massive scale many of the distinctive aspects of Irving's thought and practice. In the Apostolic Church the number of apostles was not limited to twelve and the ritual and vestments were absent, but the office and function of the fourfold ministry was derived from the same Scripture passages and was the same in authority and rule as in the Catholic Apostolic Church. The Assemblies of God, the Elim and the Independent Churches differed from each other only in detail and were all practically identical to Irving in all they taught and practised concerning the spiritual gifts.[28]

During the early years of this century most of those who had heard of the strange goings-on in Topeka, Los Angeles, Tonypandy, Kilsyth, Monkwearmouth and other early Pentecostal revival centres, dismissed them all as madness and wild ravings. The same had been said of Irving and, like the events in the West of Scotland and at Regent Square Church in 1830–32, it was thought that it would soon die out. But between the wars it became evident that so far from being a passing wave of religious emotionalism, the Pentecostals were establishing themselves as among the fastest developing movements in Protestantism. In America it was found that, between 1926 and 1936, traditional Churches had lost 8 per cent of their membership while the Assemblies of God had gained 208 per cent and the whole Pentecostal movement had gained 264 per cent.[29] Their growth in other countries was equally startling.

Since the last war, leading churchmen of all denominations have had to reckon with the fact of the presence of a world movement which now claims fifteen million souls. To many brought up in traditional Protestantism, the beliefs and experiences of the Pentecostals are as distasteful as Edward Irving became to most of his contemporaries but others recognize in the growth of this ecclesiastical phenomenon a power and vitality that older traditions lack.[30] Whatever other Christians think, Pentecostalism now stands as a 'third force' in world Christianity.[31]

Irving attempted to defend himself at the bar of the courts of the Church of Scotland. That he did do so was not the result of madness or even lack of judgement. It was due to his ever-optimistic nature which passionately desired to renew the waning life of the Church he loved, and thought to do so by converting her to the truth as it had been revealed to him. Neither can he be dismissed as one who was unbalanced or deluded. All his writings during his last years show a lucid and ordered mind unfolding a complete theological system which can now be clearly understood as cogent and coherent in the light of the theology and experience of the twentieth-century Pentecostal movement.[32] Irving can now be seen as a John the Baptist, for church history has shown him to have been the forerunner of all those who believe in Christ as the Baptizer with the Holy Spirit, the 'initial evidence' or 'standing sign' of whose ministry is the speaking with other tongues.[33] He can also be regarded as a Luther, for, in standing *contra mundum*, on the Word of God against the ecclesiastical hierarchy, he was instrumental in initiating a spiritual movement which is now being seen by many to be a second Reformation.[34] He may also be compared to a Knox in exile in that, although he is still without honour in his own country and among his own people, he would immediately leap from obscurity to theological prominence, should the Church of Scotland begin to take seriously the challenge of Pentecostal doctrine and experience.[35]

Irving today can be understood as the first Reformed-Pentecostal theologian. He is one of the few to whom it is given to uncover new systems of Scriptural truth that prove themselves subsequently to be a blessing and inspiration to millions. Because of the Pentecostal analogy and comparison that now exists and which must be the basis of any future assessment of his person and work, almost everything he wrote and everything already written about him must be reconsidered.

His writings on the Holy Spirit in relation to the new humanity of Jesus Christ, correspond to his writings on the two controversies which led to his trials and deposition; first, over the human nature of Christ and second over the gifts of the Holy Spirit. His understanding of the former was preliminary and preparatory to his understanding of the latter. His doctrine and experience of the latter confirmed and authenticated the former. These two doctrines are today separated by the gulf between the Reformed and the Pentecostal Churches but in his system they are reciprocal and mutually interdependent corollaries of one Trinitarian Christology. Karl Barth has acknowledged Irving as a forerunner of those who in recent years, like himself, teach that Christ assumed fallen human nature[36] but he does not teach the Baptism with the Holy Spirit with the 'initial evidence' or 'standing sign' of speaking with tongues,[37] nor does he speak of the gifts of the Spirit in any detail.[38] Irving has also been acknowledged as a fore-runner by those who today teach and experience the baptism and gifts of the Spirit,[39] but the Pentecostals have no explicit teaching on the nature of Christ's humanity.[40] Irving's Christological position would thus appear to be unique and deserves the attention which it has so far not received.[41]

This study is designed to show the development of his thought on these two related and interdependent doctrines. How did he formulate his thought on each of them? How did he come to see them in relation to each other? What was the nature of that relationship? What was his final 'Pentecostal' synthesis of them in doctrine, experience and discipline? What was the precise ecclesiastical and theological response to his teachings? What were the actual arguments put forward in the debates on these issues? What was the result of these controversies? These are the questions which this book begins to try to answer.

The method of this reconsideration is historical. Irving's Christo-logical writings have been put into their context and have been treated consecutively. They have been explained as far as possible by his own theological narratives in which he gives his own comments and explanations of the formative influences on his thought. Much of what has already been written about this aspect of his work has been spoiled by the intrusion of interpretative categories which have been alien and inappropriate to the subject-matter. At the height of his troubles he lamented 'Will men never take a man's word for his faith, but always be drawing conclusions concerning it according to their own oblique and erroneous minds.'[42] It is the hope and the intention of this book to take Irving's word for his faith and, as far as possible to let him speak for himself.

PART ONE

I

The Sermons on the Incarnation

Irving is First Suspected and then Accused of Heresy.
1825 to 1828

EDWARD IRVING began his ministry in the Caledonian
Chapel, Hatton Garden, Holborn, on 'the second Sabbath of
July 1822'.[1] His call had been signed by fifty members.[2] By the
end of his first year in London he had emerged from 'the shade of
that happy obscurity'[3] into the sunlight of ecclesiastical and national
fame. To his great astonishment his preaching had attracted 'every
rank and degree of men, from the lowest, basest of our press hirelings,
up to the right hand of royalty itself'.[4]

Soon the church, which seated five hundred, became too small to
hold the crowds and in May 1823, earlier plans to build a National
Scotch Kirk, which had been abandoned, were revived under the
impetus of the desire to accommodate the rapidly growing congregation.[5]

Towards the end of 1825, Irving delivered a series of sermons on
the doctrine of the Trinity,[6] which were very well received:

> Those discourses were delivered when his popularity was at its
> zenith, and received by all with the greatest applause, and produced
> in multitudes an effect which has abidden to the present time.[7]

The doctrine of the Trinity was the first major teaching which he
gave after his ministry had become established as the most outstanding
in London:[8]

> The doctrine especially of the blessed Trinity, and the offices sus-
> tained by the Persons thereof in our salvation, I desire, for my Church

25

and for myself, to acknowledge, was then opened to us, and remained no longer, as it is to most, a believed but unknown mystery.[9]

It was these sermons on the Trinity, on which he worked with a view to publication during the next two years, which came to be called the sermons on the Incarnation.[10] He was planning to have them published, 'being moved thereto by the request of the Elders and Deacons, expressing the general wish of the Flock'.[11] They were to form the first of three volumes entitled *Sermons, Lectures, and Occasional Discourses* and subtitled *The Doctrine of the Incarnation Opened in Four Sermons*. They were to form the *first* volume by the special request of his congregation 'because they had found the Sermons on the Incarnation the most profitable to their souls'.[12] It was after these sermons had been printed and while the second and third volumes were in the process of being printed that certain events which had occurred during the previous months caused him to withhold the publication of the first volume. He had become suspected of heresy regarding his understanding of the human nature of Jesus Christ.

A few months before the preparation of the sermons on the Incarnation, in March 1827,[13] Irving had preached a sermon to a new society for the distribution of Gospel Tracts. Some of his audience on that occasion took exception to his use of the term 'sinful flesh' with reference to the human nature of Jesus Christ. They made this known to a certain Rev. Mr. Cole. This was the origin of the first suspicions of heresy:

> It is said to have been in the delivery of this oration, that some of Mr. Irving's hearers became astounded on hearing it declared, that the body or humanity of the adorable Redeemer, the beloved Son of God, was 'sinful flesh' – that the Eternal Word took hold of human nature in its fallen state, with much to the same effect. These things being mentioned to the Rev. Henry Cole, a clergyman of the Church of England, resident in the vicinity of London, he was petrified with astonishment at the intelligence and to satisfy himself as to the truth of the report, that gentleman determined to avail himself of the first opportunity of attending the place of worship, where Mr. Irving then statedly exercised his ministry, and hear for himself what this new doctrine was.[14]

Mr. Cole's desire to hear Irving preach was not fulfilled until six months later. It was not until the evening of Sunday 28th October, 1827 that he visited the newly opened National Scotch Church in Regent Square on the way home from his own service and heard the last twenty minutes of the sermon. He was horrified to hear Irving refer to the human nature of Jesus Christ as 'that sinful substance'. He described what he heard in a letter to Irving which he published afterwards:

> You were declaring, 'That the main part of his victory consisted in his overcoming the sin and corruption of his human nature.' You stated, 'That he *did* not sin.' 'But' you said, 'there was that SINFUL SUBSTANCE against which he had to strive, and with which he had to conflict during the whole of his life upon earth.'[15]

He was so upset by what he heard that he waited behind after the service in order to speak privately with the minister. He wanted to find out whether or not he had understood exactly what had been meant by what had been said. The letter he addressed to Irving tells of their conversation in the vestry:

> My address and questions, and your answers, were as follows: 'I believe, Sir, a considerable part of the conclusion of your discourse this evening has been upon the Person and Work of Jesus Christ.' You answered in the affirmative. – I added, 'If I mistake not, you asserted that the human body of Christ was *sinful substance*.' You replied, 'Yes I did.' – I continued, 'But is that your real and considerate belief?' You answered 'Yes it is, as far as I have considered the subject.' And here you produced a book, which I believe was some national confession of faith, to confirm your faith and assertions: in which you pointed out to me these words, (if I mistake not,) 'The flesh of Jesus Christ, which was by nature mortal and corruptible.' – Upon which I continued with amazement, 'But do you really maintain, Sir, that the human body of Jesus Christ was sinful, mortal and corruptible?' You replied, 'Yes, certainly. Christ (you continued) *did* no sin: but his human nature was sinful and corrupt; and his striving against these corruptions was the main part of his conflict. Or else (added you) what make you of all those passages in the Psalms, "Mine iniquities have taken hold upon me that I am not able to look up: They are more in number than the hairs of my head, etc., etc." ' – I answered with astonishment, 'But surely, Sir, by all those passages are represented the agonies of the blessed Saviour under the number and weight of all his people's sins imputed to and transferred upon him.' – 'No, No! (you replied) I admit imputation to its fullest extent, but that does not go far enough for me.

Paul says, "He hath made him to be sin for us, who knew no sin." Imputation was not the faith of the primitive saints, but introduced by councils which were held after the times of the Apostles.' – I observed, 'But, if, as you have already allowed, Christ did no sin, how can those passages in the Psalms refer to any sins, as being his own sins?' You replied, 'I will tell you what it is, and what I mean. Christ could always say with Paul, "Yet not I, but sin that dwelleth in me." ' – 'What! Do you mean, then, (I replied) that Jesus Christ had that "law of sin in his members" of which Paul speaks, when he says, "I find another law in my members warring against the law of my mind, and bringing me into captivity to the law of sin in my members?" ' 'Not into captivity (you replied); but Christ experienced everything the same as Paul did, except the "captivity." ' – 'This, Sir, (I observed) is, to me, a most awful doctrine indeed.' And after making other remarks upon the awfulness of the doctrine, and asking you once or twice if such was your deliberate and considerate belief, which you answered in the affirmative, I put this final question to you, – 'Do you then, Sir, really believe, that the body of the Son of God was a mortal, corrupt, and corruptible body, like that of all mankind? The same body as yours and mine?' You answered 'Yes! just so: certainly: that is what I believe.'[16]

Mr. Cole left Irving after this conversation and did not return. During the following weeks he composed the letter from the introduction to which the above extracts have been taken. He listed Irving's errors, which he then went on to refute, under four headings:

I. That the body of Jesus Christ was sinful, mortal and corruptible substance.

II. That by the passages in the Psalms, 'Mine iniquities have taken hold upon me, so that I am not able to look up, they are more in number than the hairs of my head, etc.' and the like, we are to understand, not the sins of Christ's people imputed to, or transferred upon him; or, not those only, but his own sins and iniquities, from the corruptions of his own flesh.

III. That Jesus Christ could always say with Paul, 'It is no more I that do it, but sin that dwelleth in me;' and, 'I see another law in my members warring against the law of my mind.'

IV. That the Body of the Son of God was a sinful, mortal, corrupt and corruptible body, in all things the same as that of the writer and the REV. EDWARD IRVING.[17]

Mr. Cole had this letter published at the end of December 1827.[18] Irving assumed that it would not attract much serious attention but he was soon proved to have been wrong in this assumption. It not only attracted immediate and widespread notice but was also acclaimed on all sides as a fair statement of orthodoxy. He was astonished to find it receive such universal acclaim and horrified to find himself called a heretic:[19]

> I shall never forget the feeling which I had upon first hearing my name coupled with heresy; so much did it trouble me, that I once seriously meditated sending a paper to the *Christian Observer*, in order to contradict the man's false insinuation. But I thought it better to sit quiet and bear the reproach.[20]

As the 'great outcry against the doctrine'[21] grew like a sudden storm around him, he decided not to try to defend himself in the pages of the *Christian Observer*. Instead, he allowed only the second and third volumes of *Sermons, Lectures and Occasional Discourses*, that is, *On the Parable of the Sower, Six Lectures*, and, *On Subjects National and Prophetical, Seven Discourses*, to be published as planned in January 1828. The first volume, on the Incarnation, he withheld from publication while he considered adding a further two sermons to it in which he would set out the doctrine more fully in a controversial as well as in a dogmatical way:

> The stir which was made in divers quarters, both of this and my native land, about this matter, as if it were neither the orthodox doctrine of the church, nor a doctrine according to godliness, shewed me, who am convinced of both, that it was necessary to take controversial weapons in my hand, and contend earnestly for the faith as it was once delivered to the saints. I perceived now, that the dogmatical method which I had adopted for the behoof of my own believing flock, would not be sufficient when publishing to a wavering, gainsaying, or unbelieving people; and therefore it seemed to me most profitable to delay the publication until I should have composed something fitted to reestablish men's minds upon this great fundamental doctrine of the church, – which having done, I resolved to insert the same as two other sermons; the one upon the method of the Incarnation, and the other upon the relations of the Creator and the creature, as these are shewn out in the light of the Incarnation.[22]

After some months' reflection, he began to compose these two projected sermons. During the late summer and autumn of 1828 he records his progress on them in letters to his wife.[23] By late autumn he had them finished and printed. They were added to the original four sermons as numbers three and six. He dated the dedicatory letter to his congregation 10th November and the book was published later that month as the first volume of *Sermons, Lectures and Occasional Discourses: – The Doctrine of the Incarnation Opened in Six Sermons.* Of this book he said '. . . there is much more to God's glory in that volume than in all my other writings put together',[24] and it was in the first of his two extra sermons (that is, number three) that he contended most earnestly 'for the faith as it was once delivered to the saints'. This sermon is called 'The Method of accomplishing the Mystery, is by taking up the Fallen Humanity into the Personality of the eternal Son of God.' It is in four parts 'I. The composition of Christ's person. II. The Universal Reconciliation wrought by his Death, and the Particular Election ministered by his Life in Glory. III. The removal of the Law, and the bringing in of Grace. IV. Conclusions.'[25] This sermon is his first extensive statement of the controversial and dogmatical point at issue. He gives a summary of its contents in the Preface to the volume:

> The point at issue is simply this; whether Christ's flesh had the grace of sinlessness and incorruption from its proper nature, or from the indwelling of the Holy Ghost. I say the latter. I assert, that in its proper nature it was as the flesh of his mother, but, by virtue of the Holy Ghost's quickening and inhabiting of it, it was preserved sinless and incorruptible. This work of the Holy Ghost, I further assert, was done in consequence of the son's humbling himself to be made flesh. The Son said, 'I come:' The Father said, 'I prepare thee a body to come in:' and the Holy Ghost prepared that body out of the Virgin's substance. And so, by the threefold acting of the Trinity, was the Christ constituted a Divine and a human nature, joined in personal union for ever.[26]

He believed that this had always been the orthodox faith of the Christian Church and that this was expressed in Article xxi of 'The (Scots) Confession of Faith and Doctrine' of 1560 where it said '. . . as the eternal godhead hath given to the flesh of Christ Jesus (which of its own nature was mortal and corruptible) life and immortality. . . .' He also believed that any doctrine which made out that Christ's flesh was inherently immortal and incorruptible and did not therefore need the sustaining power of the Holy Spirit, was a 'pestilent heresy' which made void the doctrines of 'atonement, redemption, regeneration, the work of the Spirit, and the human nature of Christ.'[27] He went on to say that he was not monothelite in his understanding of either the person or the work of Christ:

With all this I hold the human will of Christ to have been perfectly holy, and to have acted, spoken, or wished nothing but in perfect harmony with the will of the Godhead; which to distinguish it from the creature will, he calleth the will of the Father; for that there were two wills in Christ, the one the absolute will of the Godhead, the other the limited will of the manhood, the Church hath ever maintained as resolutely as that there were two natures. These two wills, I maintain, were always concentric or harmonious with each other, and the work achieved by the Godhead through the Incarnation of Christ was neither less nor more than this, to bring the will of the creature, which had erred from the Divine will, back again to be harmonious with the Divine will, and there to fix it for ever. This is the redemption, this is the at-one-ment, which was wrought in Christ, to redeem the will of a creature from the oppression of sin, and bring it to be at one with the will of the Creator. All divinity, all Divine operation, all God's purpose, from the beginning to the ending of time, and throughout eternal ages, resteth upon this one truth, that every acting of the human nature of Christ was responsive to, and harmonious with, the actings of the Divine will of the Godhead.[28]

He then said that it was 'a calumny' and 'a hideous lie' for him to have been represented by Mr. Cole and others as having said that Christ was 'unholy and sinful because we maintain that he took his humanity completely and wholly from the substance, from the sinful substance of the fallen creatures which he came to redeem'.[29] These were unjustified inferences and were the very opposite of what he had said. He believed that Christ's whole life was a continual victory over the world, the flesh and the devil:

He was passive to every sinful suggestion which the world through the flesh can hand up unto the will; he was liable to every sinful suggestion which Satan through the mind can hand up to the will; and with all such suggestions and temptations I believe him beyond all others to have been assailed, but further went they not. He gave them no quarter, but with power Divine rejected and repulsed them all; and so, from his conception unto his resurrection, his whole life was a series of active triumphings over sin in the flesh, Satan in the world, and spiritual wickedness in high places.[30]

This, he said, was the 'honest and true statement of the issue', and he pleaded that his work might be read without prejudice. He confessed that in a book of nearly six hundred pages dealing with such a complex doctrine, he might not always have expressed himself without a fault. He strongly denied, however, that he had written anything against the truth of God, the holiness of Christ's soul or body, or the doctrines of atonement, substitution, imputation and satisfaction.[31]

Now that he had committed himself extensively to print on the subject of controversy, his critics had ample scope for more exact opposition to his views. His sermon on the Method of the Incarnation was read and condemned by most of the religious world. He discovered that the alleged charges of heresy that were levelled against him depended on his detractors having taken certain sentences from his writing out of context. He defended himself by showing that if these allegedly heretical passages were put back into their rightful context, the grounds for any exception being taken to them, were removed. He instanced two examples from passages that had been most objected to and criticized:

1. . . . we say and will maintain unto death, that Christ's flesh was as rebellious as ours, as fallen as ours.[32]

He admitted that, if this sentence had stood alone, it would have been a terrible misstatement of the truth. His critics quoted it as if it was meant to stand alone but it did not and was not meant to.[33] Put back into its context it had a completely different meaning, for the paragraph, as he wrote it, went straight on to say:

But what then? Is Christ's flesh the whole of his creature-being? No: it his humanity inhabited by the Holy Ghost, which maketh up his creature-being. And, through the power of the Holy Ghost, acting powerfully and with effect, to the resisting, to the slaying, to the overcoming of the evil propensity of the fallen man, it is, that the fallen manhood of Christ is made mighty, and holy, and good, and every way fit to express the will of the Divinity.[34]

When it is put back into its context, the first sentence can be seen as a good description of what it was that the Son of God had to overcome through the power of the Holy Spirit. He then gives his second example of the extrapolatory procedure of his critics:

2. His flesh is the fit medium between the powers of darkness and the

powers of light. And why fit? Because it is linked unto all material things, devil-possessed, while it is joined in closest union with the soul, which in Christ was God-possessed in the person of the Holy Ghost.[35]

The epithet *devil-possessed,* by a mistake of punctuation had been made to qualify *it,* that is, Christ's flesh, instead of *material things.* It would still have been an open question grammatically whether or not this changed the meaning, if the sentence was taken out of context. But if the whole passage is read, it is impossible to come to such a conclusion. The whole paragraph and the whole argument of which it is a part, is a lengthy and detailed demonstration of how it was that Christ's flesh was always redeemed from the power of evil by his soul or will.[36] This is how the offending sentence reads in context:

It now remaineth to examine how the Holy Ghost bringeth the body into this harmony with God. This difficulty must be met again, and not avoided. A sinful world, sinners such as those around me, want to know how they are to be reconciled, how their reconciliation hath been accomplished in Christ. We are in earnest and we are not to be shuffled out of our salvation by any subterfuges: therefore tell us plainly, how this great work was accomplished. By the grace of God, I will tell you. The Holy Ghost took up his residence in the soul of Christ; God had given the world unto the devil, and the devil had his residence in the fallen world around. The flesh of Christ was the middle space on which the powers of the world contended with the Holy Spirit dwelling in his soul. His flesh is the fit medium between the powers of darkness and the powers of light. And why fit? Because it is linked unto all material things devil-possessed, while it is joined in closest, nearest union unto the soul, which in Christ was God-possessed, in the person of the Holy Ghost. His flesh is the fit field of contention because it is the same on which Satan hath triumphed ever since the fall. Here then, in the flesh of Christ, is the great controversy waged. Through this, Satan presented his temptations of appetite, of sight, of pride, trying him with lust (desire) of the flesh, with the desire of the eye, with the pride of life. This did he at the very outset of his ministry, not that he had not done it before, or was not to do it after, or did not do it ever, but that it was then done in a manifest and notorious manner, that it might be capable of record and of tradition; and that such dreams might be prevented as I am now reproving, and that it might be for ever manifest and indubitable, that the Son had no favour, and that Satan had no let or hindrance in this great and terrible conflict. And when, at the end of his ministry, he said, 'The prince of this world cometh, and findeth nothing in me,' he solemnly declareth, that during the whole of the fiery conflict which he had endured, and unto which he alone was conscious, Satan had never been able to make a lodgment, or gain a hold in his flesh; that though free to come in all his might, he had ever been repelled, as he was repelled in the wilderness, that his flesh thus oppressed, thus hideously oppressed, had never been able to sway his will, upholden in its stedfastness by the Holy Ghost; that the might of the Holy Ghost in his soul had been able to reconcile unto God the inveterate obstinacy and stubborn rebellion of flesh and blood; that for once the law of the flesh had not been able to drag down a soul to perdition; that for once a soul had been able to draw up the flesh into reconciliation with the will of God; that all his life long the will of the flesh had been successfully withstood by the will of the Spirit, yea, that the will of the Spirit had enforced the flesh to do it unwilling service. All this is signified by the expression which he used immediately before his agony, 'Satan cometh, but findeth nothing in me.'[37]

Put back into its context, it becomes clear that Irving's meaning is exactly the opposite of that which his critics make it out to be. This lengthy paragraph from which the mistaken epithet 'devil-possessed' comes, not only makes Irving's meaning plain regarding the refutation of alleged heresy but also gives an example of his understanding of the relationship between the constitution of the person and the triumph of the work of Jesus Christ, – the organic connection between the incarnation and the atonement.[38]

2

Our Lord's Human Nature

Irving Replies to his Critics: Opposition Grows. 1829

THROUGHOUT THE year 1829, hostility to Irving's understanding of the human nature of Christ, continued to grow in England and in Scotland. In spite of this and the publication during the summer of *A Refutation of the Heretical Doctrine Promulgated by the Rev. Edward Irving, respecting the Person and Atonement of the Lord Jesus Christ,* by Mr. James Haldane, and of the *Sermons on Various Subjects* by Dr. Andrew Thompson,[1] he published nothing further for the time being except two articles for the first two issues of *The Morning Watch.* This magazine was a new quarterly journal representing the thought of the Albury Conference on Prophecy which had met for the first time the previous November.[2] For the opening number in March he wrote 'On the Human Nature of Christ' and for the June issue 'On the True Humanity of Christ'. In these articles he went into a detailed defence of his belief that the substance of the human nature of Christ was, in itself, sinful, and justified his position from the writings of the Fathers and the Creeds of the Church.[3]

Towards the end of the year some of his friends persuaded him to republish these articles separately in the hope that they might help to change the mind of the ecclesiastical public on this subject, especially in Scotland.[4] He did not republish them as they were but used them, together with excerpts from the third sermon on the Incarnation, as the basis of a new tract which he called *The Orthodox and Catholic Doctrine of Our Lord's Human Nature.* It was published in January 1830. In this précis of his earlier writings he stated the Scriptural basis for his understanding of the nature of Christ's flesh; justified it by the authority of the Apostolic, Nicene and Athanasian creeds and the Confessions of the Church of Scotland;[5] answered objections to his understanding of the miraculous conception, the atonement and the value of Christ's sufferings; and showed how the doctrine was fundamental to the doctrines of the Father, the Son, the Holy Spirit, the Scriptures, union with Christ, regeneration and holiness.

In the Preface to this work he gives a synopsis of his teaching. He says that the reader must understand that when he calls our Lord's human nature *sinful* 'I am defining the qualities of that *nature* which he took upon him, and demonstrating it to be the very same in substance with that which we possess.'[6] He said that most of his opponents believed that 'the substance of the human nature underwent a change in the miraculous conception' whereas he believed that it did not undergo any change until the resurrection:

> We hold that it received a Holy-Ghost life, a regenerate life, in the conception: in kind the same which we receive in regeneration, but in measure greater, because of his perfect faith: which perfect faith he was enabled to give by being a Divine Person, of one substance with the Father. . . . This is the substance of our argument, – that his human nature was holy in the only way in which holiness under the Fall exists or can exist, . . . through inworking or energizing of the Holy Ghost.[7]

Consideration of Christ's unity with us in the one flesh had raised a metaphysical question for him regarding the constitution of individuality or personality which he felt he was now able to answer. He asked 'Where lies . . . that which I denominate *I myself*?'[8] He used to think 'that the community is in the flesh, and the personality is in the soul'. But he had now come to realize 'that if there is not a community in Christ's soul with us, the community in his flesh is really nothing but an appearance'. He now maintained that whatever anyone understood by man's personality, Christ's human nature in itself had community of flesh and soul with it. He then defined what he understood by the personality and how this affected redemption:

> I incline to believe that the personality is a property superinduced by God upon that community of body and soul which we inherit, being that which connects every man with Himself. . . . For certain, Christ had a body and soul of man's substance, without thereby having a human person: and therefore we can assert the sinfulness of the whole, the complete, the perfect human nature, which he took, without in the

least implicating him with sin: yea, verily, seeing he subdued those properties which it had in itself and made it holy, we assert him to be the only Redeemer of man from sin.[9]

In this way Irving explained how he came to see how it was possible for Christ to have had a human body *and soul* and yet to have been without sin. He elaborated on this by distinguishing between His human nature and His person. Sin in a nature is not the same as sin in a person:

> Whenever I speak of the flesh of Christ, I mean, except when the contrary is expressed, the whole creature part, which is not a person, but a substance; a substance which we must describe by its properties of sinfulness and darkness and deadness, in order to understand the wonderful work of redemption which Christ wrought in it. What was holy, was his Person; and from that came redemption into the nature.... Sin, in a nature, is its disposition to lead the person away from God; sin in a person, is a yielding thereto. All creation is sinful. . . . The Person of the Son of God was born into it, he restrained, withstood, overcame this co-operation of a sinful creation, conquered the conqueror, and won it back to God. . . . This is the great theme which we maintain.[10]

He then restated the difference between his position and that of his opponents. In the Preface to the Sermons on the Incarnation he had said that the difference of opinion was between those who believed that Christ's flesh was inherently sinless and his own belief that it was sinless 'from the indwelling of the Holy Ghost'. Although he had gone on to say that 'from his conception unto his resurrection, his whole life was a series of active triumphings over sin in the flesh, Satan in the world, and spiritual wickedness in high places,' he realized that this needed amplification. He drew out the difference between those who only believed that Christ was identified with us in origin, and his own belief that during His whole life Christ was one with us in all our liability to sin:

> They argue for an identity of origin merely; we argue for an identity of life also. They argue for an inherent holiness; we argue for a holiness maintained by the Person of the Son, through the operation of the Holy Ghost. They say, that though his body was changed in the generation, he was still our fellow in all temptations and sympathies: we deny that it could be so; for change is change; and if his body was changed in the conception, it was not in its life as ours is. In one word,

we present believers with a real life; a suffering, mortal flesh; a real death and a real resurrection of this flesh of ours: they present the life, death and resurrection of a changed flesh: and so create a chasm between Him and us which no knowledge, or even imagination, can overleap.[11]

The publication of this tract did nothing to change the mind of ecclesiastical opinion or help his cause. It only made his situation worse by giving further documented evidence of his alleged heresies. Hostile publications continued to appear and in particular in *The Edinburgh Christian Instructor* from the pen of Marcus Dods (the elder). In January 1830, in the first of three articles reviewing *The Doctrine of the Incarnation Opened,* various articles in *The Morning Watch* and other publications on Christ's human nature, he launched an erudite attack on those who believed that Christ had assumed fallen humanity in order to redeem it. In his two articles on Christ's humanity in *The Morning Watch,* Irving had displayed considerable scholarship in support of his opinion. Now Dods displayed an equal amount in support of the opposite view.[12] Irving believed his position 'to have been the orthodox faith of the Christian Church in all ages',[13] but Dods thought that he had promulgated 'a doctrine which never was heard of within the pale of the Church'. To his learning Dods added sustained invective:

> In order to prove their position that Christ took a fallen human nature, they (i.e. Irving and company) . . . produce a quotation from Augustine, in which there is not the most distant allusion to the question, never once hinting that the Father strongly maintains, both here and elsewhere, that Christ took human nature in its unfallen state. All the helpless imbecility of ignorance, which they may justly plead in their own favour, cannot exculpate them in this case any more than in others. Ignorance should be modest and diffident. It should not riot in all the wantonness of insult, and support its insolence by something worse than even ignorance and insolence combined. We do not bid these gentlemen blush. But if the saints in heaven are permitted to see what is going on on earth, what will be the feelings of Augustine, and of the many others whom they have quoted, when they see themselves arranged side by side as witnesses against the truths which, while living, they loved, and were willing to pour out their blood to defend – to see themselves cited as witnesses in support of a doctrine which never was heard of within the pale of the Church, – which was never maintained by any man professing Christianity, Socinians alone excepted![14]

38

By the time he wrote his second article, for the February issue of *The Christian Instructor,* Dods had read Irving's new tract. In that and in his third article in March he censured this new publication as heavily as his earlier writings.[15] The redoubled outcry which the publication of *The Orthodox and Catholic Doctrine of Our Lord's Human Nature* provoked, caused Irving to reconsider every detail of its form and content in case his reasoning or his writing had been inaccurate, but he could find no fault with it and saw no reason to alter it in any way.[16] He could see no basis for the criticisms that were made against it. He had never said that Christ's flesh had sinned and had explained what he meant by the term 'sinful flesh' when applied to Christ in the Preface and in Part I. He had never said that Christ was guilty of original sin. On the contrary he had devoted the section on 'The Miraculous Conception' to proving the opposite. Neither had he denied the atonement. He had affirmed the doctrine in the section on 'The True Nature of Atonement'. Nor had he denied the merits of Christ's sufferings in the section on 'The Value of Christ's Sufferings'. Other charges could be answered by simply putting the condemned quotations back into their context as already instanced. The more fantastic allegations against him, such as that he taught that Christ was first generated and then regenerated, he could only explain 'by the charitable supposition that they have never read my book, and made up their judgement of it from slanderers'.[17]

He felt that there were no grounds for any of these charges. He had written with clarity what he considered to be the true doctrine of Christ's human nature and had answered every objection. As opinion hardened on both sides, his horror of being branded a heretic was balanced by the glory of being persecuted for righteousness' sake. He had said of his first controversial essay:

> Now, I glory that God hath accounted me worthy to appear in the field of this ancient controversy, which I hold to be the foundation-stone of this edifice of orthodox truth.[18]

And for this, his second, even more controversial publication, he thanked the God of truth:

> Who had enabled me to put forth such a bold and uncompromising statement of the true faith of our Lord's human nature. If I had to write it over again, I question sometimes whether I durst speak out

39

so plainly against the opposers of the truth, whom at that time I had thought to be only a few schismatical and misled men, but alas! whom I now find to be a very numerous body of the ministers of the Church of Scotland.[19]

3

Opinions on our Lord's Human Nature

Confrontation: Irving Separates from, and is Condemned by, the London Presbytery. 1830

THE NUMBER of ministers who opposed the truth as Irving saw it, was growing rapidly and in the spring of 1830 they began to voice their opposition officially through the courts of the Church. It was not at first against Irving himself that legal questions were directed, but against two young men who had accepted his teaching, the Rev. H. B. Maclean and the Rev. A. J. Scott.[1] The Rev. Hugh Maclean had come under Irving's influence when he was minister of the Scots Kirk at London Wall. He had recently been inducted to the parish of Dreghorn in Ayrshire and had very soon been presented with a petition by members of his congregation because of his alleged heresy regarding the doctrine of the humanity of Christ. This petition was taken first to the presbytery, then to the synod and finally to the General Assembly. The Rev. Alexander Scott was a licentiate who had been assistant to Irving at Regent Square for the previous two years. On 20th April, while he was undergoing his trials for ordination to the Scots Kirk at Woolwich, objections were raised as to his orthodoxy by the Presbytery of London.[2]

Stimulated by the opposition which was beginning to express itself thus formally against his friends and followers, and in particular to help Hugh Maclean, in an attempt to prevent the success of his ecclesiastical persecution, Irving wrote his third work on the humanity of Christ. This was called *The Opinions Circulating Concerning Our*

41

Lord's Human Nature, Tried by the Westminster Confession of Faith.
It was published in May 1830 during the sitting of the General Assembly.[3] In this tract he says that there were three opinions circulating concerning Christ's human nature, his own and two others with which he disagreed. After stating what they were he went on to test them against the Westminster Confession, Chapter viii, which spoke of the Mediator. In this examination he showed that the Westminster Confession agreed with his own understanding. Summarizing the two opinions with which he disagreed he stated them briefly to be:

> First, that the nature of Christ was the nature of Adam as created and uninjured by the fall, and not his mother's, but Adam's, as distinguished from her's, and that he was not mortal and corruptible, nor in any way subject (though liable) to our infirmities. Secondly, that the nature he took was indeed his mother's, but so wrought upon in the generation as to be purged from sin, and this all independent of the working of Christ, and before he would have any thing to do with it in any way.[4]

Put even more concisely, these two views were 'either that His nature was intrinsically better than ours, or that it underwent a physical change before its assumption into the person of the Son.'[5] In contradistinction to these, he put forward his own opinion:

> The opinion, in contradiction or amendment of which the other two have originated, is, that our Lord took the same nature, body and soul, as other men, and under the same disadvantages of every sort, that his flesh was mortal and corruptible, and passive to all our temptations; that his soul was joined to his flesh according to the same laws, and under the same conditions, as ours is, and liable to be tempted by the objects of a fallen world, acting upon and approaching it, through his flesh, just as ours is, – in one word, that his human will had lying against it, and upon it, exactly the same oppressions of devil, world, and flesh, which lay against and upon Adam's will after he had fallen, and which lies upon every man's will unto this day. And yet, though 'tempted in all points like as we are', and 'in the likeness of sinful flesh,' and 'made in all things like unto his brethren', the power and holiness of incarnate Godhead was such as to sanctify his body from first to last, and to sustain it holy; so that all his life long 'he presented his body a living sacrifice, holy and acceptable, and proved what was that holy and acceptable and perfect will of God'. This great work of doing the will of God in a body, whereby we are sanctified through the offering thereof, is due, they who hold this opinion affirm, to the

act of the Son taking our nature, and acting, in our proper manhood, perfect faith upon the Father; to the act of the Father anointing him with the Holy Ghost above measure; to the act of the Son of Man using the Holy Ghost, thus bestowed, against the whole multitude of our temptations; to the act of the Holy Ghost empowering the infirmity, sanctifying the unholiness, quickening the mortality, and in all respects perfecting the human nature which he took, flesh and soul, at all times, so that he could be called the Holy One of God from his conception to his resurrection; although, between these two periods, he was flesh, enduring our conflict, our death, and all the curse, and all the law, which our sin had introduced; so that he could even say, 'He that hath seen me hath seen the Father', 'Satan cometh and hath nothing in me', 'I and my Father are one'.[6]

This publication, like the other two, did nothing to prevent his, by now vast unofficial opposition from continuing to form itself into official action. The questions that had been raised concerning the orthodoxy of Sandy Scott, led to a private conference and to a committee being set up to look into the matter. On 4th May this committee drew up a brief general statement to which Irving, who was a member, found he could agree.[7] It was hoped that a doctrinal compromise had been reached:

> By this statement those members of Presbytery who were opposed to Mr. Irving conceived that they had struck at the very root of his peculiar sentiments and their hope was that if he did not formally recant his error, he would at least in future preach a sounder and more wholesome doctrine.[8]

He continued to preach as before, holding that he was in no way contradicting the statement which he had agreed to. But the Presbytery, turning now from Scott to him, was not pleased with this and at a meeting on 20th July, it was proposed that the court should 'take into consideration certain writings on the subject of our Lord's human nature which had been published by one of its members'.[9] Irving objected to this on the grounds that Jesus's ruling on offences (*Matt.* 18:15) had not been complied with. His objection was accepted and the matter was dropped.[10]

It was not until the Presbytery meeting of 20th September that the matter was raised again. The Rev. James Millar gave notice that at the next meeting he would call attention to Irving's tract *The Orthodox and Catholic Doctrine of Our Lord's Human Nature.* This he did on 19th October and after some debate carried his motion 'that the Presbytery should obtain satisfaction regarding certain statements of the work in question'.[11] Irving was the one dissentient voter and voiced his protest loudly against this resolution.[12] After making a final plea, which was rejected, he walked out of the court 'appealing my case to the Church of Scotland, who alone had the rightful authority over me and my flock'[13] and withdrew himself from the jurisdiction of the Presbytery. He gave his own account of his action:

> I then rose the second time, and signified to them what I could, and what I could not, submit to the adjudication of that body of three ministers and as many elders, from whom I had no appeal. Every thing which affected my conduct amongst them as a brother I would submit to free censure, and rebuke if necessary, but nothing affecting my standing as a preacher and ordained minister of the Church of Scotland, and as the minister of the National Scotch Church in London, who, by trust-deed, must be ordained by a presbytery in Scotland, and not by the presbytery of London. It was argued that I stood wholly and entirely at their tribunal; and when I perceived that there was nothing for it, but either to give up my standing as a minister of Christ to the judgement of these six men, or to dissolve my voluntary connection with them, I resolved of the two evils to choose the latter, and not to submit the authority of the Church of Scotland to the verdict of any six men in Christendom.[14]

During the next month the committee appointed to examine Irving's tract met to discharge its remit. On 30th November it reported its findings to the Presbytery. It had been unanimously agreed that he had been found guilty of heresy on four charges.[15] These were: 1. That he had made Christ out to be guilty of original sin.[16] 2. That he had not only misrepresented, but held up to scorn the doctrine of sanctification.[17] 3. That in his tract 'The great and precious doctrine of redemption is also made void.'[18] 4. That in his tract 'The doctrines of Imputation and Substitution, as they are commonly understood, are opposed and denied.'[19] The conclusion of the report was that this book contained 'errors subversive of the great doctrines of Christianity, and that it was dangerous to the welfare of the Church of Christ'.[20] The Presbytery accepted the report and proceeded against him:

44

The Presbytery having adopted this report of its committee, and having thrice summoned Mr. Irving to return to its jurisdiction, and finding that he neglected to submit himself, declared him to be no longer a member of the court, nor capable of being admitted thereto until he should recognize its authority and openly renounce those errors to which he had given public notoriety.[21]

Irving read through the report and discovered that all the excerpts from his book which had been condemned had been misrepresented and misunderstood because they had been taken out of context. By this process of extrapolation the committee had concluded that he had *meant* the opposite of what he had *said* on these four major doctrines, in spite of his 'direct disavowal and demonstration to the contrary'.[22] The only possible way 'to rebut the odious charges' was 'simply by giving the whole of the passages which they have garbled' and this he proceeded to do.[23]

Now that he had separated himself and been separated from the London Presbytery, Irving was in an independent position. His standing as minister of the National Scotch Church might have been precarious but for the unanimous support of his Kirk Session throughout his troubles. At a meeting on 15th December they voiced their wholehearted agreement with his teaching and disagreement with the proceedings of the Presbytery in a written declaration of faith which they published and circulated to all the parties involved:

We solemnly declare – That we utterly detest and abhor any doctrine that would charge with sin, original or actual, our blessed Lord and Saviour Jesus Christ, whom we worship and adore, as 'the very and eternal God, of one substance and equal with the Father; who when the fulness of time was come, did take upon Him man's nature, with all the essential properties and common infirmities thereof, yet without sin', – 'very God and very man, yet one Christ, the only Mediator between God and man', who in the days of His flesh was 'holy, harmless, undefiled, and full of grace and truth'; 'who through the eternal spirit offered himself without spot to God'; 'the Lamb of God that taketh away the sin of the world'; 'a Lamb without blemish and without spot'; in which offering of Himself 'He made a proper, real, and full satisfaction to His Father's justice in our behalf.' . . . And, finally, we do solemnly declare that these are the doctrines which are constantly taught in this church, agreeably to the standards of the Church of Scotland and the Word of God.[24]

4

Christ's Holiness in Flesh

A Final Statement of Irving's Teaching on the Nature of Christ. 1831

IT WAS in the months following his separation from the London Presbytery that Irving wrote his fourth and final work on Christ's humanity. It was called *Christ's Holiness in Flesh, The Form, Fountain Head, and Assurance to us of Holiness in Flesh* and was published in the spring of 1831. It was in three parts: 1. 'The Fact and Form of Our Lord's Holiness,' in which he proved from Scripture that Christ was originally, constitutionally and actually holy in our flesh, and showed that God testified to this and what all men gained by it. 2. 'Illustrations from Scripture,' in which he amplified part 1, referring especially to *Romans* 6, 7 and 8, *II Corinthians* 3:3; 4; 5:16–21; *I Peter* 2:21; 3:18; 4:12 and *I John*. 3. 'Conclusions of Doctrinal Truth and Practical Holiness,' in which he examined the article of faith of the Church of Scotland which says 'That the Son of God took human nature of the substance of His mother, which (human nature) was wholly and perfectly sanctified by the Holy Ghost in the act of conception and was upholden in the same state by the same power of the Holy Ghost; and underwent no process or progress of sanctification as it needed none'. Clause by clause he demonstrated that, contrary to what might have been expected from one who was now an 'execrated heresiarch', his views agreed with this accepted deliverance of the Church.[1]

The Preface to this, his last attempt to clear himself and justify his theology, did not give a summary of his aim and method. Instead he gave the lengthy narrative which has been used as the basis for this part of the present study. Such a summary was not necessary since his aim, as in his other writings, was to clarify his position and to refute his critics and his method was still by Scriptural exposition and appeal to the standards of the Church. This tract was distinguished from the others only by the extent to which he had been able to amplify what he meant by Christ's 'whole life' being 'a series of active triumphings over sin in the flesh, Satan in the world, and spiritual wickedness in high places'.[2] His extended expository method had enabled him to explain in detail what he meant by Christ having not merely 'an identity of origin' but 'an identity of life also' with us and to expand fully the understanding of his belief that Christ 'all his life long' had 'presented his body a living sacrifice, holy and acceptable, and proved what was that holy and acceptable and perfect will of God'.[3] It was here more than in his earlier writings that he did 'present believers with a real life; a suffering, mortal flesh; a real death and a real resurrection of this flesh of ours'. He found the key passage to this understanding of the identity of Christ with us in a 'whole', 'real', life, in *Colossians* 2:11-15:

> 'In whom also ye are circumcised with the circumcision made without hands, in putting off the body of the sins of the flesh by the circumcision of Christ: Buried with him in baptism, wherein also ye are risen with him through the faith of the operation of God, who hath raised him from the dead. And you, being dead in your sins, and the uncircumcision of your flesh, hath he quickened together with him, having forgiven you all trespasses: Blotting out the hand-writing of ordinance that was against us, which was contrary to us, and took it out of the way, nailing it to his cross: And having spoiled principalities and powers, he made a show of them openly, triumphing over them in it.'

This passage is a perfect expression of the truth that 'Christ's flesh and ours are one and the same in all natural laws and capacities, needing the very same power of God to sanctify it, and capable of the same sanctification by that power.'[4] It is the perfect expression of the meaning of the text 'Always bearing about in the body the dying of the Lord Jesus,' and shows that in Christ's death all the enemies in our flesh were put to death:

> Where his circumcision is made equivalent to the cutting off of our superfluity of naughtiness, the body of sins of the flesh; his baptism is our burial and resurrection to a new life; his nailing of the flesh to the cross nails these carnal ordinances of the law, and spoils all

principalities and powers which were wont to accuse us through the law, and master us through the flesh; and we believing that all these benefits were wrought out by Christ for all flesh, do enter into the same benefits, and are brought into a condition of living the life of Christ.[5]

It is in this way that Christ is identified with us not merely in origin but in life. Those who say that all these benefits of Christ were done for us 'in the supernatural generation' have to explain why Paul never once mentions that event but speaks always of 'circumcision, baptism, the cross, and the resurrection'. At His miraculous conception He only received the *power* to do these things:

> In that act he received the power, the agency of the Holy Spirit to do them, but the doing of them was not then, but at three several acts; circumcision shewed that he had the body of the sins of the flesh to cut off, and baptism that he had it to bury, and the cross, that he had flesh under the curse to crucify, and resurrection, that he had mortal flesh to take out of the hands of principalities and powers of darkness, and his receiving the various testimonies of God, especially the resurrection, shews, that he had never failed to do all these things for flesh most perfectly, *ever* presenting it holy unto God.[6]

The doing of these things for us by Christ in our flesh was not all at once at His conception, but 'at three several acts'. These three separate acts, according to Paul, are circumcision, baptism and the cross – and – resurrection. In all these acts, and especially in the resurrection, God testified that Christ had always preserved his flesh holy and 'proved what was that holy and acceptable and perfect will of God'. God testified to Christ's perfect holiness in many passages of Scripture and in every one of these the agent of his holiness is the Holy Spirit. The Holy Spirit is the only agent who can work holiness in the creature, and the reason why he is called Holy is 'because the part and province of holiness belongeth unto Him'.[7]

Irving had always maintained that 'His human nature was holy in the only way in which holiness under the Fall exists or can exist, . . . through inworking or energizing of the Holy Ghost.'[8] Applying this to the 'several acts' of Christ's 'identity of life' with us, he arrived at the presentation of what he meant by 'a real life' of Christ. For 'all his life long' and especially at each of these 'several acts', it was the Holy Spirit who was the power or the agent who enabled Him to act 'perfect faith upon the Father'. The Holy Spirit had a part to play 'all his life long' and especially in each of these 'several acts' whereby Christ lived a holy life in our flesh:

> That part which the Holy Ghost took in his generation sealed him holy, devoid of all original corruption, free from all offence in the sight of God. Then being circumcised, he became a debtor to keep the whole law, and being come to the water of baptism, God signified that he had kept the law of love these thirty years without one fault by sealing him with the Holy Ghost, and again pronouncing him his well beloved Son, in whom he was well pleased. And now, having perfected holiness according to the law, he was made the depository of the Holy Ghost for mightier uses, even for the uses of witnessing God's own almighty power over, and in the midst of his own creation. At the baptism of Christ, manhood made a step above its original creation, was taken into an inner chamber of the divine purpose, and called upon to be the hand and voice of God in commanding and doing the Creator's business, as well as his servant, in obeying the Creator's laws. In one word, to be the residence of God, his house to dwell in, his tongue to speak, his hand to act. This ministry Christ went forth upon after he had been baptized with the Holy Ghost, and he was sealed as having never failed in it, by the power, after his resurrection of breathing on his disciples and imparting the Holy Ghost, and after his ascension, of baptizing them with the Holy Ghost.[9]

The reality of Christ's holy life in our flesh is to be found in His acting perfect faith to his Father in human flesh by means of the power of the Holy Spirit. How this happened is expressed by these events or acts. The identity of His life with us is in the flesh for 'there is not *my* flesh and *thy* flesh, but FLESH'.[10] In this way Irving was able to speak of the events of Christ's life as real without lapsing into the errors of progressive sanctification or adoptionism. Much of this tract is devoted to setting up a detailed expository framework which enabled him to speak in this way of Christ without falling into these and other errors. In the process he replied to the various criticisms which his earlier writings had received. Referring to the charge that he believed 'that our Lord's nature needed or underwent a process or progress of sanctification'[11] he said:

> Men, more injurious than charitable, have inferred, that because sanctification is progressive in the believer, therefore, to call Christ a head of sanctification, is to believe it to have been progressive in him

49

also. Will men never take a man's word for his faith, but always be drawing conclusions concerning it according to their own oblique and erroneous minds. I do not believe that sanctification was progressive in the Lord.[12]

Christ's human nature did not need to undergo a process or progress of sanctification, as he showed extensively throughout the tract. But this did not mean that He did not really go through the process and progress of all the stages of a man's life. His sanctification was not a process or a progress because He always sustained His manhood perfectly holy through all the stages of His life. It was because He did so that He is the perfect, holy redeemer of man from all evil. Irving expanded on this in terms of Christ's original, constitutional and actual holiness and God's testimonies to this:

All flesh kept the law in Christ, and at his baptism all flesh was buried in its grace, the law hath no demands upon flesh any more. . . . From the time of his baptism with water and the Holy Ghost, he became the man of the spirit, and was the man of the law no longer; and now his work was to contend with spiritual wickedness in all these forms, with Satan personally, with demons inhabiting men, with diseases, storms and tempests and every created thing. Formerly he was putting his flesh under the law, and by his legal conformity, did present flesh without one uncleanness, and now having used the flesh for God's glory, having redeemed his body from under the law, he receiveth the adoption of Son of God publicly at his baptism, and is now to use his body for the more glorious end of commanding and subduing the rebellious creation, both visible and invisible, which also was an original design in the creation of man, to have dominion. But before the man can receive dominion over the outward world, he must first use dominion over his own flesh, and bring it into accordance with the mind of God. This having to do completely and perfectly through all the stages of a man's life, through all the offices of man from childhood to mature manhood, always and alike perfect, though growing in wisdom and in favour with God and man, he is put in trust with the spirit, and his twelve legions of angels ready harnessed at his word. And this inexhaustible strength of God, the holy man Jesus is required to wield as God doth wield it. Having far more than a giant's strength, he is to shew what weakness and affront, and persecution he can himself personally bear; what bounty, and grace, and goodness he can bring upon that land and upon those people who are ever doing him wrong. And all the power of man, whether actually enjoyed by Adam, or to have been enjoyed if he had stood, being now put upon Jesus the second man, having occupied as God himself wished, yea, delighted to behold, he hath accomplished man's work completely and hath but to die in order to rise again with the long expected, long promised reward of immortality and life. Thus did the Lord Jesus present his body spotless upon the cross, – thus did he present in his words and actions the very life of God in flesh, thus did he bring forth the new form of the spiritual man in all his power and patience, in all his suffering and glory, – thus did he perfect holiness in the fear of God, – and thus did he redeeem the soul and the body of man from all evils, and, notwithstanding of all the temptations of the devil, the world and the flesh, did in all things what was well pleasing in the sight of God.[13]

This excerpt and the previous one are typical expressions of the fulfillment of Irving's earlier desire to 'present believers with a real life; a suffering, mortal flesh; a real death and a real resurrection of this flesh of ours' and to explain *how* Christ had 'an identity of life' with us.[14] In his earlier tract he had also said that an intelligible and unquestionable statement was called for which would show that the Holy Spirit did not play a subsidiary part in the whole of Christ's work:

I confess myself totally unable to see any part which the Holy Ghost had in this greatest work of the Trinity, – bringing the Son into the world, and by him redeeming all creation from the power of the devil, – if either of these two errors we are contending against be maintained, namely, that Christ had an unfallen nature, or that he had a human nature rendered intrinsically and inherently holy of itself by the miraculous generation. On the last hypothesis, the Holy Ghost had a hand in the generation of the substance by mixing his Divine nature with it, which is heresy; or by a new work of creation, which I have shewn above to be little better. But was the work of redemption or incarnation finished in the act and instant of the miraculous generation? Certainly in the person of Christ it was not finished till his resurrection; in the Church it is not finished yet; in the world it is not yet begun. Now what we want is such an intelligible and unquestionable statement of the acting of the Holy Ghost in this work from first to last; as shall shew him acting no subsidiary part, but that very part which is proper to him as a co-equal consubstantial person of the blessed trinity. We have the Father ever active in supporting the fallen creature; we must also have the Holy Ghost ever active in some equally continuous and necessary way of action.[15]

In *Christ's Holiness in Flesh* he gave just 'such an intelligible and unquestionable statement of the acting of the Holy Ghost in this work from first to last' and demonstrated explicitly what he had stated implicitly when he demanded that the Holy Spirit be shown to have an equality with the Father and the Son and be 'ever active in some equally continuous and necessary way of action'. The second half of this paragraph from *The Orthodox and Catholic Doctrine of Our Lord's Human Nature* is a declaration of this intent which he succeeded in carrying out in *Christ's Holiness in Flesh* and which summarizes his final and most extensive reflections on this subject:

And this we exhibit from the first in his generation, which put Holy-Ghost life into the human substance; then in his holy life, which was the life of a regenerate man, a continual Holy-Ghost life (*Luke* 1); in his miracles, and knowledge, and wisdom, which was by the anointing of the same Holy Ghost (*Isa.* 11:1, 62:1, etc.); in his spotless, guiltless death, which was by the same Holy Ghost (*Heb.* 9); in his resurrection and ascension unto glory, which was by the same Divine power (*Eph.* 1); in his uniting to himself every one of the Father's election, and feeding them, and sanctifying them and glorifying them, which is by the same Spirit, by the same life which he received of the Father (*John* 6). Throughout I see the Godhead of the Father, Son, and Holy Ghost acting to the redemption, sanctification, and eternal glorification of the substance of manhood, with all its dependencies of creation; and yet there is no mixture of the uncreated essence of Godhead with the creature, no confusion, nor conversion, nor change of any sort.[16]

PART TWO

5

The Second Sermon on Baptism

THE FOUNDATION stone of the National Scotch Church, Regent Square was laid on 1st July, 1824.[1] The building was completed three years later and was opened for public worship on 11th May, 1827.[2] It was 'immediately before the first sacrament thereafter' that Irving found himself 'called upon to open to my people the subject of the sacraments'.[3] He preached a series of sermons on the sacrament of Baptism, in the second of which, called 'The Sealing Virtue of Baptism', he gave an exposition of the text 'Repent and be baptized every one of you in the name of Jesus Christ for the remission of sins, and ye shall receive the gift of the Holy Ghost.' (*Acts* 2:38, 39.)[4] After dealing with the first part of the text, that is, repentance and remission of sins, he moved on to consider the meaning of 'and ye shall receive the gift of the Holy Ghost'.[5] He said that receiving the gift of the Holy Spirit was traditionally understood to mean 'the inward gift of sanctification and fruitfulness' but not 'the outward gift of power' which was thought to have ceased after the close of the age of the apostles. He said that he could not see why the baptized Church should not still receive the complete gift of the Holy Spirit 'as it had been received by Jesus Christ when he ascended into glory and which was poured out upon his Church on the day of Pentecost' and why this gift should not still be in operation in the Church 'in all the ways recorded in the book of Acts and the apostolic letters'. He could find no text in Scripture to the contrary:

> The other part of the dispensation of the grace of God under which the baptized are brought is expressed in these words: 'And ye shall receive the gift of the Holy Ghost.' By which, they say, we ought to understand, not the outward gift of power which hath ceased, but the inward gift of sanctification and fruitfulness, which all believe to be co-essential in the salvation of a sinner with the work of Christ itself.

But for my own part, I am inclined to understand both; for I cannot find by what writ of God any part of the spiritual gift was irrevocably removed from the Church. I see, indeed, that she hath lost the power which heretofore made her terrible as an army with banners; so also hath she lost the bright and glorious raiment which made her fair as the moon and clear as the sun; but why she may not hope, yea assuredly believe, to have the former, when the Lord shall see it good, as well as the latter, is what I cannot see, the one being truly as supernatural a work of God as is the other.[6]

This, he said, had become obvious to him from the plain meaning of Scripture. Many texts clearly indicated this. For instance: 'Because that on the Gentiles also was poured out the gift of the Holy Ghost: for they heard them speak with tongues and magnify God' (*Acts* 10:45, 46) and Paul's list of the Spirit's workings: 'But the manifestation of the Spirit is given to every man to profit withal. For to one is given by the Spirit the word of wisdom; to another the word of knowledge by the same Spirit; to another faith by the same Spirit; to another the gifts of healing by the same Spirit; to another the working of miracles; to another prophecy; to another discerning of spirits; to another divers kinds of tongues; to another the interpretation of tongues: but all these worketh that one and the selfsame Spirit, dividing to every man severally as he will.' (*I Cor.* 12:7–11.) The absence of these operations of the Spirit should not prevent the expectation of them. There is no Scriptural authority for dividing up the gift of the Spirit into that which is extraordinary and that which is ordinary, 'and, upon the strength of this arbitrary division, to say the former was never intended to be continued, but the latter only'.[7] The real reason for the absence of the extraordinary is lack of faith. In the early days of the Church, her faith was great and so therefore was her possession of the Spirit. But gradually over the years, her faith waned and so the outward evidence of the Spirit began to disappear. By turning away from her full inheritance in Christ, she turned God's bounty into His judgement:

> I will never cease to use the withdrawal of these gifts as an argument of our being under the judgement and the wrath of God; while I regard that account of the matter with which we content ourselves – that the extraordinary have been withdrawn from us, but the ordinary remain – as a poor shift to remove the blame off from our shoulders, and as making an unworthy use of the Divine purpose and intention.[8]

He saw a parallel between the decline and fall of the Jewish state and the apostasy of the Gentile Church. He felt that it should be taken as a matter for deep humility and the cause for repentance 'that we have been brought into this state of impotency, which argues a like state of unholiness'.[9] For inward holiness and outward power are the two expressions of 'the dispensations of the Spirit unto his Church'. He was convinced that all the baptized were still 'baptized into the fulness of the spiritual gifts' and that according as God is pleased to distribute them, the operations of the Spirit as in *I Cor.* 12:7–11, are for every baptized person for 'these are the signs of the Spirit's presence'.

He then went on to speak of 'the inward gift of sanctification and fruitfulness'. The fruit of the Spirit is 'love, joy, peace, long-suffering, gentleness, goodness, faith, meekness and temperance'. (*Gal.* 5:22, 23.) He illustrated this further from *Eph.* 5:9; *Rom.* 8:12 and 9–18. The sermon then moved from exposition to application.

Since baptism is 'that solemn transaction of the Church, whereby she doth introduce believers, and the children of believers, into the inheritance of the Holy Ghost'[10] it was clear that his congregation and the Church at large had been deprived of these things because of their 'unbelief in that great and gracious promise of the Holy Ghost' which Christ received for all men at His ascension and which He wished to give to all those on whom 'His Father hath bestowed faith to receive it'. This is 'the sum and substance' of sound theology:

> That the Lord Jesus Christ, in virtue of His incarnation and humiliation to the death, hath received from the Father the gift of the Holy Spirit, – regeneration, resurrection, and eternal life, with all power in heaven and in earth; which now lie all treasured up in Him, not for selfish enjoyment, but for right welcome communication unto every one who hath received faith from the Father to apprehend and possess them.[11]

We know that the Father wants to give us faith because He has sent His Son to save sinners and after bringing Him through the experience of sinners, He has exalted Him and has 'put into His hands this infinite store of righteousness and power for the express purpose of distribution to the Church.'[12] Since we have been sealed into His Church by baptism, what is there to prevent us praying to the Father for faith that the gift of the Holy Spirit may be received from Christ?

And being thus taught that it is of God's good purpose to set His seal upon a Church, and perceiving that seal to be baptism, with which we have been sealed, what letteth or hindereth, what moveth not, what stirreth not up to draw near to the Father with all humble request and reverend acknowledgment of His only will, His sovereign right to save or to destroy; and to entreat him with all earnestness to have mercy upon us, and grant us faith, that we may receive the Holy Spirit from the hands of Christ, and so testify to the glory of the Father and the Son?[13]

Such prayers are bound to be answered because He loves to give the Holy Spirit to those who ask Him.

This was the first time that Irving had articulated his belief in the supernatural manifestations of the gifts of the Spirit. He says that from that time onwards he was firm in his conviction about these things:

From that time onwards I never ceased to believe that the spiritual gifts and the spiritual office-bearers as they are enumerated in Scripture (*I Cor.* 12:4–11; *Eph.* 4:7–17; *Rom.* 12.:6–9; *Pet.* 4:10, 11, etc.), together with the various supernatural methods of operation recorded in the Gospels and the Acts of the Apostles, are not accidental and temporary occurrences of a miraculous kind for certain special ends and occasions, but substantial and permanent forms of operation proper to the Holy Ghost, and in no wise to be separated from Him or from the Church, which is his chosen residence and temple, the 'body of Christ', and 'the fulness of Him who filleth all in all'.[14]

This affirmation of faith is misleading. It was only true with qualifications, reservations and hesitations. It was his custom when preaching to 'go regularly'[15] through a doctrine following a lectionary or doctrinal theme over many Sundays. He was a systematic, expository and doctrinal preacher.[16] He had preached this sermon as one in a series on the doctrine of Baptism and it was only in that context that he had touched on the subject of spiritual gifts at all. It was only as he applied himself to the meaning of *Acts* 2:39, that the matter presented itself to him. Having dealt with it, he continued with his baptismal theme and did not return to it nor preach on it again as a topic in itself. The reason for this was that the conviction he had here expressed regarding spiritual gifts had clashed with another conviction even closer to his heart and had produced a conflict in his mind which he could not resolve. This other conviction was his belief that, because of her unfaithfulness, the Gentile Church was under the judgement of God and that because of this the gifts of the Spirit had been withdrawn.[17] He expressed this contradictory belief in the same sermon:

> That it was a part of the Divine purpose to bring the Gentile Church under this deprivation of the Holy Ghost, as he formerly did bring the Jewish Church under blindness and deafness to the voice of their prophets, there can be no doubt: but, in like manner as they are continually rebuked, and were at length cast out from being the Lord's people, for this very cause, so do we underlie a present rebuke; and it ought to be the continual argument of the preachers of the truth, and to form the grounds of continual admonition and warning of judgement speedily about to come.[18]

Irving's understanding of the apostasy of the Gentile Church was closely linked to his belief in the imminence of the Second Advent.[19] One sign of God's judgement on the unfaithful was 'this deprivation of the Holy Ghost'. This was also a sign of the nearness of the Lord's return. According to these two doctrines, the gifts of the Spirit would not be restored to the Church until the millennial advent and reign of Christ, in spite of the fact that the Scriptures made it clear to him that they were the permanent endowment of the baptized Church. Irving is being more honest when he speaks of the real dilemma in which he found himself, in the following passage:

> But while I was convinced so long ago of the undoubted right which the Church hath in all the manifestations of the Holy Ghost made by Christ and his apostles, and that her unfaithfulness was the only cause for their disappearance, it was not so clear to me that they would be restored again anterior to the time of his second advent, when all things shall be reconstituted (*Acts*, 2:21), and the complete inheritance shall be brought to us, whereof this seal of the Spirit is only the earnest and the first-fruits (*Eph.* 1:14). For though I saw clearly and beyond question that this, like all 'the gifts and callings of God, is without repentance' (*Rom.* 11:29) on his part, it was then doubtful to my mind whether or not the Church of Christ, like the Jewish nation, might not have been ejected from her rightful possessions, and left to famine and misery of spiritual good until the times of refreshing shall come from the presence of the Lord and he shall send forth Jesus Christ, 'which before was preached unto us' (*Acts*, 3:19, 20).[20]

He admitted that if he had applied himself to the Scriptures concerning 'the resolution of this doubt', he would have seen that he was wrong to have allowed his convictions regarding the Gentile Apostasy or the Second Advent to come between him and the explicit teaching of such passages as *John* 14, 15 and 16 and such texts as 'He that believeth in me, the works which I do shall he do also and greater works than these shall ye do, because I go to the Father' (*John* 14:12) and 'These signs shall follow them that believe; In my name they shall cast out devils; they shall speak with new tongues; they shall take up serpents; and if they drink any deadly thing, it shall not hurt them; they shall lay hands on the sick, and they shall recover.' (*Mark* 16:17, 18.) It was quite clear from such promises that all these operations were always and immediately available to the faith of every believer.

With this dichotomy unresolved, there could be no advance in his thinking. The question remained unanswered for the next three years. In the meantime he became absorbed in 'the full preaching of Christ's coming in our flesh, and his coming again in glory'.[21] Of this period he wrote:

> Being occupied with the ministry of these two great truths – Christ's union with us by the one flesh, and our present union with him by the one Spirit – I had not made sure in my own mind, nor taught my people to look or to pray for the restoration of the spiritual gifts, but confined myself to the confession of our sins and the sins of our fathers, for which they had ceased, and to the bewailing of our low and abject state before the Lord.[22]

6

The Evidence of the Work
of the Holy Spirit in the
West of Scotland

1828 to 1830

IN THE summer of 1828, while on a preaching tour in the West
of Scotland, Irving met a young licentiate of the Church of
Scotland, Alexander J. Scott, son of the Rev. Dr. Scott of Greenock.[1] He was looking for a missionary assistant to help him with 'The
Mission of the National Church, Regent Square' which had just been
instituted as a further work of outreach to the neighbourhood and to
London Scots.[2] After some hesitation based on doctrinal uncertainty,
Sandy Scott accepted an invitation to fill this post and began work in
August of that year.[3] Irving described him as 'a most precious youth –
the finest and strongest faculty for theology I ever met with'.[4] During
the two years he spent as missionary at Regent Square, he exercised
his strong faculty for theology on Irving, particularly with respect to
his belief that the spiritual gifts should still be in operation in the
Church. Irving agreed with him that this should be so, but his other
theological presuppositions prevented him from believing that it
could or would be so. He was impressed but unmoved by his discussions with Scott:

> He was at that time my fellow-labourer in the National Scotch
> Church, being our missionary to preach to the poor of this city; and
> as we went in and out together, he used often to signify to me his con-
> viction that the spiritual gifts ought still to be exercised in the Church;
> that we are at liberty, and indeed bound to pray for them, as being
> baptized into the assurance of the 'gift of the Holy Ghost', as well as of

'repentance and remission of sins' (*Acts*, 2;38). When I used on these occasions, to propose to him my difficulty, lest for our father's transgressions we should have been adjudged to the loss of our inheritance until our Redeemer should come, he never failed to make answer, that though we were baptized into the one body, the Church, we were called to act thereon upon our several responsibilities as persons; that the promise is to every believer personally, who, receiving of the same, do by their several gifts constitute the body and membership of the Church. Though I could make no answer to this, and it is altogether unanswerable, I continued still very little moved to seek myself or to stir up my people to seek these spiritual treasures.[5]

While Irving remained in this parlous condition, aggravated by Scott's precocious theological faculty, certain events were taking place in parts of the West of Scotland, which, as they were communicated to him, began to move him more than theological debate and which were eventually to have a decisive influence on his thought and action.

During the spring of 1828 in Port Glasgow, Renfrewshire, a young man named James Macdonald received a conversion experience while alone at prayer in his house.[6] A few weeks later his twin brother George also testified to having been converted to saving faith in Jesus Christ.[7] They were followed in this at intervals by their sisters. As ship builders they were not well versed in theology and at first their knowledge of doctrine was very limited. They read no book but the Bible and were soon convinced from the Scriptures of the following doctrines:

1. Assurance; from the text 'Believe in the Lord Jesus Christ and thou shalt be saved.' They knew they were believers and therefore felt assured of their salvation.
2. God's universal love. The love which they had received made them love and desire the salvation of all men. They could not think that the author of this love desired less.
3. The real humanity of Christ. This was taught them from the book of Psalms when they realized from the New Testament references that the Psalms had been the experience of Christ.
4. Christ's millennial advent and reign. They could not help seeing this from many Scripture passages.
5. The continuance of the miraculous gifts of the Spirit in the Church This they also saw in the Scriptures.[8]

The first two of these doctrines were associated with the ministry of John McLeod Campbell, who had been preaching Assurance of Salvation and the Universal love of God since his ordination to the parish of Row (Rhu) near Helensburgh in 1825. At that time opposition was growing to his views and he was soon to be brought before the courts of the Church for heresy on both these points. The last three of these doctrines were associated with the ministry of Irving, as has already been shown. Because of this, the Macdonald brothers were soon regarded as disciples of Campbell and Irving and were considered to be doubly heretical. Irving's views were well known in the neighbourhood because of his recent preaching tour and Campbell's word had 'leavened all that land':

> Prayer and worship, in the spirit of what seemed a recovery of the true Gospel message, became the first interest of many households and groups; 'thousands were converted, and a confidence in God was awakened in them such as they had never before experienced'. 'Mr. Campbell's new light,' writes a contemporary reviewer, 'created no small stir round the Gareloch and all over the land. There was an awakening of religious life there, which got its first impulse from the Row-kirk. Greenock, Glasgow, Edinburgh thrilled as with the gush of a fresh spring-tide. On the southern shore of the Clyde estuary at Port Glasgow, across the water from Roseneath, lived another family which had been deeply moved by this religious revival. The heads of the family were twin brothers, George and James Macdonald.[9]

During the summer of 1828 another young man called James Grubb, who was lying ill with an incurable disease, received a conversion experience with the assurance of salvation. From then on, from his sick bed, he exercised a remarkable ministry of evangelism and spiritual discernment, until he died.[10] There was also a friend of the Macdonald's who, before dying in the summer of 1829, testified to having seen a vision of the glory of God.[11] Irving had met James Grubb in May 1828 when on the same preaching tour during which he had been introduced to Sandy Scott. He was kept informed of the details of these events by one of his deacons who came from that district and who heard regularly from his relatives there. He gives his own account of his knowledge of these events:

> There appeared about this time, in the death-bed experience of certain holy persons, very wonderful instances of the power of God's

63

Spirit, both in the way of discernment and utterance, and also apparent glory. They were able to know the condition of God's people at a distance, and to pray for the very things which they needed; they were able to search the hearts of persons in their presence; they were above measure strengthened to hold out both in prayer and exhortation. In one instance, the countenance shone with a glorious brightness, as if it had been the face of an angel; they spake much of a bright dawn about to arise in the Church; and one of them, just before death, signified that he had received the knowledge of the thing that was about to be manifested, but he was too far gone to give it utterance. It came like a halo over the soul of the departing saint, to cheer him on his way; but it was not intended for communication.[12]

These things were confirmed by Sandy Scott who was on holiday at his father's manse in Greenock in the autumn of 1829 and who, after enquiring into the details of these events, 'was stronger than ever in his conviction that the gifts of the Holy Ghost would be restored and that speedily'.[13] During his stay there, Scott shared his belief in the availability of the manifestations of the Spirit to all believers, with 'some of the godly people in those parts'. Among these was a young woman called Mary Campbell from Fernicarry on the Gareloch, whose sister Isabella, like James Grubb and the others noted, had recently died after a short life of great holiness which had attracted much attention and even veneration.[14] Mary was also known for her piety and she too was lying seriously ill from the same consumption. When Scott visited her he tried 'to convince her of the distinction between regeneration and baptism with the Holy Ghost',[15] telling her that the former came from the incarnation and the latter from the glorification of the Son of God but although, as Irving well knew, his 'power of statement and argument . . . is unequalled by that of any man', he failed to change the decided convictions of this 'woman of very fixed and constant spirit'.[16] Before he left her however, he urged her to reread the Acts of the Apostles with the distinction he had made in her mind and not to reject what he believed to be the truth of God before giving it serious consideration.

It was in December that she did eventually read, not Acts, but John 14, 15 and 16, with Scott's distinction in mind and saw all that she read in a completely new light. She saw for the first time that the human nature of Christ was in itself the same as every man's, and that His holiness was not inherent but sustained by the Son of God acting

faith on it by the Holy Spirit. This was what Irving had believed and
and taught in all his writings on the human nature of Christ since
1825:

> She saw the truth of our Lord's human nature, which in itself was
> no other than our own, and derived the virtues of immaculate holiness
> and superhuman power from no passive quality, but from an active
> operation thereon of the Son of God by the Holy Ghost. She came to
> see what for six or seven years I had been preaching in London, that
> all the works of Christ were done by the man anointed with the Holy
> Ghost, and not by the God mixing himself up with the man. The person
> is the Son of God; the bounds which he hath consented to speak and
> act in are the bounds of mortal manhood; the power by which, when
> within these narrow bounds, he doth such mighty things, against and
> above the course of nature, death, and hell, is the power of the Holy
> Ghost; and the end of the whole mystery of his incarnation is to show
> unto mortal men what every one of them, through faith in his name,
> shall be able to perform; as it is written in the first of these chapters,
> 'Verily, verily, I say unto you, He that believeth on me, the works
> which I do shall he do also, and greater works than these shall he do,
> because I go unto my Father' (*John*, 14:12).[17]

The effect of this discovery so thrilled and excited her that she
could scarcely sleep for thinking about it. The text which kept going
through her mind was 'How God anointed Jesus of Nazareth with the
Holy Ghost and with power, who went about doing good, and healing
all that were oppressed of the devil; for God was with him.' (*Acts* 10:
38). She soon saw the implications of this:

> She straightway argued, if Jesus as a man in my nature thus spake
> and thus performed mighty works by the Holy Ghost, which he even
> promiseth to me, then ought I in the same nature, by the same Spirit,
> to do likewise 'the works which he did, and greater works than these'.[18]

She wrote a letter to Irving on 16th January, 1830 in which she
expressed her joy at the realization of this truth, its implications and
finally its application to all and especially to herself. Irving describes
the contents of this letter:

> It contains the first overflowings of a soul filled with the glorious
> truth, that every baptized man should, through the indwelling of the
> Spirit of Christ and the presence of the Comforter, shew forth the same
> signs and wonders as Christ did, 'that the Father might be glorified in

the Son'; as it is written (*Mark*, 16:17), 'And THESE SIGNS shall follow them THAT BELIEVE: in my name they shall cast out devils; they shall speak with new tongues; they shall take up serpents; and if they drink any deadly thing, it shall not hurt them; they shall lay hands on the sick, and they shall recover.' This letter is remarkable as containing the true view of bodily suffering as a manifestation of Satan's power in this sinful flesh of ours, which Christ took in order to cast him and keep him out of it. With these emphatic, and, in her own case, prophetic words, the letter concludes: 'You cannot conceive the effect which this view of suffering has upon me. I am indeed most painfully exercised in mind when I think of it, and am sometimes forced to exclaim, why should I, seeing I am a daughter of Abraham, be so long bound to the *devil*? Pray for me, my dear friend, in reference to this thing.'[19]

Mary Campbell continued to rejoice in this new understanding of Scripture and in the possibility that it might affect her experientially. In February and March she was planning to be a missionary although physically her health was still deteriorating.[20] She spent much time in meditation and prayer. On Sunday 30th March, one of her sisters and her friend had been spending the day at Fernicarry in prayer and fasting. Their prayers were especially for the restoration of spiritual gifts. In the evening they went upstairs to have a time of prayer with Mary:

> They had come up in the evening to the sick chamber of their sister, who was laid on a sofa, and, along with one or two others of the household, they were engaged in prayer together. When, in the midst of their devotion, the Holy Ghost came with mighty power upon the sick woman as she lay in her weakness, and constrained her to speak at great length, and with superhuman strength, in an unknown tongue, to the astonishment of all who heard, and to her own great edification and enjoyment in God.[21]

Some days later James Macdonald, on the other side of the Clyde at Port Glasgow, was 'endowed with the power of the Holy Ghost' and through his ministry, first his sister Margaret and then Mary Campbell were miraculously and immediately healed. Another of the Macdonald sisters gave an account of these events:

> For several days Margaret had been so unusually ill that I quite thought her dying, and on appealing to the doctor, he held out no hope of her recovery unless she were able to go through a course of powerful medicine, which he acknowledged to be in her case impossible. She

66

had scarcely been able even to have her bed made for a week. Mrs. —— and myself had been sitting quietly at the bedside, when the power of the Spirit came upon her. She said 'there will be a mighty baptism of the Spirit this day', and then broke forth in a most marvellous setting forth of the wonderful works of God, and as if her own weakness had been altogether lost in the strength of the Holy Ghost, continued with little or no intermission for two or three hours, in mingled praise, prayer and exhortation. At dinner time James and George came home as usual, whom she then addressed at great length, concluding with a solemn prayer for James that he might *at that time* be endowed with the power of the Holy Ghost. Almost instantly James calmly said, 'I have got it.' He walked to the window and stood silent for a minute or two. I looked at him and almost trembled, there was such a change upon his whole countenance. He then with a step and manner of the most indescribable majesty, walked up to Margaret's bedside and addressed her in those words of the twentieth psalm, 'arise and stand upright'. He repeated the words, took her by the hand, and she arose; then we all quietly sat down and took our dinner. After it my brother went to the building yard as usual, where James wrote over to Miss Campbell commanding her in the name of the Lord to arise. The next morning, after breakfast James said, I am going down to the quay to see if Miss Campbell is come across the water: at which we expressed our surprise, as he had said nothing to us of having written to her. The result showed how much he knew of what God had done and would do for her, for she came as he expected, declaring herself perfectly whole. Rumour of all that had passed soon got abroad, and for two days our house was scarcely ever empty of visitors. Satan was busy also, trying to create confusion, and mar the work of God, and unhappily too far succeeded in some, to our grief but especially that of James, than whom no one could more anxiously watch against the minglings of the devil and the flesh.[22]

Mary Campbell gave her own account of her healing in a letter written on her recovery:

On the Saturday previous to my restoration to health, I was very ill, suffering from pain in my chest and breathlessness. On the Sabbath, I was very ill, and lay for several hours in a state of insensibility. Next day I was worse than I had been for several weeks previous (the agony of the Saturday excepted). On Tuesday I was no better. On Wednesday I did not feel quite so languid but was suffering some pain from breathing and palpitation of my heart. Two individuals who saw me about four hours before my recovery, said that I could never be strong; that I was not to expect a *miracle to be wrought upon me*: it was not long after until I received dear brother James Macdonald's letter, giving an account of his sister's being raised up, and commanding me *to rise and walk*. I had scarcely read the first page when I became quite overpowered, and laid it aside for a few minutes; but I had no rest in my mind until I took it up again, and began to read. As I read every word came home with power, and when I came to the command to arise, it came home with a power which no words can describe; it was felt to be indeed the voice of Christ; it was such a voice as could not be resisted; a mighty power was instantaneously exerted upon me: I felt as if I had been lifted from off the earth, and all my diseases taken from off me at the voice of Christ. I was verily made in a moment to stand upon my feet, leap and walk, sing and rejoice.[23]

A few evenings later, on Friday 18th April, George Macdonald spoke in tongues. He was followed by James. The next night they spoke in tongues again and also interpreted.[24] James Macdonald recorded these events in a letter the next day, Sunday 20th April:

On Friday evening while we were all met for prayer, utterance was given to George in an unknown tongue, and next to me. It is manifestly out of ourselves: *we have no more power over it than a trumpet has over its sounds*, – I mean control as to forming the words; for the spirits of the prophets are subject to the prophets, in as far as they can refrain from speaking. On Saturday Mr. C. came over, and my mouth was again opened. He said, it is written 'pray that ye may interpret'; he accordingly prayed. I was then made to speak in short sentences which George interpreted one by one. The first word of interpretation was 'Behold he cometh – Jesus cometh.'[25]

Meanwhile Irving in London was continuing to preach 'Christ's coming in our flesh, and his coming again in glory'.[26] He was now nearing the climax of the controversy on the former while his understanding of the latter kept him from expecting or praying for the restoration of spiritual gifts. He had been informed of the earlier 'very wonderful instances of the power of God's Spirit, both in the way of discernment and utterance and also apparent glory'. Scott had told him of his increased 'conviction that the gifts of the Holy Ghost would be restored, and that speedily'. He had received letters from Mary Campbell telling him of her acceptance of his understanding of the relation of the Spirit to the human nature of Jesus Christ. Yet the news of the actual restoration of the gifts, while

68

causing him great joy, came as something of a shock and a surprise, as he and his congregation continued 'the bewailing of our low and abject state before the Lord'.[27]

> Thus we stood, when the tidings of the restoration of the gift of tongues in the West of Scotland burst upon us like the morning star heralding the approach of day, and turned our speculations upon the true doctrine into the examination of a fact.[28]

He said that when he heard this news he felt like parents who, after believing that their family had been lost at sea for many years suddenly heard of children who had been discovered on an island 'answering in feature and in form, in age and in number, to the dear offspring whose loss they had so long lamented'.[29] He was filled with 'joyful hope', 'trembling anxiety' and the desire for 'earnest and careful search'. Although he did 'rejoice with great joy' when the tidings were read to him, coming as they did 'through a most reliable channel', he was anxious not to trust any evidence that he had not been able to authenticate himself. He had not yielded to the arguments of his own preaching or to the theological acumen of Sandy Scott. Since the acceptance of this news would mean not only a readjustment of his own theological schema but also possibly a revolution in the Church, he was determined to be particularly cautious and careful in his investigations before he gave his approval.[30] Of this news he went on to say:

> I felt it to be a matter of too great concern to yield up my faith to anything but the clearest evidence, and at the same time of so great importance as not to leave a stone unturned in order to come at the truth; for if it should turn out to be true, I perceived at once that it would revolutionize the Church and make such an upturning as the world had not seen. I had the amplest means of obtaining information, first from eye and ear witnesses, men of reputation, elders of the church, then from many of the most spiritual members of my flock, who went down to see and hear, and finally from the gifted persons themselves.[31]

7

Confirmation of the Evidence

Summer 1830

DURING THE summer, Irving continued to receive information from those involved. 'Eye and ear witnesses, men of reputation, elders of the church' who he knew in the area of Port Glasgow and the Gareloch, kept him posted as he endeavoured to leave no 'stone unturned in order to come at the truth'.[1] There was plenty of information to be passed on because manifestations continued to be in evidence at prayer meetings in the Macdonald's house and at large gatherings in Helensburgh at which Mary Campbell wrote in tongues and prophesied.[2] These activities produced something of a national sensation and much literature began to be published about them. Large crowds gathered from all over the country. One of the Macdonald sisters wrote on the 18th May 'Ever since Margaret was raised and the gift of tongues given, the house has been filled every day with people from all parts of England, Scotland and Ireland.'[3] In Helensburgh it was recorded that Mary Campbell had attracted 'merchants, divinity students, writers to the Signet, advocates' and 'gentlemen who rank high in society come from Edinburgh'.[4] It was an issue of spiritual importance and all felt called upon to decide for themselves whether or not these gifts were genuine. Many came to the conclusion that they were pretentious counterfeits but many more did not. The Rev. Robert Story who was the parish minister at Roseneath and who knew the Campbell family intimately, went to visit Mary especially to judge for himself.[5] After doing so he wrote to the Rev. Dr. Thomas Chalmers, Professor of Divinity at Edinburgh who was eager for a first-hand opinion, 'I am persuaded you will be prepared to conclude that these things are of God and not of men.'[6]

Irving received reports of all these things from his friends in the area. He then received further information from 'many of the most spiritual members of my flock, who went down to see and hear'.[7] Towards the end of August a party of six of his members led by Mr. John Bate Cardale, a solicitor, travelled North from London and spent three weeks in Port Glasgow to see and hear for themselves.[8]

They met the increasing number of those who had received spiritual gifts and attended numerous prayer meetings at which the gifts were in operation. At the time of their return, Irving was on a preaching tour in Ireland.[9]

When he returned he discovered that 'Mr. Henderson and Dr. Thompson are fully convinced of the reality of the hand of God in the west country work, and so is Mr. Cardale.'[10] Mr. Cardale gave a very favourable report on all they had seen and heard. It was published in the December issue of *The Morning Watch*. After describing the manner and matter of the gifts which he witnessed in operation and the lives of the gifted, he gave a testimony to both:

> These persons, while uttering the unknown sounds, as also while speaking in the Spirit in their own language, have every appearance of being under supernatural direction. The manner and voice are (speaking generally) different from what they are at other times, and on ordinary occasions. This difference does not consist merely in the peculiar solemnity and fervour of manner (which they possess), but their whole deportment gives an impression, not to be conveyed in words, that their organs are made use of by supernatural power. In addition to the outward appearances, their own declarations, as the declarations of honest, pious, and sober individuals, may with propriety be taken in evidence. They declare that their organs of speech are made use of by the Spirit of God; and that they utter that which is given to them, and not the expressions of their own conceptions, or their own intention. But I had numerous opportunities of observing a variety of facts fully confirmatory of this. . . .
>
> In addition to what I have already stated, I have only to add my most decided testimony, that so far as three weeks' constant communication, and the information of those in the neighbourhood, can enable me to judge (and I conceive that the opportunity I enjoyed enabled me to form a correct judgement), the individuals thus gifted are persons living in close communion with God, and in love towards Him, and towards all men; abounding in faith and joy and peace; having an abhorrence of sin, and a thirst for holiness, with an abasement of self and yet with a hope full of immortality, such as I never witnessed

71

elsewhere, and which I find nowhere recorded but in the history of the early church: and just as they are fervent in spirit, so are they diligent in the performance of all the relative duties of life. They are totally devoid of anything like fanaticism or enthusiasm; but, on the contrary, are persons of great simplicity of character, and of sound common sense. They have no fanciful theology of their own: they make no pretensions to deep knowledge: they are the very opposite of sectarians, both in conduct and principle: they do not assume to be teachers: they are not deeply read; but they seek to be taught of God, in the perusal of, and meditation on, his revealed word, and to 'live quiet and peaceable lives in all godliness and honesty'.[11]

Shortly after Mr. Cardale and his party returned to London, the lay theologian Thomas Erskine of Linlathen arrived in Port Glasgow to assess the movement. He stayed for six weeks in the Macdonald's house and took part in the daily prayer meetings, witnessing many spiritual manifestations. He had visited them briefly before as early as May and had declared himself to be 'more overpowered by the love, and assurance, and unity seen in their prayers and conversations than by the works'.[12] He now expressed his opinions of what he had experienced in a tract *On the Gifts of the Spirit* which he published before the end of the year. His findings were favourable:

> Whilst I see nothing in Scripture against the re-appearance or rather continuance of miraculous gifts in the Church, but a great deal for it, I must further say that I see a great deal of internal evidence in the West Country to prove their genuine miraculous character, especially in the speaking with tongues. . . . After witnessing what I have witnessed, I cannot think of any person decidedly condemning them as impostors, without a feeling of great alarm. It is certainly not a thing to be lightly or rashly believed, but neither is it a thing to be lightly or rashly rejected. I believe that it is of God.[13]

Erskine amplified this further in a book which he published the following year called *The Brazen Serpent, or Life coming through Death*. In this he affirmed extensively from the Scriptures that miraculous gifts were 'the permanent endowment of the Church' and that 'had the faith of the Church continued pure and full, these gifts of the Spirit would never have disappeared'. He also reaffirmed his own testimony of his experience in Port Glasgow:

> The world dislikes the recurrence of miracles. And yet it is true that miracles have recurred. I cannot but tell what I have seen and heard. I

have heard persons, both men and women, speak with tongues and prophesy, that is, speak in the spirit of edification, exhortation, and comfort.[14]

It was not until the following year that Irving was able to get first-hand information 'from the gifted persons themselves'. By that time he had long since decided that these manifestations were genuinely of God. Indeed he had already decided in their favour before he received Mr. Cardale's official report or read Erskine's tract. His direct contact with those involved together with the testimony of 'eye and ear witnesses' had been enough to convince him. The later reports and meeting with Mary Campbell came only as confirmation. The extensive information which he had already received had enabled him to overcome his theological objections and to yield his faith up to what he took to be the clearest evidence. The conviction expressed in his second baptismal sermon could no longer be repressed by his contradictory understanding of the Gentile Apostasy and the Second Advent. The evidence before him was too authentic and was in accordance not only with his latent belief in spiritual gifts, but also with his expressed convictions regarding the human nature of Christ for which at that moment he was suffering severe opposition in the Church. The testimony of Mary Campbell and the Macdonalds had turned his 'speculations upon the true doctrine' of the human nature of Christ 'into the examination of a fact'.[15] The development of Mary Campbell's theological understanding which led up to the manifestations of the Spirit in her, confirmed independently by the parallel understanding and experience of the Macdonalds, had made him face the implications of his own teaching on the human nature of Christ.

If the evidence of the gifts of the Spirit should be authenticated by reliable witnesses, then he could not doubt that 'the outward gift of power' should, could and would be manifested in all believers. To do so would be to doubt that understanding of Christ's humanity for which he was about to be arraigned. Mary Campbell and the Macdonald brothers had applied 'what for six or seven years' he 'had been preaching in London' to their condition. Their application of this understanding of the word of God had resulted in manifestations of the works of God. Irving saw that in this way his 'speculations upon the true doctrine' of Christ's humanity had been turned 'into the examination of a fact'. It was his doctrine of the human nature of Christ that stood or fell by the results of the examination of this fact. This was why he 'felt it to be a matter of too great concern to yield up' his 'faith to anything but the clearest evidence'. 'For if it should turn out to be true' then his 'speculations upon the true doctrine' of Christ's human nature would have been validated and authenticated. The arguments which had been put forward by Scott had been 'altogether unanswerable' but still had not moved him. Scott had distinguished between regeneration and baptism with the Holy Spirit and had stressed the texts that indicated that the latter as well as the former was promised 'to every believer personally, who, receiving of the same, do by their several gifts constitute the body and membership of the Church'.[16] His influence on Mary Campbell had been considerable and yet these insights had only been a preparation for the reception of the truth about the reality of Christ's human nature that had come to her as she read *John* 14, 15 and 16. This was the decisive element in her testimony. It was also the decisive factor for Irving and the one that broke down his theological presuppositions which were inconsistent with it and forced them to come into line. Arguments based on the Scriptural authority for the baptism with the Holy Spirit or on the promise of 'the outward gift of power' to every believer, could be fitted into his system of thought regarding the Gentile Apostasy and the Second Advent, and could be effectively rejected. But an argument based on his own beleaguered and almost universally denounced doctrine of Christ's humanity could not. Irving had not thought through the implications of the latter and the time which he took to decide whether or not the spiritual manifestations were of God was also used to adjust himself to the shock of realizing that he must make Mary Campbell's theological conclusions his own or go back on his most dearly held truth regarding the nature of the flesh which Christ assumed. He was therefore not rationalizing his own failure to resolve the conflict which the preaching of his second baptismal sermon had produced or his inability to yield his faith up to the 'unanswerable' propositions of Sandy Scott, when he came to see that his 'full preaching of Christ's coming in our flesh, and his coming again in glory' over the past three years, had been the necessary and essential preparation for the restoration of the gifts of the Spirit.

As he appropriated the implications and consequences of his own theology of Christ's humanity from the thought and experience of Mary Campbell and the Macdonalds he was glad that the dichotomy in his thinking had not been resolved earlier and that because of this he had been led, over a considerable period of time, to develop and to defend the very doctrine which now proved to be decisive in the preparation of the way for the reception of spiritual gifts. Over the past three years he *could* have been convinced from other Scriptural insights:

> But the way had to be prepared by the full preaching of Christ's coming in our flesh, and his coming again in glory – the two great divisions of Christian doctrine which had gone down into the earth, out of sight and out of mind, and which must be revived by preaching before the Holy Spirit could have anything to witness unto; for he doth not witness to any system of man, Calvinistic or Arminian, or to any ordinance of man, Episcopalian or Presbyterian; but to Jesus, who suffered for us in the flesh, who shareth with us his life and power, and cometh with us in glory.[17]

8

The Church's Holiness and Power

THERE WERE many who believed that these manifestations were of the devil or were psychic delusions. Even Sandy Scott could not bring himself to decide that they were definitely of God in spite of his powerful convictions that such things were to be expected. John McLeod Campbell remained reserved and sceptical[1] but Irving had found that the evidence that had come to him by the early summer was sufficient to convince him. His own doctrine assured him of the soundness of the central conviction of Mary Campbell and the Macdonalds regarding the nature of Christ's humanity. He now saw that the manifestations confirmed and vindicated what he regarded as this Orthodox and Catholic truth. On 2nd June he wrote 'The substance of Mary Campbell's and Margaret Macdonald's visions or revelations, given in their papers, carry to me a spiritual conviction and a spiritual reproof which I cannot express.'[2]

Later in the summer he expressed the conclusions he had come to in an article for the September issue of *The Morning Watch* called 'The Church, with her endowment of Holiness and Power' in which, for the first time, he began to develop the thoughts he had mooted in 1827.[3] He reaffirmed all he had then said about 'the outward gift of power' expanding on it with detailed exposition of *Mark* 16:17, 18 and *I Cor.* 12. In spite of his title he speaks little about the Church's endowment of holiness. Holiness is the gift that comes from Christ's life and death and resurrection. Power is the gift that comes from His ascension and glorification, through His reception of the Holy Spirit and outpouring on the day of Pentecost. We have the completeness of the former but only the first fruits of the latter.[4]

These first fruits are to be found in many places in the New Testament and particularly in the two passages selected here for special consideration. In the first of these the signs or actings of Christ which are a foretaste 'of that perfect and complete acting in which He is to go forth when He comes to redeem the body and to redeem the inheritance',[5] are the casting out of devils, the speaking with new tongues, the taking up of serpents, the drinking of deadly poisons without harm and the laying hands on the sick and their recovery. These five signs are indicative of Christ's lordship over all creation:

> For in creation there is no more than these five parts: the pure spirit; the embodied soul of man, the animal creation, and the inanimate world, of all which sin hath taken possession, and over all which Christ hath obtained superiority, to reconstitute them in that way which shall for ever demonstrate the being and attributes of God.[6]

Irving says that his idea of the Church is based on the apostolic teaching of 'the body of Christ' and his understanding of its endowment from the text 'the fulness of Him that filleth all in all.' (*Eph.* 1:23)[7] The whole purpose of redemption is to enable God to purchase for Himself a body in and through which He might show forth His holiness and power:

> The whole mystery of redemption is God's obtaining for Himself such a complete organ of expression and of action in the finiteness of which the attributes of His own infinite being might be truly and fully expressed. To procure for Godhead such a fit organ, the Son and Holy Ghost do, without departing or separating from the Godhead, which is impossible, take connection with the creature, and from a portion thereof do constitute that most seemly and adequate Shechinah of the Eternal God.[8]

The second passage considered, *I Cor.* 12, is all about the meaning of the unity and diversity of the membership of the body of Christ. The members of the body are 'the manifestations of the Spirit'.[9] Paul enumerates these gifts. The first is the word of wisdom and the second is the word of knowledge 'whereof the former refers to mysteries of doctrine which needed exposition; the latter to events, whether past, present, or to come'.[10] The Church of Scotland has preserved both these in her offices of minister and teacher; 'would that the rest had been as carefully preserved!'[11] The next gift is faith, not saving faith for that is something different but 'it is the strong confidence in

Christ's power, in the presence of which power it is done, and without which it cannot be done'.[12] The fourth is 'gifts of healing'. This is for the confirmation of the preached word:

> The word preached is, that Christ hath redeemed men from the power of death; and in sign thereof we do in His name heal all manner of diseases, and upon occasion raise the dead, (as is recorded both of Peter and Paul): and the conclusion is, that the name of Christ is indeed able to effect these things preached. The sign is part and parcel of the thing preached, and by being so confirms it. It is not an appeal to blind power, but it is an appeal to Jesus to confirm the truth preached, by giving a sign of His possessing this power which we preach Him about to perform.[13]

Next comes 'the working of miracles'. A miracle is the turning back of and resistance to the power of nature. Nature has been distorted and misused by Satan. Miracles turn nature back to its pre-fall grace and goodness 'that men might know that cause and effect is only an appointment or permission of God while it pleases Him'.[14] If only men would realize that 'the laws of the material world are not necessary but under the control and in the hands of our merciful Redeemer' there would not be 'the present entire unbelief of a miracle being ever again':

> This power of miracles must either be speedily revived in the Church, or there will be a universal dominion of the mechanical philosophy; and faith will be fairly expelled, to give place to the law of cause and effect acting and ruling in the world of mind, as it doth in the world of sense.[15]

The only check to this would be 'to stop the sun, like Joshua; to make him travel back, like Isaiah; to walk upon the water, like our Lord; or to handle the viper like the apostle Paul'.[16] People today even doubt or deny 'the existence of a will the cause of itself'. Cause and effect dominates all and God is thought of 'merely as a Great First Cause'. Nothing can stop this and 'dethrone this monster from the throne of God' except 'the reawakening of the Church to her long-forgotten privilege of working miracles':

> The miracle-workers in the Church are Christ's hand, to show the strength that is in Him: the healers of diseases are His almoners, to show what pity and compassion are in Him: the faith-administrators are His lion-heart, to show how mighty and fearless He is: and the

utterers of wisdom and knowledge are His mind, to show how rich and capacious it is.[17]

The next gift is prophecy. Paul gives the whole of *I Cor.* 14 to prophecy and regards it as very important. He says that it should be coveted above all other gifts. This is the same gift as that 'which was ministered by the Old Testament prophets'. It is 'the faculty of shewing to all men their true estate in the sight of God, and their nearness to His judgements, and the way of escape; the faculty of doing for persons what they did for kingdoms and cities; foretelling being a part, but only a part of it'.[18] The next comes discerning of spirits. Paul says in *I Cor.* 14:29 'Let two or three prophets speak and let the others discern.' No one person has all the gifts and within the body the prophet needs to be tested by those who have the gift of discernment:

> The prophet needed the guardianship of the discerner of spirits, and the discerner of spirits the instruction of the prophet: the one brought the precious metal from the heavenly treasury, the other essayed it, lest it should have contracted any defilement or intermixture in the transmission.[19]

There are two tests which the discerner must apply to any prophetic utterance. One is that given by John, whether the spirit of the prophet would confess that 'Jesus Christ is come in the flesh' and the other is given by Paul and is whether he would say that 'Jesus is the Lord'. It was very ominous that these were the two points for the holding of which Irving was being prosecuted:

> It is very ominous, that these are the two very points for which we are now being persecuted by many, who deny Christ to have had flesh with the law of flesh; and deny that His lordship is of this earth – alleging that, when Satan shall have served himself of it, it is to be destroyed. I have no doubt whatever that these are doctrines of devils, and that they bespeak a revival of Antichrist in the bosom of the Church.[20]

The next gift is 'divers kinds of tongues'. Irving had carefully studied the gift of tongues. He was sorry that this gift had been 'the occasion of so much scoffing and blasphemy to many'.[21] What was this gift for? He could see that it had three functions. First, it was like an ambassador's commission. Paul spoke in tongues more than all of

79

them (*I Cor.* 14:18,) and he was the greatest missionary. It was a seal for mission.

> And what an assurance to a man's heart, and confirmation to his faith, to have his mission thus ascertained to him, and sealed by the Holy Ghost! Methinks it would be more effectual than a salary of a thousand pounds by the year from the most notable of our missionary societies.[22]

Secondly, tongues shows the unity of Christ with His members. God is seen to be in them 'of a truth, when that power within . . . doth testify to no other person but to Christ'.[23] Union with Christ is an important doctrine. Tongues bears upon this doctrine. Who but God can keep up communication 'between the Father's throne and the world'? How can the limited substance of Christ's soul, which is out of the world, be yet in the world, in the souls of men? only by means of another Being, the Spirit 'proceeding from Christ to the bounds of all space and time, and able to unite them into oneness with Him'. He is of one substance with Christ and is also a person:

> And thus is the Divinity and the Personality of the Comforter made to appear through this great truth of Christ the inhabiter of His people; which, again, is proved by His using their organs in a way in which they themselves are not able to do. Moreover, this power of Christ in the Spirit to speak all the diversities of speech, shows him to be the fountain-head of speech, the Word, by whose endowment man is a word-speaking creature.[24]

Thirdly, tongues shows 'That a person is something more than that community of reason which he doth occupy as the tenant of Him whose name is the Logos, or the Reason.'[25] For *I Cor.* 14 shows clearly that even when the reason is inactive and nothing is understood, a man is edified (v. 4) and is still speaking to God (v. 2):

> What a deep subject of meditation were a man thus employed in secret converse with and enjoyment of God although his reason be utterly dead![26]

The ninth and last gift is the interpretation of tongues which is closely connected with tongues itself. It is not translation. Irving imagines what it would be like if there was an order of tongues speakers and an order of interpreters in the Church. How glorious it would be to hear them:

The unknown tongue, as it began its strange sounds, would be equal to a voice from the glory, 'Thus said the Lord of Hosts', or 'This is my Son, hear ye him'; and every ear would say, 'Oh that I knew the voice'; and when the man with the gift of interpretation gave it out in the vernacular tongue, we would be filled with an awe, that it was no other than God who had spoken it. Methinks it is altogether equal to the speaking with the trumpet from the thick darkness of the Mount, or with a voice as thunder from the open vault of heaven. The using of man's organs is indeed, a mark of a new dispensation, foretold as to come to pass after Christ ascended up on high, when He would receive gifts and bestow them on men, that the Lord God might dwell, might have an habitation, in them. Formerly the sounds were syllabled we know not how, because God had not yet prepared for Himself a tent of flesh; which he accomplished to do first in Jesus of Nazareth, and is now perfecting in His Church, who are His temple, in whom He abideth as in the holy place, and from whom He speaketh forth His oracles in strange tongues. The strange tongue takes away all source of ambiguity, proving that the man himself hath nothing to do with it, and leaves the work and the authority of the word wholly in the hand of God.[27]

Speaking in tongues was the 'greater thing' which Jesus promised would be done by believers.[28] It was the power of God, to blaspheme which was to blaspheme against the Holy Spirit. This was a new thing and God did not even manifest Himself in Christ in this unequivocal way. This was because Christ was a witness to the Father and not to Himself:

Christ came to do the Father's will in our condition, that we in the like case might be assured of power and ability through Him to do the same. He was the prototype of a perfect and holy man under the conditions of the Fall, that we, under those conditions, might know there was power and will in God that we should all be perfect and holy. This being accomplished, and Christ ascended up on high, God sets on foot another work, which is to testify that honour to which man had become advanced in the person of the Son of man, and in all other persons who by faith should be united to Him. . . . In the incarnation, Christ's identity with the fallen man was shown, yet without sin: in the Church, Christ's identity with God is shown, the power and glory of God in Him are exhibited, that all men might believe in His name. This gift of tongues is the crowning act of all. None of the old prophets had it, Christ had it not; it belongs to the dispensation of the Holy Ghost proceeding from the risen Christ: it is the proclamation that man is enthroned in heaven, that man is the dwelling-place of God, that all creation if they would know God, must give ear to man's tongue, and know the compass of reason. It is not we that speak, but Christ that speaketh. It is not in us as men that God speaks; but in us as members of Christ, as the Church and body of Christ, that God speaks. The honour is not to us, but to Christ; not to the Godhead of Christ, which is ever the same, but to the manhood of Christ, which hath been raised from the state of death to the state of being God's temple, God's most holy place, God's shechinah, God's oracle, for ever and ever.[29]

This passage concludes the main portion of this article in which *Mark* 14:17, 18, and *I Cor.* 12, have been examined in detail in order to answer the question 'How much of that power, which Christ hath received, is it befitting to Him and the Father to put forth by the Church in this the day of His absence?'[30] The operations of the Spirit as they have been enumerated and studied, are 'the first-fruits of that complete power of the Spirit which she shall possess when the body shall be redeemed from the corruption of the grave'.[31] Irving has some final remarks to make on the reason for the absence of these signs in the Church. He repeats the conviction which he expressed on this subject in his baptismal sermon, that their absence is due to faithlessness. Having studied this further he is prepared to say that these things have decayed but not altogether ceased:

> If they ask for an explanation of the fact that these powers have ceased in the Church, I answer, that they have decayed just as faith and holiness have decayed; but that they have ceased is not a matter so clear. Till the time of the Reformation, this opinion was never mooted in the Church; and to this day the Roman Catholics, and every other portion of the Church but ourselves, maintain the very contrary. Moreover, it is only of later days that anyone hath dared to assert that the gifts of prophecy and healing are no longer to be looked for. Read the lives of the Reformers, of the Puritans, of the Covenanters, written by sound and zealous Protestants; read the histories of the Church written more than fifty years ago – our Petrie, for example – and show me whether these writers hold it blasphemy to say that a man may be, and hath been, gifted with both these gifts, especially that of prophecy? Who has not heard of the prophecies of Huss, and of Wishart?[32]

The faithlessness of the Protestants regarding the spiritual gifts is shown in their creeds and articles of faith which have 'leant to the side of their being ceased'. This is even more evident in 'the spirit of their doctrine' and in their preaching which shows a great ignorance of the doctrine of the Second Advent of which these things are signs:

> And I would say, that this gift hath ceased to be visible in the Church, because of her great ignorance concerning that work of Christ at His second coming, of which it is the continual sign; because of her most culpable ignorance of Christ's crowned glory, of which it is the continual demonstration; because of her indifference to the world without, for preaching to which the gift of the Holy Ghost is the continual furnishing and outfit of the Church. Since the Reformation little else has been preached besides the baptismal and eucharistical gift, the work of Christ's death unto the justification and sanctification of the believer. The dignity and office of the Church, as the fulness of the Lord of all, hath not been fully preached, or firmly held, and is now almost altogether lost sight of. Church government, bickerings about the proper form of polity, and the standing of the civil magistrate to the Church and in the Church, have been almost the only things concerning the Church which have come into question among Protestants.[33]

Those who believe that 'Jesus Christ is come in the flesh' and that 'He will come again in glorious majesty to judge both the quick and the dead' also believe the Scriptural teaching on 'the permanent endowment' of 'the outward gift of power'. These believers can also discern that God has begun to put forth a new spring time in His Church through the restoration of these gifts of the spirit.[34] These who so believe have been 'prepared by the full preaching of Christ's coming in our flesh, and his coming again in glory'. Irving's exposition in this article hinges on the realization that the manifestations of spiritual gifts are signs of the former and foretastes of the latter. On the basis of this sound theological understanding and having made 'earnest and careful search' with 'joyful hope' and 'trembling anxiety' he was now prepared to yield his faith up to what he considered to be the clearest evidence that a revival had indeed begun to break out in their midst which was of the Lord:

> They called Methodism and Evangelicalism a revival: I have always maintained that, though better than downright Pelagianism, they were far behind the Reformation; which itself was only the beginning of a glorious work, strangled in its cradle. But now I see a revival worthy of the name – a revival of doctrine, of discipline, of holiness. Christians are beginning to speak their native language of faith and

truth and to endure their prerogative of being partakers of the Lord's sufferings. And if this revival proceed, it cannot but show itself in all those essential functions for which the Church was constituted; of which one is, to enjoy and hold forth a first-fruits of that power which Christ is to act out in the day of His appearing.[35]

By the end of the summer of 1830 Irving had come to see that the manifestations of the gifts of the Spirit had not been withdrawn until the Second Coming of Christ because of the apostasy of the Gentile Church but were continual signs and demonstrations of Christ having come in the flesh and were continual foretastes of His imminent reappearance. He had also come to the conclusion that the manifestations in Port Glasgow and round the Gareloch were of God. He had therefore committed himself to defending a movement and a doctrine which was causing even greater national excitement and controversy than that of the humanity of Christ for which he was in the process of being called to account by the Scots Presbytery of London.

PART THREE

9

The Gifts of the Holy Spirit

DURING THE autumn of 1830, after the return of Mr. Cardale and his party from Port Glasgow, prayer meetings were started in various private houses in London 'for the outpouring of the Holy Ghost'. These meetings were greatly encouraged by the miraculous cure of Miss Fancourt on 20th October which was very like the healings of Margaret Macdonald and Mary Campbell.[1] Irving does not appear to have taken any part in the formation of these meetings although he had committed himself to their support. At the time he was engaged in defending himself against the charges of heresy brought against him by the Scots Presbytery of London, in separating himself from that body, in being found guilty and in having the sentence of eviction passed against him. In November he wrote a sequel to 'The Church with her Endowment of Holiness and Power' called 'On the Gifts of the Holy Ghost Commonly called Supernatural', the first part of which was published in the December issue of *The Morning Watch*.[2] In this article he continued his Scriptural expositions in order to refute those who thought that the gifts of the Spirit had been 'given only for a season, while Christianity was making way in the world'.[3] He aligned himself with those who believed that they had been given, 'like the other gifts and callings of God, without repentance and revocation'. He is convinced that 'the Church hath them now in as full right as ever, and ought to be exercising them with as great diligence, and for the very same ends, as did the apostles and primitive Christians' and that the only way this controversy can be settled is 'by an appeal to the Word of God'.

The first text he takes from *Psalm* 68 which is quoted by Paul in *Eph.* 4: 'Thou hast ascended on high, thou hast led captivity captive: thou hast received gifts for men; yea, for the rebellious also, that the Lord God might dwell among them.'[4] This passage answers the question: What is the 'end and purpose of God in the giving of these gifts to Christ, and Christ's end in giving them to us'?[5] It shows that the answer is 'For a habitation of the Lord God . . . to construct for God a place to dwell in . . . to prepare God a tabernacle, or house, or habitation.' It is that all might be builded 'into a holy temple in the Lord, in whom even you are built into the house, for habitation of God in the Spirit'.[6] This habitation, tabernacle, house and temple is the Church, His body, which contains the fulness of Christ. Since 'the gifts . . . are men',[7] the Church is more than just a witness to God's revelation:

> The Church is to be not only the container of the manifested God, but she is the actor of His works, and the utterer of His wisdom; and to accomplish this, Christ, when He ascended up on high, received the Seven Spirits, the fulness and completeness of the vital, active Godhead. This is His occupation in heaven, to build the spiritual temple of the Lord out of the materials which He hath impregnated with His own life. And the Church is this temple; we are it; we on earth are it. The idea and the end of the Church is to be such a thing.[8]

What has happened since the ascension? Has Christ or the Spirit failed? Have we succeeded in defeating his purpose or is the Church still this building of God?:

> Christ hath either failed to do His Father's will since His ascension, or the Spirit hath failed, or the materials have succeeded in defeating the Architect; or else the Church is this building of God, where God is heard in His manifold wisdom, and seen in His various actings: His wisdom, in this membership having the word of wisdom; His knowledge, in this membership having the word of knowledge; His truth, in this membership having the gift of faith; His health, in this membership having the gift of healing; His supremacy of spirits, in this membership having the discernment of spirits; His voice, in this membership having the gift of tongues; and His understanding, in this membership having the interpretation of tongues.[9]

Whether the Church is thought of as a house or a body it is all the same. If a human body is required in all its parts in order to house a human spirit, how much more will this apply to the housing of Christ's Spirit.

The second text which Irving goes to is *Isa.* 8:18: 'Behold, I and the children whom the Lord hath given me are for signs and for wonders in Israel from the Lord of hosts, which dwelleth in Mount Zion.' This verse is seen as a type of Christ and the Church in *Heb.* 2. Some have said that 'signs and wonders' cannot be equated with 'miraculous endowments' and only refers to the relation of believers to an unbelieving world. Irving thinks otherwise:

> I count it good here to observe, that in no instance doth the expression 'signs and wonders' signify in Scripture anything but supernatural acts and appearances. In proof of which I refer to these passages: *Matt.* 24:24; *Mark* 13:22; *John* 4:48; *Acts* 2:22, 43; 4:30; 6:8; 7:36; *Rom.* 15:19; *II Cor.* 12:12; *Heb.* 2:4; in all of which the words used here in the Septuagint for 'signs and wonders' occur as the ordinary and constant form of words for supernatural demonstrations of the power of God: nor is there a single instance to the contrary in all the Scriptures.[10]

Having established this, the reason why these supernatural powers are given in this passage must be noted. This is found in v. 14 where it says 'and he shall be for a sanctuary.' Like the passage from *Psalm* 68, the reason for these 'signs and wonders' is for the preparation of a sanctuary in Mount Zion 'even the new Jerusalem, the city of God, which hath the glory of God, and is God's tabernacle, being also the bride of the Lamb, the completeness of the elect, or Church of the living God'.[11]

But this text speaks primarily of the relation of the prophet to his children. In *Heb.* 2:13 this is seen as a figure of the intimate relation between Christ and his disciples. This is a 'stronghold of the truth of Christ's unity with us in flesh, and in mortal flesh'[12] for he goes on immediately to say 'Forasmuch then as the children are partakers of flesh and blood, he also himself likewise took part of the same; that through death he might destroy him that had the power of death, that is, the devil; and deliver them who through fear of death were all their lifetime subject to bondage.' (vv. 13–15) Irving has come to the place where he can express for the first time his new realization that his belief that Jesus Christ assumed fallen humanity in order to redeem it, was inseparable from the belief that the reception of the complete gift of the Holy Spirit was the inheritance of all in Christ. The latter was the necessary inference and corollary of the former. His exposition for the former had rested heavily on such passages as *Heb.* 2. Now his exposition for the latter had come to the same passage. This is a new synthesis of 'two great truths – Christ's union with us by the one flesh, and our present union with him by the one Spirit'[13] which hitherto he had not expressed and until a few months before had seen but not believed. *Hebrews* 2 had showed him already that Christ shared our flesh. Now that he had come to believe that the gifts of the Holy Spirit were definitely the permanent endowment of the baptized Church and of individual believers he could see the implications of this in the same chapter. He speaks of this relationship:

A relationship of such strength and endearment will not be mentioned in our prophet for mere accidental or casual purposes, but for some high and solemn end: and what is this? It is expressed in these words, 'are for signs and wonders'; which expression, as we have shown above, in all cases signifies supernatural acts and appearances. As His children, therefore, we with Him are called to be for signs and wonders – that is, to minister the supernatural manifestation of the power of God; to be the hand of God for action, as we are His house for habitation; to be the body in which dwelleth the Spirit of God in all goodness and righteousness and truth; in which, also, and in all the members of which, God himself worketh all signs and wonders and mighty acts in the sight of men.[14]

This being so, what is the link between this supernatural action and our being Christ's children? This is his answer:

The answer is, That the children ever exhibit the powers and faculties of the Father. Now Christ is our Father, not as the mortal man, but as the risen man; not as flesh and blood, for we are not born again of flesh and blood, but as the quickening Spirit who begetteth us for God. Our new life holdeth of his risen glory. . . . Forasmuch, then, as we are the children of the heavenly man, we should exhibit the form and feature and power and acts of the heavenly man, of the Son of God, of Him in whom dwelleth the fulness of the Godhead bodily. Now, His actings as the risen man are entirely and altogether supernatural, whether you look at them in the inward man of the heart renewed by His power, or in the outward demonstration which He is to make when He shall come again to destroy the course of this present evil world, to raise the dead, to cleanse away sin, and other mighty acts to do, which are not within the laws of nature, but above them all. We, then, as His children, begotten from above into His heavenly image, ought to put forth, in order to prove our sonship, some features of the supernatural, not only in the way of a holy will triumphant over the law of sin, and a word triumphant over the law of falsehood, but of a mighty power triumphing over the law of sickness, infirmity, and death: in one word, we should put forth a first-fruits of that power which He Himself will put forth in the day of His appearing.[15]

Irving had here expressed the fact that he had now appropriated Mary Campbell's theological development which had been communicated to him the previous January and which for her had been the decisive element in her preparation for receiving the gift of tongues. After it had come to her 'that all the works of Christ were done by the man anointed with the Holy Ghost'[16] which was what Irving had been preaching in London 'for six or seven years', she had gone on to make the inference that Irving, for the reasons given earlier, had not yet made:

> She straightway argued, if Jesus as a man in my nature thus spake and thus performed mighty works by the Holy Ghost, which he even promiseth to me, then ought I in the same nature, by the same Spirit, to do likewise 'the works which he did, and greater works than these'.[17]

He had seen that 'the children are partakers of flesh and blood' and that 'he also took part of the same'. Now he saw and believed that the children are partakers and demonstrators of the supernatural powers of the risen, ascended and glorified body of Christ. He had now connected these two truths. 'Christ's unity with us in the flesh' is expressed in the children ever exhibiting 'the powers and faculties of the Father' while the proof of our sonship is in the putting forth 'a first-fruits of that power which He Himself will put forth in the day of His appearing'. He was now entering in to the fulfilment of his earlier theological speculations. His second baptismal sermon was still in his mind as he went on to say that at our baptism we have promised to us not only remission of sins and the consequent admission of holiness but also the gift of the Holy Spirit as in the prophet Joel 'for the purpose of demonstrating that we are children of the risen Christ, members of the glorified and omnipotent Head.'[18] Unlike his baptismal sermon he speaks of the reception of 'the outward gift of power' for the first time as 'the baptism of the Holy Ghost'. This was the same endowment for the disciples as for Christ. His understanding of our union with Christ is thus carried a stage further:

> Therefore also the apostles and disciples were not permitted to go and preach until they had received that heavenly baptism. Their word

must first be instinct with heavenly power, before it can convert men unto God. So also it was with Christ himself; He undertook not His public ministry till He had received the baptism of the Holy Ghost; and to that baptism Peter referreth His miraculous power and doings; 'That word (I say) ye know, which was published throughout all Judea, and began from Galilee, after the baptism which John preached; how God anointed Jesus of Nazareth with the Holy Ghost and with power; who went about doing good and healing all that were oppressed of the devil; for God was with him,' (*Acts* 10:37, 38). Then, also, He began to make disciples; then His word began to be spirit and life. Till that time He was merely the holy man under the law; . . . from that time forth He became the holy man baptized with the Holy Ghost, putting forth the first-fruits of His celestial glory. And we, being baptized with the same Holy Ghost, are required in this life to put forth the same first-fruits of our celestial glory; and our words, like His words – being in truth His in us – should be spirit and life. This, now, is the answer to the question. How are these signs and wonders connected with the relationship of children? The answer is, because the child is like his Father, and puts forth a first-fruits of his Father's power.[19]

Irving goes on to ask, What are the uses for which Christ and His children are gifted? He finds from *Isa.* 8:19, that the answer is, for saving people from going to spiritualists, necromancers and those who worshipped devils and to overcome forces of spiritual darkness.[20] They were to provide a supernatural ministry to the Jews which, if it was rejected, would lead to their exile.[21] They were also to serve 'as God's own witness to the words which the ministers of His Son declare.'[22] This was proved not just in the power, but in the demonstration that it was a good and merciful power, which men could discern from a loving God. It is not enough just to believe in miracles:

> The witness of God, with the word of Christ, standeth in a certain description of miraculous works, and not in miraculous works in general; gospel works, the counterpart of gospel words; and therefore proving that it is one and the same God who doth the one and speaketh the other. Of what kind these are we learn from the catalogues of them in the New Testament so frequently referred to.[23]

These particular gospel works, show 'Christ to be the Redeemer from sin, by actually freeing some person from some of the bondages of sin'.[24] For Christ is 'the Redeemer from all bonds of Satan' and

92

all these 'signs and wonders' are 'a token and a part' of that redemption:

> Unless men, therefore, be left so far to themselves as to say, that God hath ceased to testify to the work which Christ performed in the flesh – of casting Satan out; of redeeming all flesh from death, and disease its precursor; of restoring the animal and the vegetable world, and all creation, to their sinlessness, innocency, and subserviency to mankind; – unless men be disposed to say, that they know God hath ceased to be at any pains or charges, in giving Testimony to this work of His son, they have no ground for believing that the age of miracles is past; and if they say, they know the mind of God to have changed in this matter, we ask them for the source of their knowledge; and till they produce this, we must look upon them as unfaithful witnesses of God and of Christ, fraudulent messengers between them and the world.[25]

Irving does not believe that miracles have been totally absent from the Church. Many try to make this out in order to justify their claim that the age of miracles is past. But granting that this has been largely the case, he says that the reason for it is 'that there hath been no testimony to the great work of Christ's redemption such as to be worthy of being so sealed into'.[26] He sees the signs and wonders as seals which confirm the testimony to the great work of Christ's redemption. In his baptismal sermon he had said that the Church's 'state of impotency . . . argues a like state of unholiness'.[27] This thought is now carried further on the basis of the deeper insight he has had into the relationship between the inner and the outer work of Christ. Miracles have been largely absent because there has been no testimony to the inner work of regeneration and sanctification of which they are the outward seals and confirmations. This is so because the Church does not believe that Christ redeemed our flesh. The London Presbytery, representing the majority of the ecclesiastical world, was in the process of rejecting his understanding of Christ having redeemed flesh in the flesh. His friend John McLeod Campbell was in the process of being deposed for preaching the love of God to all men. Maclean and Scott were to be similarly dealt with. This is the context in which he saw how these rejected truths were related. It is not just that the Church denies the possibility of the miraculous gifts of the Spirit. Behind that is the denial that Christ has come in the flesh and has redeemed that flesh. Since the miraculous gifts of the Spirit are seals and confirmations of that redemption of flesh, then there can have been no testimony to this redemption to be sealed in these miraculous ways:

Now I frankly avow my belief, that there hath been no preaching of the resurrection and redemption of the flesh, and of the world, in the Protestant Churches within my memory; and a very poor testimony of the redemption of the soul from sin – an Arminian, Pelagian, or particular – redemption doctrine, and not a Christian one; – preaching for the honours of a system, or articles, or of confessions, more than for the honour of Christ; certainly no preaching of Christ glorified, possessed of the Seven Spirits of God; of Christ to come and redeem the world from the usurpation of wickedness; of Christ to come and raise all the dead, to glorify this Church, and to cast the wicked into hell. These are the realities of Christ's consummate work, which being preached, God seals with a first-fruits of the very thing declared; but these have no more in an open manner, been declared in this island, or, I may say, in Christendom, since the first three centuries, than in regions which the gospel hath not visited; and so there has been nothing to seal to. The seal to the preaching of this time, is a good living, a good name with the world, a reputation for learning and eloquence. 'Verily it hath its reward.' But as the liberty of preaching shall awaken, and the full voice of its glory heard, its true seal will be given, which is from men, casting out of the synagogue, persecution and death; from God, 'the doing among them the works which none other man did'. 'And all this will they do unto you, because they know not the Father, nor' Christ. If they knew the Father, they would know the Father's works, and love the manifestation of them, and desire it: if they knew Christ, they would speak of His glory, and desire His appearing.[28]

10

The Baptism of the Baptizer

THE PRAYER meetings which had been started in various
private houses to pray for 'the outpouring of the Holy Ghost',
continued to meet throughout the winter. In the early days of
1831 Irving wrote *Christ's Holiness in Flesh* as a final statement of his
understanding of the humanity of Christ. As well as those aspects of
this tract which were mentioned in the first part of this study, there
was further evidence of his uniting his earlier insights regarding
Christ's human nature with his more recent understanding of spiritual
gifts. He continued to reflect on the implications of this, especially with
reference to the baptism with the Holy Spirit. In the article which he
had just written, there are indications of the same thoughts as appear
in his tract, as in 'Till that time (His baptism) He was merely the holy
man under the law'; and in 'from that time forth He became the holy
man baptized with the Holy Ghost'.[1] Indeed the whole of this tract is
permeated with the expression of insights arising from this holding
together of these reciprocal doctrines. The result was a statement of
what he had meant when he had said 'They argue for an identity of
origin merely; we argue for an identity of life also. . . . In one word,
we present believers with a real life; a suffering, mortal flesh of ours.'[2]
This has already been noted in Part I in terms of His holy life on earth
and the communication of His holiness to us through the Spirit. It
was noted then what Irving had managed to achieve. Now it is possible
to see how he managed to achieve it. For the purposes of the historical
method of this study, only those stages of Christ's life on earth up
until His resurrection were then instanced. But Irving also went on
to draw out the implications of our being partakers of Christ's power
as well as His holiness. The coming together of these two streams of
his thought is once again evidenced as he considered the relationship
of Christ's baptism with the Holy Spirit to ours. In the section

'Conclusions of Practical Holiness' he sums up his understanding of how the holiness of Christ's flesh removes the whole of man's sinfulness, that is '(1) The guilt of Adam's sin; (2) The want of original righteousness; (3) The corruption of our whole nature', and of nature itself.[3] Man in Christ, Christ the second Man, has presented satisfaction to God in all these points – 'A clean and guiltless soul, a whole man, renewed after the image of God, and nature reclaimed to the service of God.'[4] It has been noted how Irving detailed his understanding of the 'real life' of Christ with regard to His holiness. He now detailed the same with regard to His power:

> So far, therefore, as the soul of man is concerned, it was presented unto God, in an acceptable and an accepted state, even as he made it, in its full maturity of wisdom and knowledge, perfect in love and perfect in obedience, on the morning of Christ's baptism. And that morning, in the baptism with the Holy Ghost, God, for the first time, since Adam was banished out of Paradise, found a man in all points proved by the law and perfect without sin; but lo! now it is no garden meeting and converse of friend with friend, but entering into the heart, and taking possession of the inward parts.... Oh! what an advance manhood made that morning of the baptism of Christ, at Bethabara, beyond Jordan! But still though God did thenceforward inhabit with his own mighty power and sweetest delectation all the inward parts of a man, so as to take his soul for his temple, still man's outward part, flesh, the body, together with its dependent visible world, was not yet irradiated or blessed with any particle of God's favour, because it had not as yet vanquished death and corruption, and the grave.[5]

Christ was Spirit – quickened and anointed at his baptism. From that time He became the spiritual man. He still had to fight and overcome the 'principalities and powers' of evil, and death itself, before He could ascend to that glory which we shall fully share with Him, but of which we now only receive an earnest or foretaste. This is part of the fruit of Christ's holiness in the flesh:

> For the present therefore, we must be content with the enjoyment of God upon the throne of our hearts, as the Father of our spirits, as the inhabitant of our souls, in which to make the sweet influence of his presence to be felt, and through which, when it pleaseth him to express the mightiness of his power in healing the sick, or working miracles, or speaking with tongues, or discerning spirits, or other such gifts, super-human and divine, which do all belong to this blessed baptism,

whereunto Christ hath introduced us. For baptism, Christ's ordinance, containeth two things, the working away of our sin, and the baptism with the Holy Ghost; the former holding of redemption and satisfaction, the latter holding of the new acquisition which our nature made on the morning of Christ's baptism. I present, therefore, unto every man in Christ, not only deliverance from the old offence of Adam, with all its train of consequences, but also the new inheritance of the Holy Ghost, as a Spirit of power, the earnest of an inheritance whereof Adam's was only a type. This is a part of the fruit of Christ's holiness in the flesh which is little thought of. Men have been so much disturbed of late about the thoughts of their own safety, that they have little time to consider the new gratuities which their deed of pardon containeth.[6]

At His baptism, Christ became the spiritual man. After His ascension he became the Spirit-quickener. This is the meaning of 'the first man was made a living soul the second man was made a quickening spirit'. Christ's superiority over Adam lay in His having been made a Spirit-quickener. In 'The Church, With Her Endowment of Holiness and Power', Irving had expounded *Mark* 16:17, 18 and *I Cor.* 12 in order to demonstrate what those first-fruits of power were that the Church should be putting forth. In 'On the Gifts of the Holy Ghost, commonly called supernatural', from his exposition of *Psalm* 68:18 and *Isa.* 8:18, his understanding of children sharing the Father's power as well as His holiness in flesh, had become focused for the first time on the baptism with the Holy Spirit. He now saw that the former were foretastes of the 'high uses and offices' of the latter. These were the fruits of Christ's holiness in flesh. They were the 'new gratuities which' our 'deed of pardon containeth'. In a final summary, he unites these developments of his thoughts:

> Now this Spirit-quickening was manifested forth in Christ at his baptism, from which time he became the spiritual man; and after his ascension into glory, he became the Spirit quickener. He then began to baptize with the Holy Ghost. Of this baptism, we have already declared, that every mortal man is an heir, and every believer a possessor, whether he may have stirred up the gift or not. It is as much of the essence of a true faith to believe in Christ as the Baptizer with the Holy Ghost, as it is to believe in him as the Lamb of God which taketh away the sin of the world. For with one and the same breath was he announced in both characters by his appointed forerunner and herald, John the Baptist. And it is as much the prerogative of Christian baptism to confer the communion and fellowship of the Holy Ghost, as he was

poured out on the day of Pentecost, as it is to confer the forgiveness of sins which was purchased for us upon the cross with Christ's most precious blood. But this baptism with the Holy Ghost being possessed, and every baptized person is responsible both for the possession and the use thereof, it is still only an earnest of the things which are about to be, when the church being raised in her glory, shall enter into the possession of her God and of her inheritance. . . . Of the high uses and offices to which he shall promote the raised saints in that day and for ever, the manifestation of the Spirit, or the gifts of the Holy Ghost, were intended for an earnest. These are wisdom to rule, and govern, and administer all things as God himself would; and knowledge of his inmost mind, and of all creation's use and destination; both of which gifts God shall put forth by us and not otherwise, in that eternal age of blessedness: and there is faith in God, such as shall draw forth from him the full power of his strength to remove mountains, if need be, and to work all other miraculous works, for the demonstration, that in us abideth God the supreme power and cause of all things, that God worketh by us the reformation and re-establishment of this distressed world; whose diseases to heal, there is the gift of healing, whose possessed chambers to deliver from spiritual wickednesses, there is the discernment of spirits, and to announce the undoubted presence of God within us, there is the gift of tongues. These are all but stirrings and movings of that Spirit of redemption and power, which we shall completely possess when we are raised from the dead.[7]

11

Prophecy and Tongues

ON 30th April, 1831 the expectations of those who had been meeting for prayer began to be realized when Mrs. Cardale 'spoke with great solemnity in a tongue and prophesied'.[1] She thus became the first member of Regent Square Church to do so. At this time Irving was very anxious about the cases of John McLeod Campbell, Sandy Scott and Hugh Maclean which were due to come before the General Assembly of the Church of Scotland the next month. So he started an early morning prayer meeting from 6.30 to 7.30 a.m. at the church in order to pray that the General Assembly might not decide against his friends. At this meeting prayers were also offered for the manifestation of the gifts of the Spirit. It is estimated that a thousand people attended. Irving gives his account of it:

> We met together about two weeks before the meeting of the General Assembly, in order to pray that the General Assembly might be guided in judgement by the Lord, the head of the Church. We cried unto the Lord for apostles, prophets, evangelists, pastors and teachers, anointed with the Holy Ghost the gift of Jesus, because we saw it written in God's word that these are the appointed ordinances for the edifying of the body of Jesus. We continued in prayer every morning, morning by morning, at half past six o'clock; and the Lord was not long in hearing and answering our prayer.[2]

The Lord may have soon answered their prayers for spiritual gifts but He did not answer their prayers for the General Assembly which displayed a spirit both 'rancorous and ruthless'[3] in its judicial proceedings. It deposed McLeod Campbell, withdrew Scott's licence to preach and sent Maclean back to his Presbytery there to be deposed. It also ruled against Irving in spite of his own magnanimous sentiments expressed on 26th May 'I cannot think of the Church being led to give judgement against me, or against the truth, or to bind me up

99

from my natural liberty and right in my own country.'[4] When he had separated himself from the London Presbytery the previous October he had said that he would appeal his cause to the Church of Scotland, 'who alone have rightful authority over me and my flock'.[5] He had said that he would not 'submit the authority of the Church of Scotland to the verdict of any six men in Christendom'. But his sanguine reverence for his mother Church was shattered by these unexpected decisions. The Assembly's action against him was expressed in their receiving a 'Report upon Books and Pamphlets containing Erroneous Opinions' and in their approving a motion to the effect that if he should appear in Scotland, the Presbytery of the bounds should be required to find out if he were the author of these books and take the necessary action.[6] The Assembly, who he had admitted alone had rightful authority over him, had 'stoned her best prophet'[7] and proved itself in his eyes as heretical a body as the London Presbytery. He was stunned, grieved and angered by these decisions against his friends and himself and by the Church's 'deliberate rejection of the highest light vouchsafed to her'.[8] Like Thomas Erskine who witnessed the proceedings, he believed that 'an evil thing had been done in the land' and foresaw further disasters overtaking the Kirk as a result.[9]

While he pondered some fitting response to this terrible news from Edinburgh, he published the second half of 'On the Gifts of the Holy Ghost Commonly Called Supernatural' in the June number of *The Morning Watch*.[10] From the title it might have been supposed that he would go on to speak further of all the gifts mentioned in *I Cor.* 12 but he does not. He concentrates on the gifts of tongues and prophecy, especially as they are spoken of in *Isa.* 28 and *I Cor.* 14. The immediate reason for this was that, as in all the other writings which have been considered, he was carrying out no academic or scholarly exercise, but was appropriating the Scriptures that applied to the situation in which he found himself. Mrs. Cardale had spoken in tongues and prophesied at the prayer meeting in her own home. Others were soon to follow. Although the General Assembly's meetings were over, the early morning prayer meeting was continuing and was attracting a very large number of people. As pastor and teacher in this context it was vital that he should apply himself to the Word of God to understand for himself and for his people the apostolic injunctions regarding the gifts of the Spirit, but especially tongues and prophecy. In doing this he followed Paul from chapter 12 to chapter 14 of *I Cor.* He continued to see these things in the light of the full revelation of God in Christ by the Spirit and began by emphasizing that even those who agreed with him that the extraordinary gifts were meant to be always in evidence had not yet realized just how closely this subject impinged on their whole understanding of the Gospel. This wider theological significance justified the depth of his study as much as its relevance to the immediate scene:

> The subject of the gifts commonly called extraordinary, and rashly conceived of as given for a local and temporary end, is one of far greater importance than the advocates of either opinion have dared to conceive, or, at least, have ventured to express; being, as I judge, connected in the closest manner with the edification of the Church in love and holiness; with her witness among the nations for their conversion unto Christ; with the glory of God, as the Creator of the human soul for His shrine, agent, and interpreter; with the glory of Christ, as the head of the Church, subordinating all the members to Himself for the use of the Creator; with the glory of the Holy Ghost, as the very life and mind and substance of Godhead, inhabiting, informing and manifesting forth the being of God, in such wise as that the Church should be God's manifested fulness, the fulness of God, who filleth all in all.[11]

The subject of the extraordinary gifts was very important because it was closely connected with all these other doctrines, particularly with the glory of God, the glory of Christ and the glory of the Holy Spirit. If the controversy over the nature of Christ's humanity had not obscured the other features of his *Sermons on the Incarnation* then, next to his section in Sermon III on 'the Universal Reconciliation brought by his Death,' which echoed the allegedly heretical views of McLeod Campbell, the place he gave to the glory of God in his system would have been most worthy of note. Sermon II considered the question, What is the purpose or end of the Incarnation. The answer given is 'The end of the mystery of the Incarnation is the glory of God.'[12] Of these Sermons in general he had said 'there is much more to God's glory in that volume than in all my other writings put together'.[13] There was also much more about God's glory. In Sermon I he had explained how it was in God's will from all eternity 'to make known unto his creatures, for their greater information, delight, and blessedness, . . . the grace and mercy, the forgiveness and love which he beareth towards those who love the honour of his Son, and believe in the word of his testimony'.[14]

The immediate cause of the Incarnation was the fall of man, but the first cause was in God himself 'who worketh all things after the pleasure of his own will, and to the praise of his own glory'.[15] God foresaw the fall and provided for it. This is 'the mystery of the Lamb slain from the foundation of the world' (*John* 17:24) 'who verily was foreordained before the foundation of the world, but was manifest in these last times for you' (*I Peter* 1:20) and 'his own purpose and grace, which was given us in Christ Jesus before the world began; but is now made manifest by the appearing of the Saviour' (*II Tim.* 1:9) show 'that the beginning or origin of the mystery of the Incarnation, that the eternal Word should take unto himself a body, is the holy will and good pleasure of God'.[16] Adam forestalled the purpose of God by eating of the tree of the knowledge of good and evil and by thus becoming 'as one of us'. This sin postponed but did not alter the original will of God to reveal and manifest Himself to the creature. Only now, since the fall, this revelation and manifestation must include the overcoming of sin and death in the flesh. In Sermon II he showed how the original purpose of creation which was fulfilled in the Incarnation, was the manifestation of the glory of God:

> This manifestation of himself is the one end of creation, and of redemption, and of restitution; and I may also add, it is the one end of the permission of sin in the world, of an apostasy in the Church, and of reprobation through eternity, – I say the chief and only end of all is the declaration of the essential glory of the Godhead.[17]

The glory which Christ brought to the Father was through His works, His powers and His holiness.[18] He rejected escape from the hour of the power of darkness in order that He might 'Glorify thy name,' by doing 'the will of him that sent me'.[19] The will of God is manifest in the work of Christ in overcoming sin in the flesh. It is the manifestation of the Father's name.[20] The glory of God is further revealed in the overcoming of death at the resurrection and again in the ascension.[21] The glory which Christ brought the Father was 'no less than the manifestation of the Godhead bodily.'[22] 'So that in Christ all the glories of the Trinity were first manifested, with all their various offices'.[23] He ends this Sermon by saying that we are called to do what Christ did. God is to be glorified in us as He was in Christ. The honour and glory of the Trinity is to be shown in us. 'Christ . . . humbled the Divinity into manhood, that he might become the very type or pattern of every Christian'.[24] His conclusion is very similar to the exhortation in his second baptizmal Sermon. It is an equally positive statement whose effectiveness was vitiated by the same caveats that prevented such expressions from being more than pulpit hyperbole:

> Whatever, therefore, the Son of man did in the days of his flesh to honour and glorify God, he expecteth us to continue and carry forward till he come again. Yea, not only expecteth it, but hath provided us with the power to fulfil it; which is our baptismal gift, when we become partakers of all the benefits of the new covenant, and enter into engagements to be wholly the Lord's. Wherefore, as the Apostle Paul did exhort Timothy to stir up the gift of the Holy Ghost which was in him by the laying on of the hands of the Presbytery, so do I call upon every one of you, by faith, fervent prayer, and willing obedience, to stir up the gift that is in you by baptism. For which reason we should arise to the work of doing the will of him who hath sent us, even as Christ did when he was baptized by John; fearing nothing, dearly loved, doubting nothing, but surely believing that he who hath called us will also justify us, will also sanctify us, will also glorify us. And if he glorify us, then will he first glorify himself in us, by making us serviceable to the manifestation of his glory in the midst of a wicked generation.[25]

The similarity between this, his second sermon on the Incarnation, and his second sermon on baptism is very marked. The reasons why neither sermon bore fruit when they were preached were the same. Having reconsidered the latter in the light of the recent manifestations of the Spirit and the removal of his objections to the belief that 'the outward gift of power' was available to the Church and to believers this side of the millennium, he had now begun to reconsider the former in the same light. He had seen how the gifts of the Spirit were evidence of the power of God. He now saw how they were evidence of the glory of God, even as they were the manifestation of the glorification of Christ through the Spirit. That glory of the Father, the Son and the Holy Spirit which we should show and which should be shown in us, he now had come definitely to believe could and would be shown in us. His continued exposition in 'On the Gifts of the Holy Ghost, Commonly Called Supernatural' only confirmed, amplified, and fulfilled his earlier understanding that the whole of God's plan in Creation and Redemption was that He might reveal His glory to man in and through His Son the God-man Jesus Christ.

Having introduced the continuation of his article in this way, Irving went into a lengthy exposition of *I Cor.* 14 referring also to *Isa.* 28 which Paul quotes in this context.[26] He makes eleven observations about the gift of tongues: 1. 'That the gift of tongues is the stammering lips and foreign tongue, through which God communicates to men the word and the power of that glorious rest and refreshing,' which we will enter when He comes.[27] 2. It is designed to make void natural speech and eloquence 'to show that God edifies the soul . . . by direct communications of the Holy Ghost'.[28] This is 'the milk of our babyhood, the power in the word to nourish any soul'. 3. It is the expression of 'the delight, the love, the humiliation, the righteous indignation, the pity, the entreaty, or other affections with which God hath filled' the soul.[29] 4. It is the manifestation of the truth we already know 'that God feeds us by the Holy Ghost, proceeding from Christ, without any intervention of book or other person, by . . . communion'.[30] 5. That 'when this inworking of the Holy Ghost in the spirit of a man' expresses itself in English 'it becomes prophecy of one form or another, word of wisdom, word of knowledge, word of teaching, etc.'[31] 6. The Church must hear every utterance but must not accept it without discernment. All must be weighed 'in the balances of the sanctuary, which is the Word of God, opened to us by the Holy Ghost, whereof every believer hath the seal.[32] 7. Speaking in tongues brings to nothing the spiritual pretensions of the intellect of the natural man. 'It is needful, therefore, that all scribes and learned men, philosophers and statesmen, and men of worldly gifts, and all men whatsoever, should become as little children'.[33] 8. All believers should pray for this gift. They should use it for private edification and not in church without interpretation.

9. That, though it be not received, we should not be disheartened, as if we were rejected of the Holy Ghost, and had not the Holy Ghost dwelling in us: because it is but the sign of a universal truth, concerning the communication between God and man, through Christ and the Holy Ghost, without any intervention; and that this is the only way through which the weary and heavy-laden sinner can come to rest; wherefore also the Holy Ghost is called the Comforter. If any person, therefore, having laid hold of this truth, is living in the faith and enjoyment of it, he is to be assured of his salvation, and to be at peace: yet he is to desire to speak with tongues, in order to convince an unbelieving and ignorant world, who will ever be trusting to book read-

ing, or man-teaching, or self-sufficiency, or some other form of error, instead of trusting to the indwelling operation of the Spirit of Christ. The tongue is but the sign and manifestation to the unbeliever: to the believer it is a means of grace, for the end of edifying himself, that he may edify the whole body of the saints.[34]

10. Because speaking in tongues dethrones the natural gifts and faculties, it does not therefore mean that there is no place for them. Paul says that the understanding should be fruitful when it is guided by the human spirit and informed by the Holy Spirit. It has the highest place in creation.[35]

11. That the true reason why the gift of tongues hath ceased to be in the Church is, the exaltation of the natural methods of teaching above, or into copartnery with, the teaching of the Holy Ghost, the meanness of our idea, and the weakness of our faith, concerning the oneness of Christ glorified, with His Church on earth; the unworthiness of our doctrine concerning the person and office of the Holy Ghost, to knit up the believer into complete oneness with Christ, every thread and filament of our mortal humanity with His humanity, immortal and glorious; to bring down into the Church a complete Christ, and keep Him there, ever filling her bosom, and working in her members; the shortcoming of our knowledge, in respect to the gifts themselves; our having ceased to lament their absence, and to pray for their return; our want of fasting, and humiliation, and crying unto the Lord; our contentment to be without them; our base and false theories to account for their absence, without taking guilt to ourselves. Any one of these causes were sufficient, all of them are far more than sufficient, to account for their long absence from the bosom of the Church. These are the true reasons; and the commonly given reason, that they were designed only for a short time, is utterly false and most pernicious.[36]

12

The Work of the Holy Spirit in London

AT THIS stage Irving was so careful not to transgress 'the canon of the apostle' which he had just expounded, that he did not even allow the tongues-speakers to demonstrate before him privately, let alone in the early morning Church prayer meeting. Only when the gift had 'perfected itself' after a few weeks did he undertake his duty (as in *Rev.* 2) to test the spirits. It was only when the tongues in each case had been followed by prophecy that he considered that 'this gift was perfected' and went to the private prayer meetings to hear and judge for himself.[1] All those concerned were known to him personally. They were all members of his congregation except two; one of whom was in the process of joining and the other was a member of another Church. They were all leading good Christian lives. The results of this testing of the spirits was favourable:

> Here, then, I had, first, the blameless walk and conversation of persons in full communion with the church of Christ; and I had next, privately hearing the utterances, in which I could detect nothing that was contrary to sound doctrine, but saw everything to be for edification, exhortation, and comfort. There was the sign of the unknown tongue – there was the prophesying for edification, exhortation, and comfort; and beyond those, there are no outward and visible tests to which it can be brought.[2]

Irving was now placed in a very awkward position. He had led the early morning prayers for the outpouring of these gifts. The gifts had begun to appear. He had tested and tried them and had found them to be of God. What should he do next? Should he allow the

106

gifts to be exercised at the early morning meeting? For weeks he was burdened with this unique and unprecedented problem:

> Having these before me, I was still very much afraid of introducing it to the church; and it burdened my conscience, I should suppose, for some weeks. For, look you at the condition in which I was placed. I had sat as the head of the church, praying that these gifts might be poured out in the church; I believed in the Lord's faithfulness, that I was praying in the prayer of faith, and that he had poured out the gifts on the church in answer to our prayers. Was I to disbelieve that which, in faith, I had been praying for, and which we had all been praying for? When it comes he gives me every opportunity of proving it: I put it to the proof according to his own word; and I find, so far as I am able to discern honestly before God, that it is the thing written of in the Scriptures, and into the faith of which we were baptized. Having found this, I was in great strait between two. God knoweth my heart and seeth it; he knoweth how I was burdened in my heart for certain days, yea, I may say weeks; and a great burden it was, and a burden which I could disclose to none.[3]

He felt it was his duty to act, but for some time could not decide in what way. While he was in this state of indecision there were several unauthorized outbursts of prophecy in the early morning meetings in which it was proclaimed that he was quenching the Spirit by not allowing the gifts to be exercised in public. The particular words which struck home to him were 'It belongs to you to open the door – you have the power of the keys – it is you that are restraining and hindering it.'[4] The day after this particular utterance was given he decided to allow the gifts to be heard. He announced his decision at the prayer meeting the following morning:

> Next morning I went to the church, and after praying I rose up, and said in the midst of them all, 'I cannot be a party in hindering, that which I believe to be the voice of the Holy Ghost from being heard in the church. I feel that I have too long deferred, and I now pray you to give audience while I read out of the Scriptures, as my authority, the commandment of the Lord Jesus Christ, concerning the prophets.' I then read these passages, *I Cor.* 14:23 . . . and *I Cor.* 11. . . .[5]
> Therefore, reading these two passages in the presence of the people, I said 'now I stand here before you . ., and I cannot longer forbid; but do, on the other hand, in the name of the Lord Jesus Christ, the head of the church, permit, at the meeting of the church, that every

one who has received the gift of the Holy Ghost, and is moved by the Holy Ghost, shall have liberty to speak': and I pointed to those whom I had heard in private.[6]

His authorization was immediately followed by an utterance in the Spirit confirming what he had done: 'Let them speak under authority in tongues and prophesying.' Whereupon Mrs. Cardale and Miss Emily Cardale proceeded to speak in tongues and prophesy.

The first two tests had been passed, now the third test had to be applied by giving the opportunity to the congregation to judge whether the spirits of the prophets were of God. Having committed himself to the pattern of biblical authority, Irving saw that it was his duty to do this, 'for beyond question it belongeth to every man to try the spirits; it belongeth not to the pastor alone'.[7] It was everybody's duty to be on their guard against false prophets according to the Lord's injunction. Paul also told Timothy to warn the churches about those who would come 'giving heed to seducing spirits, speaking lies in hypocrisy' and John said that all the spirits must be tried by the rule 'Every spirit that confesseth not that Jesus Christ is come in the flesh is not of God.' And so Irving says: 'it belonged to me, as the servant of the Lord Jesus Christ, having tried them, to put them forth to the people that they might be tried of them'.[8] This he now did. He also intimated that he had done so when the congregation met for public worship the following Sunday and 'invited the people to come, and to witness for themselves'.[9]

This announcement was received with suspicion by certain members and with alarm by the office-bearers. The majority of the Elders and Deacons who had supported their minister unanimously against the London Presbytery six months before over the controversy of the human nature of Christ, were against him in this step he had taken and became apprehensive about further developments. James Nisbet, a loyal friend and elder, was the first to express his misgivings.[10] On 27th September, 1831, Irving replied in writing to his objections and said that he sympathized with him and did not want to press his views on anyone. He asked him to withhold his judgement against the manifestations until they had had a chance to develop and until he had listened to the biblical teaching on the gifts which at that time he was expounding in a series of mid-week lectures. Neither Mr. Nisbet nor his fellow elders were happy to wait. At a very well attended Session meeting on 21st October the matter was debated for four hours and it was discovered that all, except one who was undecided, were against his authorization of the use of the gifts at the early morning gatherings. Nevertheless, he remained 'very decided in the expression of his views' that these were of God and should not be stopped.[11]

Manifestations of tongues and prophecy continued at the prayer meetings during the next week. The suspicion of certain members and the expressed opposition of his own Session made Irving reluctant to listen to those who considered that the next step would be to introduce the gifts into the Sunday services.[12] He was still in this state of reluctance when, on the morning of Sunday 30th October, the service was interrupted and thrown into confusion by outbreaks of speaking in tongues.[13] An eye witness gave his account of this unexpected turn of events:

> I went to church and was, as usual, much gratified and comforted by Mr. Irving's lectures and prayers; but I was very unexpectedly interrupted by the well-known voice of one of the sisters, who, finding she was unable to restrain herself, and respecting the regulation of the Church, rushed into the vestry, and gave vent to utterance; whilst another, as I understand, from the same impulse, ran down the side aisle, and out of the church, through the principal door. The sudden, doleful, and unintelligible sounds, being heard by all the congregation, produced the utmost confusion; the act of standing up, the exertion to hear, see, and understand, by each and every one of perhaps 1,500 or 2,000 persons, created a noise which may be easily be conceived. Mr. Irving begged for attention, and when order was restored, he explained the occurrence, which he said was not new, except in the congregation, where he had been for some time considering the propriety of introducing it; but though satisfied of the correctness of such a measure, he was afraid of dispersing the flock; nevertheless, as it was now brought forward by God's will, he felt it his duty to submit. He then said he would change the discourse intended for the day, and expound the 14th chapter of Corinthians, in order to elucidate what had just happened. The sister was now returning from the vestry to her seat and Mr. Irving, observing her from the pulpit, said, in an affectionate tone, 'Console yourself, sister! console yourself!' He then proceeded with his discourse.[14]

After the service Irving with his elders and deacons had an interview with Miss Hall during which she again spoke in the Spirit. She urged her minister not to be ashamed of following his Master in spite of opposition. When he heard this 'Mr. Irving sunk on a chair and

109

groaned in distress.'[15] Once again he was burdened with the need to make a decision. By the evening he had decided to allow the exercise of the gifts at the Sunday worship services:

> After the subject had been thus forced on the congregation, I felt I could no longer resist; and in the evening I rose in my place, and said, that if again the worship should by those speaking with tongues and prophesying . . . be *added to* that evening, that they would understand it to be not the word of man, but, what I believed it to be, the word of the Spirit of God: and it was added to.[16]

The evening service was 'added to' immediately after he had said this by Mr. Taplin who burst forth into tongues in 'a voice that seemed as though it would rend the roof'. This was followed in English by: 'Why will ye flee from the voice of God? The Lord is in the midst of you. Why will ye flee from His voice? Ye cannot flee from it in the day of judgement.' As a result of this outburst the congregation was shocked and alarmed. When order had been restored, Irving sympathized with those who had been upset by hearing tongues for the first time. He said that he had had similar feelings at first. Nevertheless they were to understand that it was indeed the voice of the living God. He ended with thanksgiving that God's order had eventually been re-established.[17]

The next Sunday 6th November, was communion. There were no interruptions during the morning service at which a hundred new members joined the church. In the evening the assistant minister David Brown, successor of Sandy Scott, preached the sermon. The service was disturbed by two utterances in the Spirit. Irving records how he was enabled once more to keep control:

> Last night David Brown preached a mighty sermon on the 91st Psalm, bearing much allusion to the cholera, and twice over did the Spirit speak forth, once in confirmation, generally, that it was the judgement of God, once, in particular, to the scoffers. I was seated in the great chair, and was enabled by my single voice to preserve order among, I dare say, 3,000 people, and to exhort them, as Peter did at Pentecost, and commend them to the Lord. And they all parted in peace.[18]

During the week the early morning meetings were continuing to be attended by nearly a thousand people. In addition to the singing, the prayers and the exposition of Scripture, times were now regularly given for waiting 'for the Spirit to speak, which He does sometimes by one, sometimes by two, and sometimes by three'.[18] There was also a mid-week evening service at which Irving was 'preaching to thousands "the Baptism with the Holy Ghost" '.[20]

On Monday 7th November, Irving admitted that 'most of the Session dislike all this'.[21] This was an understatement. The elders had already almost unanimously expressed their dislike of manifestations in the week-day services. Their worst fears were confirmed when the Sunday services began to be interrupted. They objected in the strongest terms and considered what action they should take to curb what they took to be grave contraventions of the practice and procedure of the Church of Scotland.

During the previous two weeks the news of these events had spread round London and had been reported unfavourably in the press. The manifestations were taken to be spurious and the stories of the disturbances were greatly magnified in the telling. The general response was that they were displays of ridiculous fanaticism.[22] On 6th November, many 'scoffers' had come out of curiosity to the evening service to witness 'such astonishing novelty and sensation'.[23] On the evening of Sunday 13th November, 'crowds assembled in greater force than ever and it was said that the leading infidels of London had dispersed themselves through the church'.[24] Mrs. Hamilton, who was Mrs. Irving's sister and was married to one of the elders, was there and reported the worst uproar to date:

> In the evening there was a tremendous crowd. The galleries were fearfully full; and from the commencement of the service there was an evident uproariousness, considering the place, about the doors, men's voices continually mingling with the singing and the praying in most indecent confusion. Mr. Irving had nearly finished his discourse, when another of the ladies spoke. The people heard for a few minutes with quietness comparatively, but on a sudden, a number of fellows in the gallery began to hiss, and then some cried 'Silence!' and some one thing, and some another, until the congregation, except such as had firm faith in God, were in a state of extreme commotion. Some of these fellows (who, from putting all the circumstances together, it afterwards appeared were a gang of pick-pockets come to make a *row*) shut the gallery doors, which I think was providential – for had any one rushed and fallen, many lives might have been lost, the crowd was so great. The awful scene of Kirkcaldy church was before my eyes, and I dare say before Mr. Irving's. He immediately rose and said,

'Let us pray', which he did, using chiefly the words, 'Oh, Lord, still, the tumult of the people', over and over again in an unfaltering voice. This kept those in the pews in peace, none attempted to move, and certainly the Lord did still the people. We then sang, and before pronouncing the blessing, Mr. Irving intimated that henceforward there would be morning service on the Sunday, when those persons would exercise their gifts, for that he would not subject the congregation to a repetition of the scene they had witnessed. He said he had been afraid of life, and that which was so precious he would not again risk, and more to the like effect. A party still attempted to keep possession of the church. One man close to me attempted to speak. Some called, 'Hear! hear!' others, 'Down! down!' The whole scene reminded one of Paul at Ephesus. It was very difficult to get the people to go; but by God's blessing it was accomplished. The Lord be praised! We were in peril, great peril. But not a hair of the head of any one suffered.[25]

At the week-day service the next day Irving confessed that he regretted having gone back on his decision to allow the exercise of the gifts at the Sunday services. He had been overcome by fear for the safety of everyone the night before. He said that he would keep the implied promise he had then made by forbidding their exercise on the following Sunday evening but that thereafter he would not only allow the Spirit to be heard, but also encourage the gifted.[26]

The elders meanwhile had reacted sharply against the Sunday night confusion which appeared to them to be getting more out of hand each week. Since most of the elders were also trustees, it was resolved to hold a meeting of the trustees 'to consider what steps should be taken in consequence of the tumult and confusion of the previous Sunday evening'.[27] As elders they were under the chairmanship if not the rule of Irving, but as trustees they were not. They met on Saturday 19th November, in the vestry. Irving was present at his own request. They pleaded with him to change his policy regarding his authorization of the gifts in worship but he was quite determined not to be half-hearted in his application of what he understood to be the Word of God, as he explained:

I explained to them that I could not in this matter take any half measures, but would be faithful to God and His Word, and would immediately proceed to set the ordinance of prophesying in order, in the meetings of the church; and because I see prophesying with tongues is as much for the assembling and snaring of the hypocrite (*Isa.* 28 : 13,

14) as for the refreshing of the Saints, I was resolved that whatever class of people might come to the church at any meeting, I would not prevent the Lord from speaking then and there what it pleased Him to speak; and I pointed their attention to that part of the trust-deed which gave into my hand the regulation of everything connected with the public worship of God in the house over which they were the trustees. And after a good deal of conversation, conducted in a very friendly, and I hope, Christian spirit, I came away and left them to deliberate.[28]

Irving's intransigence gave the trustees cause for thought. The meeting was adjourned until the following week. The terms of the trust deed were now under discussion. Already there was talk of legal action although they told their minister that if they should so decide, it would not be before having had a further conference with him. All hoped that litigation would be avoided but as both sides were known formally to each other as having taken up definite and decided positions, it was now a distinct possibility.[29]

On the next day Sunday 20th November, Irving proceeded to 'set the ordinance of prophesying in order, in the meetings of the church'.[30] He admitted that he had been wrong to give his congregation an implied promise the previous Sunday night that he would not allow speaking in tongues any more in the Sunday services. Soon afterwards Miss Emily Cardale spoke in tongues and then in English: 'He shall reveal it! He shall reveal it! Yea, heed it! yea, heed it! Ye are yet in the wilderness. Despise not his word! despise not his word! Not one jot or tittle shall pass away.'[31] During the singing of the Psalm, Mr. Horn an elder and chairman of the trustees came up into the pulpit and asked Irving for permission to read out his Scriptural reasons for not believing the manifestations were of God and for why he was going to leave the church. Irving refused. Mr. Horn then went into the vestry for his hat, walked right down the church and out. There was only one elder then left on duty.[32]

The afternoon's service was attended by two 'sealings' of the Spirit. In the evening, owing to the lack of elders present and the tumult outside, Irving took upon himself the responsibility of locking the doors and keeping them locked during the service. True to his pledge of the week before, he did not allow any gifts to be used at the service, but at the end he announced that in future this would no longer apply. From then on he would allow the Spirit to speak at every service at two regular places, after the Scripture reading and after the sermon.[33]

On the 26th October, Irving had written to his father-in-law regarding the expected reaction to what was then about to burst on the congregation, 'this, I fear, will not be endured by many. But the Lord's will be done. I must forsake all for Him. I live by faith daily'.[34] On 21st November, he wrote to his sister and brother-in-law 'And if I perish, my dear brother and sister, I perish. Let me die the death of the righteous, and let my latter end be like his.'[35] This attitude of complete conviction, resignation and abandonment to his fate had communicated itself to the trustees and was borne home to them with even greater force when they reconvened their meeting on Tuesday 22nd November. It was this fatalistic attitude which made them realize the gravity of the situation. Irving had written them a letter that day in which he told them that in obedience to and with the authority of *I Cor.* 14:23, 29–31, 37 and also *I Cor.* 11 which authorized prophetesses to speak, he had made out a new order of service in which there would be a 'pause for the witness of the Holy Ghost' after the reading of Scripture and after the sermon. He claimed ecclesiastical authority for this from the first Book of Discipline, chapter twelve where there is authorized a weekly exercise for prophesying or interpreting the Scriptures. At the time of the Reformation, 'they had adopted the prevalent but erroneous notion that the office of the apostle, of the evangelist and of the prophet, are not perpetual, and now have ceased in the kirk of God, except when it pleased God extraordinarily for a time to stir some of them up again. (Second Book of Discipline, chapter 2)'. God had raised up these again in the congregation, which he was now ordering according to Scripture and the Church. He asked them not to withstand this work of God and hoped that if they were moved to do so they would confer with him again before they did so.[36]

The trustees could not accept that the minister had the right to make these regulations according to the trust-deed. The meeting was adjourned after discussion and when it was reconvened, Irving, Mr. Cardale, his solicitor and Mr. Mackenzie, the only elder on his side, were invited to attend. They did so. The trustees pleaded with their minister to withdraw his permission for the use of the gifts which they all believed to be not only unconstitutional but delusions. They were unsuccessful.[37]

114

On the Sundays following, the gifts were in operation as usual, only now that the novelty had worn off, the services were no longer attended by the crowds of hostile strangers and trouble makers.[38] At two successive Session meetings similar entreaties were made but to no effect.[39] The trustees were forced to take a firmer attitude and at a meeting on 20th December, unanimously resolved that they could not accept the order of public worship which Irving had instituted. It was against the 'discipline of the Church of Scotland, which, by the trust-deed, they are bound to see maintained'. They could not therefore 'without a most flagrant violation of their duty to the subscribers to the National Scotch Church, suffer the continuation of the order thus established'.[40] On 24th December, Irving replied to this resolution which had been intimated to him. He said he did not feel he was at liberty to deviate from the regulations for worship which he had given in his letter of 22nd November, for the Scriptural and ecclesiastical reasons given there. He believed this was a work of God and he warned them not to try to stop it:

> I most solemnly warn you all, in the name of the Most High God, for no earthly consideration whatever, to gainsay or impede the work of speaking with tongues and prophesying, which God hath begun amongst us, and which answereth in all respects, both formally and spiritually, to the thing promised in the Scriptures to those who believe – possessed in the primitive church; and much prayed for by us all.[41]

This letter finally convinced the trustees that they had no alternative but to take legal advice. It was now clear to them that only litigation could decide a case in which both parties were unshakably convinced they were right.

On the same day as Irving replied to the trustees, he also posted the first of three articles called 'Facts Connected with Recent Manifestations of Spiritual Gifts' to Mr. James Fraser, editor of *Fraser's Magazine*. This appeared in the January 1832 issue and has been used as the basic narrative for Part 2 of this study. In the introduction he says that if anyone wished to study the teaching that he had first broached in his second baptismal sermon they might do so 'more fully in a *Treatise on the Baptism with the Holy Ghost* whereof the first part was published a few weeks ago'.[42] He had been 'preaching to thousands the Baptism with the Holy Ghost' at the mid-week services earlier in the autumn. Now these sermons were published. The first recipients of this new tract had been the trustees who had each received a free copy along with his letter to their meeting on 22nd November.[43] Over the past months, his thoughts had been centring on the biblical teaching of the baptism with the Holy Ghost. This publication was meant to be the first part of a longer work but no second or third part was ever produced. Apart from the earlier references which have already been noted this was his only work on this subject. It is therefore his first and last piece of sustained reflection on this theme and, since it is also almost the last thing he published, is the climax of his writings on the topic of this study. He regarded it as 'the most glorious and blessed theme of which I have ever yet discoursed' for it was 'the very glory of God in the sight of angels and of men':[44]

> Oh, brother! this baptism with the Holy Ghost, which I am about to teach thee of, is the very glory of God in the sight of angels and of men: wilt thou not be the bearer of it? Whilst thou heard not of it, thou couldst not desire it; but now that I am about to teach it thee, I beseech thee to open thine ears, for it is the most glorious and blessed theme of which I have ever yet discoursed, or of which thou hast ever yet heard.[45]

PART FOUR

13

The Baptism with the
Holy Spirit: What it is not

IN *The Day of Pentecost or The Baptism with the Holy Ghost.* Part
1. Section 1, preached in the autumn of 1831 and published,
November, 1831, Irving introduces his subject by saying that, as
a king's herald must be listened to because he bears the king's message
so John the Baptist, herald of Jesus Christ, must be listened to. What
word does he bring from the King?[1] It is this: 'He that sent me to
baptize with water, the same said unto me, upon whom thou shalt see
the Spirit descending, and remaining on him, the same is he which
baptizeth with the Holy Ghost' (*John* 1:33). John's gospel also says
'Behold the Lamb of God, which taketh away the sin of the world.'
Other functions of Jesus are mentioned but this work of baptizing
with the Holy Spirit, is the only one that is mentioned by all the
Gospel writers. The atonement of Christ opened the floodgates of
mercy and holiness but the baptism with the Holy Ghost is 'his
nobile officium' and is:

> The *end* unto which all the other work he wrought, of keeping the
> law, of condemning sin in the flesh, of openly triumphing over devils
> in his cross, and over death in his resurrection, were the *means*.[2]

This is further borne out by the infinite superiority of the baptizer
with the Holy Spirit over the baptizer with water:

> The superior dignity of baptizing with the Holy Ghost, is further
> manifest from the superior sanctity of the Holy Ghost. All manner of
> blasphemy against the Son of Man shall be forgiven; but the blasphemy
> against the Holy Ghost shall neither be forgiven, in this world nor in
> that which is to come. And why so? Because the Son of Man is Son of

God manifested in the form of mortal life, under the infirmities, temptations, and disadvantages of this our fallen estate; but the Holy Ghost is the same Son of God manifested in the form of that eternal and Divine life which he entered into by the resurrection from the dead.[3]

The work of the Son of Man; up until the resurrection consisted in His taking mortal life and offering it as a perfect sinless sacrifice on the cross but the work of the Holy Spirit is to manifest 'that inexhaustible and glorious eternal life into which Christ entered at the resurrection',[4] which he communicated to the Church on the day of Pentecost. This life is the very wisdom, knowledge and power of God in the Church. This is the superior dignity and excellence of Christ's office as baptizer with the Holy Spirit.

> How much the life of Christ upon the throne of God is fuller, better, and mightier than the life of Adam as he was created, than the life of a poor, oppressed, yet innocent, mortal creature; so much is the manifestation of the Holy Ghost more admirable than the manifestation of the Son of Man, and the sin against the one more terrible than the sin against the other; so much also is the dignity of baptizing with the Holy Ghost a more excellent dignity than any other of all which pertain to Christ: it is his prerogative, his supremacy; which pertains to him as 'the beloved Son of God, in whom he is well pleased'.[5]

When the Son of God took our flesh and blood, the first thing He had to do was to redeem it from the power of sin by making it obey the law of God. The second thing which He had to do was to allow His holy flesh and blood to be a sacrifice to satisfy the justice of God. Having made this offering he received resurrection life, which is not Adam's life restored, but a new and far more wonderful life conferred by God, which contains His fulness. It is this life which He then received which He 'communicates to the Church by baptism with the Holy Ghost':

> Now this is the possession into which the baptism with the Holy Ghost introduceth us; this is the fountain of which we drink; this is the power with which we are anointed; this the life into which we are introduced. Not indeed manifested now in the blaze of its glory, but under the veil of this corruptible flesh; yet verily and indeed life of that life, power of that power, being of that being; 'born not of blood, nor of the will of the flesh, nor of the will of man, but of God'.

Christ's natural life was 'but holy mortal life' which ended in Him dying a spotless death, but the new life into which He entered and of which we partake in the baptism with the Holy Spirit, begins with conquering death and ends in 'the fulness of God' and the 'stature of Christ'.[6]

Scripture makes it clear that Christ did not fulfil this office of baptizing with the Holy Spirit until Pentecost, for it says of Jesus after the resurrection 'And, being assembled together with them, he commanded them that they should not depart from Jerusalem, but wait for the promise of the Father, which, saith he, ye have heard of me. For John truly baptized with water; but ye shall be baptized with the Holy Ghost, not many days hence.' (*Acts* 1:4, 5.)[7] This shows that although the Holy Spirit was in all men of faith, the prophets, the earlier apostolic acts and in the breathing of the Holy Spirit on the disciples by Jesus, nevertheless none of these constituted the act of Jesus baptizing with the Holy Spirit. This is confirmed in *John* 7:37–39 where it says 'In the last day, that great day of the feast, Jesus stood and cried, saying, If any man thirst, let him come unto me, and drink: he that believeth on me, as the Scripture hath said, out of his belly shall flow rivers of living water. But this spake he of the Spirit, which they that believe on him should receive: for the Holy Spirit was not yet given, because that Jesus was not yet glorified.' *Acts* 1:5, says that they were to be baptized with the Holy Spirit 'not many days hence'.[8] It was in fact, ten days. What happened on the day of Pentecost is shown to be this baptism with the Holy Ghost both by what took place, 'They were all filled with the Holy Ghost and spake with tongues, as the Spirit gave them utterance' and by what Peter said about it, 'Having received of the Father the promise of the Holy Ghost, he hath shed forth this which ye now see and hear.' It was also demonstrated by their power and in their witness-bearing which it had been promised they would receive from the Spirit: 'But ye shall receive power after that the Holy Ghost is come upon you: and ye shall be witnesses unto me, both in Jerusalem, and in all Judea, and in Samaria, and unto the uttermost part of the earth.' (*Acts* 1:8.) From all these texts it is quite certain that 'the great and chief work of "baptizing with the Holy Ghost", for which Christ came forth from the Father, was on the day of Pentecost accomplished to the Church'.[9] For this reason Irving has called his discourse 'The Day of Pentecost, or the Baptism with the Holy Ghost'. After these introductory remarks he begins the main study.

Part 1. *The Baptism of the Holy Ghost in the Form of Promise.*

Jesus calls the baptism of the Holy Spirit 'the promise of my Father' and 'power from on high' (*Luke* 24:49).[10] The corresponding narrative in Acts identifies 'the promise of the Father' with being 'baptized with the Holy Ghost' (*Acts* 1:4, 5). 'Power from on high' is also identified with the baptism with the Holy Spirit in *Acts* 1:7, 8.[11] Since Jesus therefore called this baptism 'the promise of the Father' and 'power from on high' Irving will examine these two names. Before he does so he states that the passage where Jesus said 'Receive ye the Holy Ghost' (*John* 20:21–23) has an equivalent meaning to His opening up of their understanding of the Scriptures (*John* 24:45) and His giving commandments to the apostles through the Spirit (*Acts* 1:2).[12] As has been already noted, it does not refer to the baptism with the Holy Spirit. In his study of what the baptism with the Holy Spirit is in promise before the day of Pentecost, Irving will speak 'first *negatively*, by showing those operations which are distinct from it, and in the order of time anterior thereto'.[13]

1. On the divers Operations of the Holy Ghost, to separate those which are not 'the Baptism with the Holy Ghost'.

The expression 'the Promise of the Father' does not mean 'which the Father promised' because Jesus added 'which ye heard of me'. It means 'the promised Father'. Christ was the Promiser. The promise, contained in *John* 14, 15 and 16, is that they will be one with the Father and be able to do all things from His indwelling. Christ promised this because He was going to the Father, in order to receive it for distribution. Peter testifies to its reception on the day of Pentecost: 'Therefore, being by the right hand of God exalted, and having received of the Father the promise of the Holy Ghost, he hath shed forth this, which ye now see and hear.' (*Acts* 2:33.) In order to know the full meaning of the expression 'the promise of the Father' Irving says 'it will be necessary to shew what part of Christ's work in the flesh was proper to the Son, and what part was proper to the Father'. Everything which is in the members must first be seen in the Head 'who is God's model of working' to whom all the members are to be conformed:

> Now, if we can discover what part in Christ's work was proper to the Father, that certainly is the thing which is assured to us in the promise of the Father; for the Father's way of working is always the same.[14]

122

When the Son of God became man, He never, of Himself, did anything 'above or beyond the proper limits and bounds of man's habitation'. Whenever He did so He always attributed it to His Father: 'The words which I speak, I speak not of myself' and 'the Father, which is within me, he doeth the works'. It is the Son's part to occupy human flesh and blood in righteousness and holiness. It is the Father's part to fill this sinless and holy Man with His own indwelling of superhuman power and knowledge:

The Father took up his abode in him immediately upon his baptism, coming in the person of the Holy Ghost in the form of a dove. Then Christ was baptized with the Holy Ghost; then he received the promise of the Father; and then also he was anointed with the Holy Ghost and with power: and from that time he went forth preaching the Gospel, and 'healing all that were oppressed with the devil, for God was with him' (*Acts* 10). Anterior to this he had done the man's perfect part, as the same is contained in the Law; he had 'fulfilled all righteousness', and 'well pleased' the Father. And this he had done, without any indwelling of the Father or baptism of the Holy Ghost, in the strength of manhood sustained by the Divine Person of the Son of God; acting continual faith upon the help of God, and fulfilling the requirements of the Law, which enforce love to God with all the heart, and love of our neighbour as ourselves. This work of perfect righteousness and satisfaction being accomplished, the Father baptizeth him with the Holy Ghost, and he becomes the holy man inhabited by the Spirit of the Almighty God, and ever after speaks of his words and actings as not his own, but the Father's, which had sent him. In virtue of his incarnation he uniteth himself with flesh; is the Person acting in it; not the inhabiter of it, but the owner of it; one with it, to continue one with it for ever, in order to do its work, to take upon him its responsibilities, to accomplish its redemption, and glorify God in having created it. And this he had accomplished, so far as the obedience of the Law was concerned, on the morning of his baptism, and in reward thereof received the promise of the Father's inhabitation; and, being inhabited by the Father, thereafter did not the work of man only, but the work of God also; spoke not the word of man only, but the word of the Father also. And after he had sufficiently shown the faithfulness and the power of the God-inhabited Man, he again descended into the arena of conflict for man's rights; and, being forsaken of the Father, was brought into the hour and power of darkness; and being in an agony and bloody sweat, in fearful swimmings and swoonings of heart, and horrors of thick darkness, which are all set forth in the Psalms, he did by this hideous passage enter into the confines and captivity of death and hades; and in manhood, bare manhood, with no more than the naked implement of manhood, he did, he the Son of God did, finish and endure all man's desert; and, receiving again the mightiest power of the Spirit, more mighty than what fell on him at his baptism, he did lead the captivity captive, and rise in the power and majesty and glory of the resurrection life, to be the dwelling-place of God for ever and ever; in whom the Father worketh and shall continue to work all his works. Incarnation, to recover man's original righteousness, is the work of the Son; and inhabitation of God thereupon, to glorify the righteous man with his own mind and power, is the work of the Father. And in these two, incarnation and inhabitation, standeth the whole work of Godhead for the redemption, regeneration, and glorification of man.[15]

The Holy Spirit is the 'substance and life' of both these operations of the Father and the Son. For neither the Father, nor the Son, does anything without the Spirit. In the work of incarnation the Spirit generates the Son a creature and enables Him to satisfy the law in perfect holiness and to complete the redemption of man in 'man's habitation'. But this work was not 'the promise of the Father' or the baptism of the Holy Spirit. 'It was all finished before the Father came to inhabit Christ with power', and the Church had received all this before the day of Pentecost as Jesus testified when He said 'I have manifested thy name unto the men which thou gavest me out of the world: thine they were, and thou gavest them me; and they have kept thy word. Now they have known that all things, whatsoever thou hast given me, are of thee; for I have given unto them the words which thou gavest me; and they have received them and have known surely that I came out from thee, and they have believed that thou didst send me'. (*John* 17:6–8.)[16] But they had not yet received the baptism of the Holy Spirit, 'the inhabitation of the Father', for Jesus went on to pray that He might be in them: 'Neither pray I for these alone, but for them also which shall believe on me through their word; that they all may be one; as thou, Father, art in me, and I in thee, that they also may be one in us; that the world may believe that thou hast sent me. And the glory which thou gavest me I have given them; that they may be one, even as we are one; and that the world may know that thou hast sent me, and hast loved them as thou hast loved me.' (*John* 17:20–23.)

The glory of Christ in which we share is 'the inhabitation and inworking of the Father'. He had a measure of it after His baptism and has it without measure since His ascension to glory. The Church's oneness with the Father is the same as that which He had during His public ministry. This is the reward which He promises consequent to our 'union of faith and love with Him as the Head of redemption and the loving Lord of all.' He speaks of it as He and His Father making their abode in those who faithfully keep His words (*John* 14:22, 24), and as Their power to answer prayers: 'If ye abide in me, and my words abide in you, ye shall ask what ye will, and it shall be done unto you. Herein is my Father glorified, that ye bear much fruit; so shall ye be my disciples.' (*John* 15:7, 8.)[17] These and similar passages contain 'the promise of the Father'. The disciples were to wait for it in the shape of the same power that Christ had received at His baptism, that they might become 'walking, speaking, acting temples of God the Father', as it says in *II Cor.* 6:16, 'for ye are the temple of the living God; as God hath said, I will dwell in them and walk in them; and I will be their God, and they shall be my people'. This operation of the Spirit is different to that which brings us to believe and stand in Christ. 'It is the consequence of union, and not the antecedence or the sustenance of it.' There are then, three operations of the Spirit, the first two of which, regeneration and sanctification, are not the baptism of the Holy Spirit. As these operations are in Christ, so they are in us because of our union with Him:

As the operation of the Holy Ghost brought Christ into manhood, which is generation; so the continuance of that kind of operation brings the elect and believing ones of the Father forth from the bosom of his counsels unto Christ; and this is regeneration, conducted properly under the hand of the Father. Being brought unto Christ, another operation of the Holy Ghost doth wash and cleanse, and feed and nourish us up in him, upon his flesh and blood; and this is under the hand of the Son, being the continuance of that which he put forth upon himself in the days of his flesh, and by which he continually resisted and overcame temptation, and presented himself holy. This Christ worketh in his members continually, and it is properly their life, their nursing, and their feeding, and their fitting to be the temples of God. Then cometh the third and last operation of the Holy Ghost, which is baptism with the Holy Ghost, bringing into the believer, thus united with Christ, the fulness of that inhabitation of the Father which Christ now enjoys for ever. And this is the coming of the Father and the Son to dwell in us, and make their abode with us: this is the thing into which we are searching under the name 'promise of the Father', or 'baptism with the Holy Ghost'.[18]

Although man never possessed this third operation of the Spirit 'until Christ was baptized with the Dove from heaven, and raised from the dead, and ascended into glory', nevertheless 'it lay wrapped up in man as a capacity; which Satan well knowing, addressed his temptation thereto, saying, 'Ye shall be as Gods.' God intended this for man from the beginning but first Satan must be overcome by man 'for by man God intended to justify himself against Satan'. Man failed, but God did not alter His original purpose. Instead, He 'set forth this other life to any one who would keep his law'. God could not give this to the wicked, for that would make Him an encourager of wickedness which it is in His nature to destroy:

> But no man did yield righteousness, until the man Jesus fulfilled all righteousness, despite of all temptations, and thus was taken into the third sphere of the Holy Ghost operation; being baptized with the Spirit, or inhabited by the Father.[19]

Further proof of the distinctness of this third operation of the Spirit is adduced from the contrast between the baptism of repentance for the remission of sins (*Mark* 1:4), of John the Baptist and the baptism of the Holy Spirit. This contrast is sustained also by Jesus and Peter as in *Acts* 11:16. 'Then remembered I the word of the Lord, how that he said, John indeed baptized with water; but ye shall be baptized with the Holy Ghost.' John's baptism went as far as Christian baptism except for the baptism with the Holy Ghost (*Acts* 2:38, 39). This is made even clearer in the story of Apollos and Paul at Ephesus (*Acts* 18 and 19).[20] It is important to realize from this that our fathers in the faith and we ourselves 'may still have been Christians, true members of Christ, washed from our sins in his blood, and changed of heart, notwithstanding we have no signs of the Holy Ghost's baptism, nor tokens of an indwelling Father, to produce'.[21] Irving believed that such had been the condition of the Church since the first three centuries; just like it was before the day of Pentecost:

> And this I believe to be the exact condition into which the church hath fallen back since the first three centuries; the same as the condition in which the church stood anterior to the day of Pentecost, with a Baptism for repentance and remission of sins, with a Lord's Supper

for union to Christ and feeding on his flesh and blood; – in which the Ephesian church was anterior to the visit of Paul, 'speaking and teaching diligently the things of the Lord . . . mightily convincing the Jews and shewing out of the Scriptures that Jesus is the Christ'; yet without baptism with the Holy Ghost, which it is Christ's chief office to bestow, the church's chief glory to possess, the Father's great desire to exhibit in the sight of the world . . . whose standing sign, if we err not, is the speaking with tongues.[22]

Having shown what the baptism with the Holy Spirit is not, Irving now goes on to show what it is.

14

The Baptism with the Holy Spirit: What it is

WHAT THEN is the baptism with the Holy Spirit? The answer simply is:

All beyond the created powers and faculties of man, which man hath ever possessed, doth now possess, or shall possess for ever.[1]

From the beginning God chose man to be His dwelling place and for that purpose made him in His own image and likeness. In so doing he did not intend to make Himself a man or to make man God or to mingle Creator and creature in any way. He meant to do it 'by the organs and faculties of that creature' putting forth 'His own surpassing beauty, supreme majesty, infinite love and almighty strength'. This original purpose 'had been long defeated by the sinfulness of man'.[2] It was only through His own Son becoming man and overcoming sin in the flesh that his initial intention could be realized. The Father inhabited the perfect man Christ and did all the marvellous things of superhuman knowledge, wisdom, demon exorcism, healing, power over the elements, raising the dead, abolishing death and the grave, love, preaching and all the other acts recorded in the Gospels:

Christ, as a creature, was a poor weak mortal; a worm, and no man. This he consented to be; this he was, in the form of a slave; but what power was given him! what liberty! what Godhead wisdom! what Godhead virtue! (*John* 3:34, 35; *Luke* 10:22; *John* 14, 10, 11). . . . The works did testify that God was with him, because they were works proper to the Creator. . . . To do these things was not man's province, himself mortal, nor Adam's at first, nor angels', nor any creature's, but only God's; and so God exhibited himself in action, through the powers and faculties of the Man Jesus. He revealed the Father in will, in thought, in word, in act. To do this, was in his case the baptism with the Holy Ghost. And what is it in ours? The same, the very same.[3]

We are to expect the same things to be displayed in us because what was done in Christ was done in Him as man. The Creator became the creature, that what had been planned for man since creation, might at last be received:

> For this end He, who was the Creator of all things, became the creature man, that in the creature man he might receive those things which had been intended for man from the time of his creation, yea, before the world was made. These purposes concerning man were not made for any other being but for man; and Christ, in order that they might be realized, became man. That his Father's infinite grace, predetermined upon this much-favoured creature, might be no more hindered or postponed, Christ himself took that creature's form, and presented the faultless subject for the Father to do all his will upon. And the same honours which Christ hath attained as man, are reserved for every man who walketh in his footsteps. . . . 'The glory which thou gavest me I have given them; that they may be one even as we are one' (*John* 17:22).[4]

To question this 'is not to understand the doctrine of the incarnation at all'. Such passages as *Luke* 10:19, 20; 12:10–12 and *John* 17:8, show that He shared 'his flesh-inheritance of the Holy Ghost' with those who believed. *Acts* 2:32, 33 shows how He shared the inheritance which He received on His ascension to glory:[5]

> There is as perfect sympathy between Christ in glory and his members on the earth, as between the head and the members of the body, between the trunk and the branches of the vine; and therefore we are not only to expect that the works which he did we shall do also, but that greater works we shall do, because he is gone to the Father, and hath received power which in this world he did not possess.[6]

We understand therefore that by the baptism of the Holy Spirit and the indwelling of the Father, the works of God, as they were manifest in Christ, are to be manifest in us and that the life of Christ is an example to the believer 'in its miraculous and divine works, as it is to him in its humility, meekness, and holiness'. Also that we may enjoy what Christ enjoyed of the Father's indwelling (*John* 15:11); and peace (*John* 14:27); and insight into His mind (*John* 14:26);

and truth (*John* 15:26, 27); and power (*John* 14:12); and faith (*Matt.* 21:21); and prayer (*Matt.* 21:22); and knowledge (*John* 16:13, 14); and all things (*John* 16:15; *I Cor.* 2:7; *I John* 2:20, 27; *Eph.* 3:19; 4:13, 15, etc., etc.).[7] There are numerous texts which indicate that the New Testament Church took for granted that it was a community of power and had possession of the indwelling Father. The most detailed of these is the list of diversities of operations of the manifested Holy Spirit, inworkings of the Father and endowments of Christ in *I Cor.* 12:4–11. The enumeration of these gifts is demonstrative of the great truth which Irving is presenting, which is:

> *That the baptism of the Holy Ghost doth bring to every believer the presence of the Father and the power of the Holy Ghost, according to that measure, at the least, in which Christ during the days of his flesh possessed the same.*
> My idea, therefore, concerning the baptism of the Holy Ghost, or the promise of the Father, is simply this, that it is a superhuman supernatural power, or set of powers, which God did from the beginning purpose to place in man, but which he accomplished not to do until his own Son had become man, and kept man's original trust.[8]

Once Christ had removed the obstacle of sin, 'Then God attained that for which he had longed', and accomplished his great purpose for making man possessor of 'all power in heaven and in earth'. As this superhuman life was always intended for mankind, so Christ, having received it, immediately began to give it to others (*Eph.* 2:4–7).[9] This superhuman endowment of divine power was within man's capacity and desire from the beginning. That is what gave reality to Satan's temptation 'Ye shall be as Gods.' It is also indicated in the creation of man 'in God's image and likeness', that He might show Himself through the same. This is not idolatry but revelation:

> Not that man might be seen to be God, but that God might dwell in, and be seen dwelling in, man. It reduces you at once to anthropomorphism, if you do not recognize the truth that God was to be seen dwelling in the image, not the image as the representative of God. An image the representative of God, is the essence of idolatry: God dwelling in that form of creature which is made to be his image, is revelation or manifestation of himself. In the very creation of man, therefore, I see the purposes of inhabitation, and endowment with attributes divine, as clearly contained, as I see it fully accomplished in the resurrection of Christ.[10]

Irving saw this foreshadowed in the cherubim, the symbol of the Church, in which God lived and from which His power proceeded.[11] Also in the prophets' miraculous powers. Also in the wonders done by the angel of the Covenant.[12] These are all types and symbols of God dwelling in man which were realized when Christ ascended to glory:

> The resurrection life, is life of God within the man; it was first consummated in Christ, and belongs to us in virtue of union with him. We have it only as a baptism till then; as he had it as a baptism from the day of his baptism until the day of his agony.[13]

'The Promise of the Father' therefore means the promise of the power of the Godhead. The promise which it was given to the prophets to proclaim was of Messiah, the Son of Man, who would redeem man and his world from evil. When Messiah comes, He also has a promise:

> He comes not only to be the end and seal of all former prophecies, but to originate a far higher and more glorious promise than they had brought; which is, the promise of the Father. They promised the Son; the Son, when he comes, promised the Father. They promise manhood's Redeemer; he promiseth manhood's Glorifier. They promise holiness in flesh, and life from the dead, through the incarnation of God; he promiseth Divine wisdom, power and glory, through inhabitation and inworking of God. Therefore he could properly say, 'The Promise of the Father, *which ye have heard of* ME' – of *him,* and not of any *former prophet* – for though the former prophets had given hints of the day of Pentecost, yet did they not speak of it as the inhabitation of the Father; 'For no one knoweth the Father, but the Son, and he to whom the Son shall reveal him.'[14]

Irving then touches briefly on the second name that Jesus gives to the baptism of the Holy Spirit, that is 'power from on high'. He says that this name fits into the same pattern of exposition which he has followed for the first one. The text 'all power in heaven and on earth has been given unto me' sums up the complete inheritance of Christ's power as Son of God and Son of Man, 'power from on high' referring to the former, a baptismal share of which we inherit through union with Him.[15]

These two sections, what the baptism with the Holy Spirit is not and what it is, can be summed up by a Trinitarian presentation of the three spheres of Divine operation:

There are, therefore, three spheres of Divine operation in man, to every one of which the Father and the Son and the Holy Ghost co-operate, and over each one of which one of the Three Persons presides respectively; so as that, in bringing man to perfection, not only the unity of the Three Persons in one substance, but also their distinctness of personality in the same, should be shewn gloriously forth. The first sphere is creation, the second is incarnation, the third is inhabitation; the former under the hand of the Father, with the co-operation of the other two Persons according to their offices; the second under the hand of the Son, with the same co-operation; the other under the hand of the Holy Ghost, with the same co-operation.[16]

He finishes this second section with a final definition of what the baptism with the Holy Spirit is:

It is an act of Christ's, whereby he doth give to his church the Holy Ghost, to dwell in them, and to work in them all the joy and consolation, all the word and power, which reside in himself; to the end that, in obeying the motions of the Holy Ghost within us, we may shew forth in the world, and to the world, the goodness of God, and the power and glory of the Son of Man, who sitteth in God's throne, and exerciseth all the power of the Father in his presence.[17]

15

The Baptism with the Holy Spirit: Further Confirmation of the Doctrine from Scripture

IN THE third and final section, *The Day of Pentecost or The Baptism with the Holy Ghost,* preached in the autumn of 1831, Irving goes on to confirm and amplify the doctrine which he has stated. He does so first by expositions of all the Old Testament promises and prophecies which are mentioned in the New and which refer to the subject. These are (1) *II Cor.* 6:16–18 and *Lev.* 26:11, 12 which show the glory of the tabernacle or temple as a type of the church with the baptism of the Holy Spirit.[1] (2) *Eph.* 4:1–16 and *Psalm* 68:18 which speak of the unity and diversity of the gifts of the Spirit bestowed by the glorified Man on his disciples.[2] (3) *Acts* 2:16–21 and *Joel* 2:28, 29 which show that the baptism of the Holy Spirit generalizes to all the members of Christ's body 'that gift of prophecy, vision, and dreams, which had resided in a few chosen and distinguished persons raised up for special occasions.'[3] (4) *I Cor.* 14 and *Isa.* 28 and 29 in which speaking in tongues is spoken of as a new form of prophecy which God had devised as a last effort to reach His disobedient people before He visited them with His judgement.[4] (5) *Luke* 4:18 and *Isa.* 61:1, 2, which speak of the anointing of the Divine reason in Christ and which comes to the Church as the gifts of 'the word of wisdom and the word of knowledge' and the capacity to receive the things of the Spirit (*I Cor.* 2)[5] (6) *John* 7:37–39 and *Isa.* 12:3; 32:15; 44:3 which emphasize that the Spirit would be given by Christ 'not by outward effusion' as in the Old Testament references 'but by inward inhabitation, inexhaustible upspringing and plentiful outpouring'. The water flowing from the rock is the type of the rivers of living waters flowing out of the belly of the believer.[6]

These are but six examples of what 'is not the subject of a few isolated texts of the Old Testament, but the burden of all the prophets, the theme of all the Psalms, and the end of all the types and symbols of the Law'.[7] The one object of prophecy is to foretell and describe this blessed condition of inhabitation:

> And being so, instead of selecting a few passages, we might have quoted and commented upon half, and more than half, of all the prophetical word and symbolical institutions of the Old Testament, as pertaining to our subject, and containing the perfection and completeness of that supernatural work of the Holy Ghost, both over mind and over matter, whereof his baptism is the first-fruits and earnest.[8]

Having dealt with these Old Testament prophecies, Irving now turns to the Gospels where the baptism with the Holy Spirit is also spoken of prophetically.

In the Old Testament, the calling and utterances of the prophets are ascribed to the word of God which came to them, but in the New Testament from the visitation of Zacharias onwards 'every one of God's communications through man is ascribed to their being filled with the Holy Ghost'.[9] This tells us that 'we are arrived at a new era in the history of God's dealings, which is the era of the fulness of the Holy Ghost.' There is plentiful information about all this in the words and works of Jesus.[10]

The first thing that must be stated is that all the words and works of Jesus Christ's public ministry are 'the manifestation at large, so far as they go, of the baptism with the Holy Ghost with which He was anointed in the form of a dove'.[11] *Luke* 4:18–22 and *Acts* 10:36–38 show that His preaching and power began after His anointing and not after His generation, birth, infancy or youth:

> It is a confusion, therefore, by no means to be permitted, to overlook this destination of the Holy Ghost, and to ascribe it all to the miraculous generation, or, as most do, to his personality as a Divine Person. The glory of his personality is seen in his deigning to become man, and keep himself so; in his willingness to receive all the virtue of a holy human life from his Father in the generation of the Holy Ghost, all the power of witness-bearing and witness-working and God-manifesting in the baptism of the Holy Ghost. . . . I hold to the position, that not in virtue of the Holy Ghost's generation, but in virtue

of the Holy Ghost's baptism, did Jesus preach with authority the word of peace, and heal all that were oppressed with the devil . . . (*John* 14:10). And that these works were not done in him of the Father in virtue of any thing proper to him as a Divine Person, but in consequence of his holy manhood and by means thereof, is manifest from the same works, yea, and greater being assured unto all who believe, in the verses immediately following: 'Believe me that I am in the Father, and the Father in me: or else believe me for the very work's sake. Verily, verily, I say unto you, he that believeth on me, the works that I do shall he do also; and greater works than these shall he do; because I go unto my Father' (vv. 11, 12) . . . (*John* 5:19, 23).[12]

The following points may be made about the life and ministry of Christ: 1. We must look to the ministry of Jesus in order to see the baptism of the Holy Spirit laid out in full.[13] We follow in His footsteps. 'He was the thing which He promised that they should be, in virtue of the baptism with the Holy Ghost; whose manner of working changeth not.'[14] We must carry ourselves after this model.[15]

2. The baptism with the Holy Spirit never violates any ties, obligations of nature or moral duties. It fulfils the law. When Jesus seemed to break the law on occasions he was only 'retrieving the law from a use of bondage into the right use of liberty'.[16]

3. This baptism never does away with our obligations to the church or to the state. Jesus paid tribute and went to the synagogue, as did his disciples (*Acts* 18:20). Even though the Church today be in the grip of Satan, we are not to act against it but are to go on quietly with Christ's work. So also with the state. We do not pull down the establishment. We bear persecution meekly as it comes and go on with our Christian testimony.[17]

4. The baptism in the Holy Spirit gives a new strength to the human will or spirit. There is as much strength given to use and administer the power as there is power itself, 'and this power was to the end of administering the supremacy of the spiritual and invisible world'.[18]

5. This last observation is confirmed by the temptation of Jesus following His baptism. Immediately after the power was given, it was tested and tried.[19] This shows also that the baptism was given for the subjection of the spiritual world, that man might have sovereignty over it:

And in virtue of this new region of sovereignty into which the spiritual baptism doth introduce men, it is, that the sin against the

135

Holy Ghost, or the abuse of this wonderful power, is so fearful and utterly unpardonable. Man's fall out of the natural supremacy was retrievable, but his fall out of the spiritual is utterly irretrievable. The one led to shocking natural sins and corruptions, such as were found exhibited in the heathen world, and are recorded in the first chapter of the Romans and elsewhere: but these are almost nothing when compared with the hideous blasphemies, satanic mockeries, unheard of heresies, and spiritual delusions, which the apostates from the primitive church fell into and practised as holy acts of religion, and palmed upon the world as the worship of God and of Christ. And I feel assured that all which then fell out is as nothing when compared with what shall yet be seen, and that immediately, in the Christian Church, when the gifts of the Holy Ghost shall have been conferred again, and with them the power of quenching, resisting, and blaspheming the Holy Ghost.[20]

6. Because of His inhabitation by God, Jesus could also communicate the whole mind and will of His Father. His authority (*Luke* 4; *John* 7:15) and wisdom He learnt from God through the Spirit and did not possess through natural powers. It is the same for us (*I Cor.* 2:9–11). Irving returns to his Trinitarian understanding of this and speaks again against those who believe that it was through His Godhead that Jesus 'got hold of God's mind'.[21] This view is not according to the truth of the Trinity:

> But that view of the subject is not according to the truth of the Trinity, which, even in the absolute Godhead, doth require that the Spirit should intercommune between the Father and the Son; but still less doth it stand with the doctrine of the Incarnation, which requireth that the Son be very man, acting and thinking always within man's bounds, and that the Holy Spirit carry on the intercourse between the absolute Godhead of the Father and the Son, thus restricting himself to the bounds of manhood. If the Son, having become man, can out of manhood reach up into the secret bosom of God, and comprehend and reveal the things therein, man is made commensurate with God; and the work of Jesus hath glorified manhood unto God, instead of revealing Godhead in man. But if Jesus, being man, can reveal no truth of God, otherwise than as the Father bringeth it unto him by the Holy Ghost, then is the limitations of manhood ascertained, and his dependence upon God for knowledge, as for everything besides, is revealed.[22]

The baptism of the Holy Spirit also gave the man Christ Jesus power over other men and over nature, animate and inanimate. It also gave him power to heal.[23] Having now looked at the example of this power in His life and ministry, Irving goes on to examine some of His words.

The first word to be considered is in the Sermon on the Mount. 1. 'Beware of false prophets . . . by their fruits ye shall know them . . . Lord, have we not prophesied in thy name? . . . depart from me, ye that work iniquity' (*Matt.* 7:15–23). Prophecy, casting out of devils and the working of many miracles correspond to the three divisions of the spiritual world. Jesus said that these powers would be revealed to have been in the hands of wicked men. Can this be so or were they possessed by false spirits? Irving thinks it could be so but it could also be demonic counterfeit. He believed that it had been so and would be so again. There were ministers of Satan who did wonders and who called themselves ministers of Christ (*I John* 4:1; *I Cor.* 12:3; *II Cor.* 11:13–15; *Matt.* 24:24).[24] He thought that the followers of Joanna Southcote were such in his day.

It was not enough to say 'show me a miracle and I will believe'. The miracle could be a wonder of Satan.[25] All such must be tested by their fruit. These passages also indicate, as in the Corinthian Church, that even these gifts, when not exercised for love, could be the occasion of much sin (also *Heb.* 6:4–6). Apostates might carry away these gifts with them and serve Satan. However mysterious or unaccountable it might seem, this passage tells us:

> That neither prophecy nor casting out of devils, nor doing of won-derful works, in the name of Jesus, is any certain proof and demon-stration of being in a saved state; nay, nor even of ever having known Jesus, or having done the will of his Father in heaven.[26]

Just as there was a Judas among the twelve, so there will be hypo-crites and backsliders among those who have received miraculous powers. Irving therefore counsels that those who have not been baptized with the Holy Spirit seek first the indwelling of Jesus and those who have, abide more closely in Him.[27]

2. The next passage is *Matt.* 12:22–38, where the Pharisees accuse Jesus of casting out devils by the prince of devils.[28] After telling them that this was not possible, He goes on to say 'If I cast out devils by the Spirit of God, then the kingdom of God is come unto you' (v. 28). This indicates 'that the casting out of devils is an infallible proof of the power of God triumphing over the power of Satan'.[29] Then Jesus

says that all forms of blasphemy will be forgiven, including blasphemy against the Son of Man, but blasphemy against the Holy Spirit will not (vv. 31, 32). This must be understood in its context which was 'the case of men ascribing unto evil agency the manifestations of the Holy Ghost'. To do this 'is to speak against God manifested in the full blaze of his power and goodness and grace'. Since there is no fuller demonstration of this Divine power to be made, there can be no forgiveness for those who ascribe these things to the devil. Irving saw a parallel situation arising in the Church of his day as the Lord restored these manifestations and men were forced to decide for or against the Spirit:

> My heart is exceeding heavy while I indite these things; for I feel assured that the time is near when the church in these lands shall be brought to this perilous test. We shall ere long have lifted up amongst us the full manifestation of the Holy Ghost, which is already present in the speaking with tongues; and when to this are added the other manifestations (and the time, I believe, is not distant), then things are come to a crisis with the church; and she must either decide for the Holy Ghost or against him, for her own salvation or her own perdition for ever and ever. It is the sense of this near and unknown crisis which chiefly moveth me to put forth these views of the baptism of the Holy Ghost; that, by the grace and mercy of God, I may do my part to prevent the overhanging ruin, and lead many, if not all, away from the brink of perdition unto the green pastures and still waters of peace and truth and love.[30]

3. The next and last passage is *Luke* 11:8–13 in which Jesus tells the story of the unfortunate traveller who asks for bread at midnight.[31] This is a parable about the persistent prayer that God will answer; especially prayer for the Holy Spirit '. . . If ye then, being evil, know how to give good gifts unto your children, how much more shall your heavenly Father give the Holy Spirit to them that ask him?' Jesus commands 'ask . . . seek . . . knock' for the Holy Spirit. We can therefore only account for our own lack of the Spirit by our failure to ask Him for it. This passage also tells us that God will give good gifts and not stones, serpents or scorpions.

There are many who have said to Irving that the gifts of the Spirit should not be sought because they might prove dangerous. There are others who, having prayed for these things and seen and heard them manifest in godly people, regard them as 'works of delusion

138

or effects of excitement'.[32] The former believe that, if we asked for bread, fish or an egg, the Lord would give us a stone, a serpent or a scorpion. The latter believe that this has already happened. This betrays an erroneous view of God:

> He will not put into our hands a weapon for harming us. Everything which we receive from him is not only in itself good, but good for us to receive; a precious talent which we may indeed abuse, but which we ought to trade with and improve for the Giver's sake, and for our own future reward in the day of reckoning.[33]

Irving begs that those who may be seeking gifts 'for the mere pride and power and notoriety of possessing them', stop doing so. But those who seek the Spirit in love, unity and holiness must 'not be afraid that God will send in its stead an evil fruit of enthusiasm, fanaticism, or diabolical delusion'.[34] They must keep their hearts and minds in Jesus, otherwise some form of evil will get in and the spiritual gift 'may become an instrument of the flesh' and end in sensuality. As Christ is Lord of the Spirit so we in Him rule in the gift and must not be ruled by it:

> The MAN Jesus is the Lord of the Spirit, and the mystery of godliness standeth in this, that the Holy Ghost hath condescended to act under the direction of man, as the Son of God hath humbled himself to become man, and God hath purposed to be bodied forth in the form of man. As it is with the Head, so with the members upholden by the Head. They also are expected under Christ to rule in the gift, and not by the gift to be overruled; and if from this personal responsibility they turn away, then do I perceive that the flesh and the gift may intermingle in frightful and hideous confusion. For what keeps down the flesh but our personal will sustained by Christ the Head? And if we, upon receiving a spiritual gift, do yield our will thereto, then is the flesh relieved from his master, and cometh in with all his natural violence to mingle in everything which we utter. With those who abandon themselves to the gift, instead of regulating its use by the laws and commandments of Jesus for the ends of love and goodness, the gift will prove hurtful and not profitable to the personal sanctification and the edification of the church. Their utterances may become worse than profitless, scandals and stumbling-blocks to the spiritual; to the carnal, occasions of mockery and blasphemy. And therefore it is an essential element of all this doctrine, that 'the spirits of the prophets are subject to the prophets'. Therefore also it is that the gift cometh in the form

of persons, 'apostles, evangelists, prophets, pastors and teachers', and not in the form of things.[35]

If a man ask God sincerely, he will receive the Spirit. We must not quench or grieve the Spirit nor despise prophesyings. We must not be suspicious of any of the gifts. It is not for us to tell God which of the gifts we should have, for He gives according to His will. Neither need we be perfectly sanctified before we ask for the gifts. The gifts go with preaching to confirm the Gospel to the believer (*I Cor.* 1:6; *Eph.* 1:13) and with baptism (*Acts* 2:38) to help the Church to make 'increase of itself in love'.[36]

Irving had now come to the end of the first part of his treatise. He had planned a second part which would deal with the fulfilment of the promise of the baptism of the Holy Spirit on the day of Pentecost and also a third part which would explain the consequences of it all. He had given an outline of these in the introduction:

> Secondly, that seeing the promise was fulfilled on the day of Pentecost, we ought most carefully to consider the record thereof, with all the passages of Scripture which cast light thereon, that we may have a complete view of the act of fulfilment. And seeing that this was to introduce a new era in the church of the greatest consequence, which no one but God's own Son in the state of glory was competent to bring in, we ought, in the third and last place, to consider this subject of 'the baptism of the Holy Ghost' in the way of its permanent effects, pointing out the new privileges, powers, and responsibilities which were thereby brought into and entailed upon the church.[37]

This plan was never carried out. Parts 2 and 3 never materialized. Part 1 was the only extensive writing that he produced on the baptism of the Holy Spirit. It was also almost the last work of importance which he wrote on this or on any subject. His literary output, which had already dropped sharply in 1831, completely dried up by the end of the following year.

16

The Complaint of the Trustees

IN JANUARY, March and April 1832 Irving published three
articles on 'Facts Connected with Recent Manifestations of
Spiritual Gifts' in *Fraser's Magazine*. The first half of the first
article contained the narrative which, as has been mentioned, has been
used as the basis of Part 2 of this study. The second half and the second
and third articles depart from the 'Facts' aitogether and give instead a
lengthy defence of the biblical authority for speaking in tongues and
extensive teaching on the subject in refutation of the numerous
criticisms that were being brought against him from all quarters of
the secular and ecclesiastical press. All the points which he touched on
he had already made in the other publications which have been looked
at in this study. It has already been noted how his other writings
came to be published and for whom they were written. In these
writings in *Fraser's Magazine* he had the opportunity of reaching
a different, more general, and he hoped, a more sympathetic public.
He states this intention in his prefatory letter to the editor:

> Your urgent request that I would permit you to publish, through
> your Magazine, some authentic account from my own pen, of the work
> of the Spirit in my church and elsewhere, in order to stay, if possible,
> the torrent of blasphemy which is sweeping through the land, and give
> reasonable and religious people the means of making up a judgement
> upon so important a matter, has at length prevailed with me; and I sit
> down faithfully to narrate what hath come under my own eye, or been
> brought to my knowledge from the most certain and authentic sources.
> For, while it is a great point of duty not to cast pearls before swine,
> nor to give that which is holy unto the dogs, it is so also to sow beside
> all waters, and especially to make known the work of the Lord among
> other classes, now that the religious world are violently rejecting it.[1]

These articles, like his earlier unsuccessful attempts to change
opinion over the controversy on Christ's humanity, did nothing to

'stay . . . the torrent of blasphemy which is sweeping through the land'. They only gave clearer indication to his opponents, if such was needed, of his own continued determination to 'die the death of the righteous' for his faith, if it was necessary, and fortified the trustees in their painful decision to institute legal proceedings against him.

In January 1832 the trustees 'being desirous of clearly ascertaining the duties and obligations imposed upon them by the trust-deed'[2] submitted a copy of the trust-deed and a statement of all that had taken place in the church during the preceding months, to Sir Edward Sugden and Mr. James Russell for their legal consideration. These eminent lawyers were of the opinion that, contrary to Irving's view, the minister, in this case, was not at liberty to do as he liked in the direction of the order of worship in Regent Square Church and that he had departed from the recognized discipline of the Church of Scotland. They also advised the trustees to act promptly against him. 'The trustees ought immediately to proceed to remove Mr. Irving from his pastoral charge, by making complaint to the London Presbytery in the manner pointed out by the deed.'[3]

On 20th February, a deputation of the trustees called on Irving with a copy of their counsel's judgement. He said he would give them his answer the following week.[4] On the intervening Sunday he intimated that he expected that he would soon be evicted from his Church. He said he was not troubled at this prospect and told those who remained faithful to the Lord to leave with him when the time came and to meet instead 'from house to house'.[5] He expressed similar sentiments in his reply to the trustees on 28th February:

MY DEAR BRETHREN, – I have read over the opinion of Sir Edward Sugden, which you were so kind as to submit to me, and I have taken a full week to consider of it. The principle on which I have acted is to preserve the integrity of my ministerial character unimpaired, and to fulfil my office according to the Word of God. If the trust-deed do fetter me therein, I knew it not when the trust-deed was drawn, and am sure that it never was intended in the drawing of it; for certainly I would not, to possess all the churches of this land, bind myself one iota from obeying the great Head and Bishop of the Church. But if it be so that you, the trustees, must act to prevent me and my flock from assembling to worship God, according to the Word of God, in the house committed into your trust, we will look unto our God for preservation and safe keeping. Farewell! May the Lord have you in His holy keeping![6]

The trustees met on 2nd March, and unanimously resolved that, since Irving had not changed his mind, they would act on their legal advice. They appointed a committee of six out of their number 'with power to call in legal assistance to prepare the complaint, and to carry the same before the London Presbytery'.[7] They met again on 12th March, to approve the complaint to the Presbytery and then immediately transmitted it, with all the other relevant documents, to the Moderator. When the Presbytery met the following day, the trustees received an unexpected setback. One of the documents which they had submitted was their statement to Sir Edward Sugden. In this there occurred the sentence 'That until the adoption of the proceedings on the part of Mr. Irving now complained of, he had uniformly conformed to the doctrines of the Established Church of Scotland.'[8] The Presbytery took exception to this because it denied their recent judgement against Irving over the humanity of Christ. So they returned the documents and told the trustees that they would refuse further consideration of the matter until they presented a statement which showed that they agreed with the former decision of Presbytery.

The trustees met on 17th March, to consider this unexpected setback. There is no record in their minute book that there was any discussion of the question as to whether they had changed their minds and now agreed with the Presbytery's decision against Irving, made fifteen months before, for they had then, as elders, signed the declaration of faith in his support on 15th December, 1830. There is only record of the simple fact that it was moved and seconded that 'the memorial as amended be presented to the Presbytery as the complaint of the trustees'.[9] Irving heard of this obstacle which had been raised by the Presbytery and of the trustees' meeting and took the opportunity of writing to them.[10] He once again pleaded with them not to stand against the work of God and prophesied judgement and disaster if they did. He said he was completely assured that God would look after him whatever happened, but he trembled at what would happen to them, to the city and to the whole land if they banished the voice of Jesus from the midst of His sanctuary:

How can you make a fashion of calling it a house of praise or prayer any longer, after having banished forth of it the voice of Jesus lifted up in the midst of the church of the saints, which is the temple of the Holy Ghost? Surely disappointment and defeat will rest upon it for ever. God will not bless it; the servants of God will flee away from it;

it will stand a monument of folly and infatuation. Nay, so much hath the Lord made me to perceive the iniquity of this thing, that I believe it will bring down judgement upon all who take part in it, upon their houses, upon the city itself in which the National Scotch Church hath, been a lamp, yea, and a light unto the whole land, and to the distant parts of the earth.[11]

This letter was minuted but not discussed. They met again on 9th April to hear that the Presbytery had 'entertained the complaint and had agreed to proceed to the proof of the same'.[12] The complaint thus amended by the trustees and received by the Presbytery, is here given in full since it is not possible to follow the case further without exact knowledge of the terms of the trust-deed and the libel:

THAT at a meeting of the congregation under the pastoral charge of the Rev. Edward Irving, held at the Caledonian Church, Cross Street, Hatton Garden, on Monday, the 19th day of May, 1823, it was unanimously resolved, that the said Caledonian Church being inadequate to accommodate the congregation attending there, means should be immediately taken for building a new church or chapel, to be called 'The National Scotch Church', and that the said new church or chapel should be in connection with the established Church of Scotland, and that the doctrines, forms of worship, and mode of discipline of that Church should be taught, observed, and practised, in the said new church or chapel, and that the said Edward Irving should be the minister thereof; and that the same should at all times thereafter be filled by a minister duly licensed to preach the Gospel by some presbytery of the established Church of Scotland, and ordained according to the rules of that Church. And also, that the said new church or chapel should be built by subscription.

THAT, at subsequent meetings of the subscribers to the said Church, duly convened and held, trustees were appointed, on certain conditions, and for certain purposes, as set forth in their deed of trust, which is herewith submitted, and to which the trustees, subscribers, and Mr. Irving, severally became parties.

THAT the trust-deed sheweth and reciteth – 'That the said trustees should, from time to time, and at all times, after the said church or chapel should be erected and built, permit and suffer the same church and chapel to be used, occupied and enjoyed, as a place for public religious worship and service of God, according to the doctrines, forms of worship, and mode of discipline of the established Church of Scotland, by the congregation of persons then or usually attendant on the ministry or under the pastoral care and charge of the said Edward

144

Irving, or such other persons as should thereafter join the said congregation, but under and subject to the orders, direction, and control of the persons in whom the management of the said church or chapel should for the time being be vested, as thereinafter mentioned, so as such orders and directions were not in opposition to, or inconsistent with, the provisions thereinafter contained, or the general scope and true intent and meaning of the trust-deed; and should permit and suffer the said Edward Irving or the person who should for the time being be appointed minister of the said church or chapel, as thereinafter was mentioned, to preach and expound the Holy Scriptures, dispense the sacraments, and otherwise officiate as minister in the said church or chapel, according to the doctrines, forms of worship, and mode of discipline, before mentioned or referred to.'

And the said trust-deed further reciteth – 'That the said Edward Irving should be the minister of the said church or chapel, in case he should be living when the same was completed, and should be then willing to accept the office of minister thereof; and that he should continue to be such minister during his life, or until he should resign the said office of minister, or be removed, in pursuance of the provisions thereinafter for that purpose contained.

'THAT in case the trustees or trustee for the time being of the said church or chapel, or the elders and deacons for the time being of the said church or chapel, being respectively heads of families and communicants in the said church or chapel, should be of opinion that the minister for the time being of the said church or chapel was unworthy or unfit to be continued in his office of minister, the persons or person so for the time being considering the minister unworthy or unfit as aforesaid, should make a specific complaint against such minister to the persons for the time being constituting the society or body commonly called or known by the name or designation of the Presbytery of the established Church of Scotland in London, and thereinafter designated by the title of the London Presbytery. That the said complaint should be made in writing, and be delivered to the President or Moderator for the time being of the said London Presbytery, who should certify thereon the date of delivery. And in case the said London Presbytery should, within one calendar month next after the delivery of such complaint, declare, by writing, under the hand of their President or Moderator, their consent to hear and decide upon the matter which should be so referred to them as aforesaid, the minister for the time being against whom such complaint should be made, should have a statement thereof in writing furnished him by the persons or person making the same, and should have notice to attend the said London

Presbytery, either in person or by attorney or agent on his behalf, at a place and on a day to be fixed upon by the said London Presbytery, so as such place be situate within the said City of London, or within ten miles of the same, and so as such a day be distant at least fourteen days from the time when such notice as last aforesaid should be delivered, and then and there to answer the said complaint.

'THAT the said London Presbytery should be at liberty, in case they saw fit, to examine the said complaints or complaint, and the said minister, and all other persons whomsoever, touching or concerning the matter so referred to them as aforesaid, either viva voce, or by interrogations in writing, and either without or upon oath; and if upon oath, an oath to be sworn before any judge in his majesty's courts of King's Bench and Common Pleas at Westminster, or a master in chancery, or before any of the judges of the Court of Session, or sheriff's deputies, or substitutes of shires in Scotland.

'THAT the award or decision of the said London Presbytery, the matter so referred to them as aforesaid, should be final and conclusive, providing the same be given in writing to the said complainants or complainant; and the said minister, under the hand of the President or Moderator for the time being of the said London Presbytery, within the space of four calendar months next after such complaint should be so made to them as aforesaid, or on or before such ulterior day or days not exceeding six calendar months from the time when such complaint should be so made as aforesaid, as the said London Presbytery (if they should deem an enlargement of the time necessary) should by writing, and under the hand of their President or Moderator from time to time appoint.

'That if the said London Presbytery should at any time neglect or refuse, for the space of one calendar month next after any matter should be referred to them as aforesaid, to declare in manner therein before mentioned their consent to hear and decide upon the same, and, having accepted such reference, should neglect to make an award therein within the time thereinbefore in that behalf mentioned, or in case there should be then no such society or body of persons as was thereinbefore mentioned, or referred to by the name or designation of the London Presbytery, it may then be referred to the seat-holders.

'THAT all matters relating to the public worship of God in the said church or chapel, and the administration of such religious rites, ordinances, and services, as should be performed or observed therein, should be left to the discretion of the minister for the time being of the said church or chapel, during such times as there should be such a minister, and to the discretion of the elders and deacons for the time being of the said church or chapel during such time as there should not be a minister, but so nevertheless that the sacrament of the Lord's Supper should be administered in the said church or chapel twice in every year at the least, and that an interval of not more than eight months be not at any time permitted between the celebrations or administrations thereof.'

Now the trustees of the said church, in discharging of the duty imposed upon and undertaken by them by the trust-deed, lay the following charges, as the subject of their complaint, against the said Rev. Edward Irving.

Firstly, THAT the said Rev. Edward Irving has suffered and permitted, and still allows, the public services of the said church, in the worship of God on the Sabbath, and other days, to be interrupted by persons not being either ministers or licentiates of the Church of Scotland.

Secondly, THAT the said Rev. Edward Irving has suffered, and permitted, and still allows the public services of the said church in the worship of God to be interrupted by persons not being either members or seat-holders, of the said church; or ministers, or licentiates of the Church of Scotland.

Thirdly, THAT the said Rev. Edward Irving has suffered and permitted and also publicly encourages females to speak in the said church, and to interrupt and disturb the public worship of God in the said church on Sabbath and other days.

Fourthly, THAT the said Rev. Edward Irving hath suffered and permitted, and also publicly encourages other individuals, members of the said church, to interrupt and disturb the public worship of God in the said church on Sabbath and other days.

Fifthly, THAT the said Rev. Edward Irving, for the purpose of encouraging and exciting the said interruptions, has appointed times when a suspension of the usual worship in the said church takes place, for said persons to exercise the supposed gifts with which they profess to be endowed.

The said trustees, in discharge of the duty imposed upon them by the trust-deed of the said church, have repeatedly urged and requested the said Rev. Edward Irving to discontinue and prevent such interruptions, and to restore the worship of God in the said church to the doctrines and forms of worship, and mode of discipline of the Established Church of Scotland, as prescribed in the said trust-deed.

But that the said Rev. Edward Irving peremptorily refuses to do so, and has laid down and established an order of worship which is now adopted and practised in the said church, encouraging these departures from the doctrine and discipline of the Church of Scotland.[13]

The trial was fixed for 26th April.

147

PART FIVE

17

The Evidence of the Witnesses[1]

THE PRESBYTERY of London met in the Scotch Church, London Wall on Thursday 26th April. The presbyters were Rev. J. R. Brown, Moderator, Rev. Dr. Crombie, Rev. J. Miller, Rev. F. McLean, and Rev. J. Macdonald, with Messrs. Birnie, Marshall and Wright, Elders. The church was packed. Many of those who had come to watch were Irving's friends. As the Moderator constituted the meeting with prayer, Mr. Taplin spoke at length in tongues and then in English telling the Presbytery that they were constituted in their own name and condemning their past proceedings. This caused considerable interruption. The Moderator restored order and the minutes of 5th April were read. The complainers on behalf of the trustees of the National Scotch Church, Regent Square were James Hargreaves Mann, James Nisbet, David Blyth and others. Irving appeared as defender with Mr. Cardale, solicitor, as his legal agent. The memorial and complaint of the trustees was then read out together with the letters which had been exchanged between Irving and the trustees during the previous months, which have already been referred to. The complaint concluded with an ambiguous reference to the other charges against Irving which had been brought before Presbytery, but which were not now before the court:

> The trustees are not remindful that there have been other charges brought against the said Rev. Edward Irving, touching certain doctrines promulgated by him respecting the human nature of our Lord Jesus Christ, and the trustees are also aware that this Rev. Presbytery has already discerned in these matters, but they restrict this their memorial and complaint to the matters set forth therein; and, having thereby made known and presented their complaint they ask and request that the said London Presbytery will forthwith take the same into their

serious consideration, so as to determine the said question, whether by such breaches of doctrine and discipline, as have been therein set forth by the trustees, and the departure from the obligation which the said Rev. Edward Irving came under when he received his ordination as a minister of the Church of Scotland, he hath not rendered himself unfit to remain the minister of the said National Scotch Church, and ought not to be removed therefrom, in pursuance of the conditions of the said trust-deed.[2]

The case opened with Mr. Mann speaking for the trustees. He said that it was laid down in the trust-deed that the church was to be and had been built as 'a church in connection with the Kirk in Scotland, in which the doctrines and forms of worship and mode of discipline of that church should be taught and practised'. Also that Mr. Irving should continue to be minister for life unless he resigned or was removed according to the terms of the trust-deed 'and those provisions were, that, if he should depart from the doctrines and views recognized by the Church of Scotland, he should be disqualified from retaining his situation'.[3]

Irving's letters to the trustees were then read out as evidence that he had so departed from the doctrines and forms of worship of the Church of Scotland. The first witness, Mr. Duncan McKenzie, an elder, was then called and examined by Mr. Mann, the Moderator and others. He said that in no case had the doctrines taught by Mr. Irving been objected to 'by any of the congregation'. As an elder he 'endeavoured to stop improper interruptions, but never these speakings'.[4] This had been his own decision, not just Mr. Irving's. As an elder he was responsible for maintaining discipline 'and, in not repressing these speakings, he did not consider that he contradicted any of the ordinances of the Church of Scotland'. He believed these utterances had been made 'In the strength and power of the Holy Ghost' and not 'by the persons themselves, in their own understanding and strength'. Then Irving asked him if the things he had seen and heard agreed with 'the things written in Scripture'? The Moderator ruled the question out of order because the question before the Court 'was not whether the proceedings were in accordance with the Scripture or not, but with the practices and ordinances of the Church'. This was greeted by hisses and disorder from the audience. There was applause for Irving when he said that 'anyone who should stand up and say, he must not bring any one article or act to the test of Scripture was wrong, whoever he might be'.⁵ The Moderator said that Irving could have appealed to Scripture in the way laid down in the Church by submitting his new doctrine to Presbytery and then to the General Assembly for its consideration. It would then, if approved, be sent down to all Presbyteries under the Barrier Act before coming back to the General Assembly for final decision. This he had not done. Irving then repeated his opinion, 'with warmth' that any court which did not allow appeal to the Scriptures was 'a court of Antichrist'. There was great applause which the Moderator suppressed. Mr. Mann said on a point of order that the trustees had not come to find out whether Irving's doctrine agreed with Scripture but simply whether he had contravened the compact he entered into with the subscribers to Regent Square Church in allowing these unconstitutional practices. The court agreed with this amid hisses from the spectators.⁶

The next witness was called. He was Mr. Edward Oliver Taplin who had been a member at Regent Square since 1826. Mr. Mann questioned him about the occasion on which he had been tempted to rebuke Irving but had been told by another in the Spirit, that his utterance was not of the Lord. How did he know when he was speaking by the Spirit of God? He said 'I *can* discern.' Mr. Cardale interrupted to ask what relevance these questions had since Mr. Mann had already said he was not there for any other purpose than to prove that the terms of the trust-deed had been infringed. Irving requested that the questions be allowed since they helped to explain the work of God. Mr. Mann continued:

How do you discern whether you are speaking by the Spirit of God or the spirit of error? – Because I am filled with love to Christ and to his church, and have joy, and peace, and strength; and, therefore, I know this is the Spirit of the Lord. Did you so feel after you rebuked your pastor? – I confess I did not; and that has led me more than everything else to believe I might be in error. Then it depends entirely on your own feelings? – If you mean in respect to myself, certainly; I read, the fruit of the Spirit is love, joy, and peace, and when I find these things within me, am I to believe it is the spirit of the devil? Could you abstain from speaking? – By quenching the Spirit, or, by resisting the Spirit. Then I am to understand that it is not super- natural? – You are to understand, if you are guided by what I believe, that it is a supernatural power; for I had it not once, and I cannot exercise it when I will; I cannot will to exercise it. Is it irresistible? If it was irresistible could it be resisted? – Did I not answer the question

153

before? Then Sir, I ask you, is it not resisting the Holy Ghost when you resist speaking? – It is; I believe it is.[7]

The Moderator then asked Mr. Taplin whether he spoke by previous arrangement with his minister. Mr. Taplin replied 'Sir, do you think we stand here knaves!' There was no collusion over the speaking in tongues. Had Irving said that those who disbelieved in these manifestations were in error? Yes; and also that there was nothing against them in the canons of the Church of Scotland. Did he have the fruits of the Spirit before these manifestations? Yes, but not so much as now. May a man have the seal of faith without these gifts? Mr. Taplin replied:

> I read, 'These signs shall follow them that believe'; but the impression on my mind is that a person may believe who has them not; I think he may. Then you think that persons may possess the seal of faith, who do not exercise these manifestations; and I ask you, is it just or Scriptural conduct to condemn any man or any church, who does not receive them? – Have I condemned any man, or any church? I did not tell you I condemned any one.[8]

Mr. Taplin refused to answer Mr. Mann's next question until he had stopped calling his own speaking in tongues that morning an 'exhibition' and 'display'. He had heard Miss Hall, Miss Cardale, and Mr. Baxter speak in Church during the Sunday services. He said that Irving had permitted their utterances and given thanks for them:

> Did Mr. Irving ever entreat the people to hear the gifted persons because they were clothed with his authority? – He has entreated his people to listen to the voice of the Spirit, not recommending the persons, but bidding them put persons out of their consideration altogether.[9]

Mr. McLean asked him what was the difference between tongues followed by English and tongues followed by the gift of interpretation. The former was analogous to 'sign and doctrine' whereas the latter was the interpretation of the tongue. He admitted that Satan could counterfeit the gifts. Were all the utterances in accordance with the doctrines of the Church of Scotland? He thought so:

> Did any of these English sentences refer to the humanity of our blessed Lord? – They have testified that he is bone of your bone, and flesh of your flesh; we are all members of his body, of his flesh, and of

his bones. That is, in all respects like fallen man? – Sin only excepted, all the infirmities of fallen man.[10]

Mr. Taplin then answered questions by the Moderator concerning authority. He said he was under the minister in these things:

> Are we to understand that you would not have uttered if Mr. Irving had not given you permission? Certainly at that time I should not . . . I do not mean the minister has authority of the Spirit, but the conscience is superior to every human authority. Do you consider there is a superior testimony given by the Spirit in those manifestations to the doctrines of Mr. Irving? – I believe Mr. Irving is directed in his ministry by the mind of the Spirit. The manifestations did not arise from my own power; it was a power upon me. In what respect are the gifts different? I believe there are different tongues, and the manner of these are different in the same way that the style of the prophets who spoke by the same Spirit is different. How do you discern this difference? – In the same manner as I discern the difference between a Frenchman, an Italian, or an Hindoo, by the ordinary method in which other tongues are distinguished. You have confessed that you do not understand these tongues; the way in which we distinguish between men of different countries is by the individual speaking the language peculiar to his country, having different forms and inflections of voice; do you mean to say you proceed on this ordinary and natural process? – I discern in the same manner as between a man speaking Welsh and Italian, but not by spiritual discernment. Is it not possible then you may be mistaken as to the difference? It is impossible they can be so near alike. Upon what grounds do you call them the gift of the Spirit? Because the Spirit speaketh them. Do you think, Sir, the Spirit speaketh gibberish? – On the day of Pentecost they were not understood but by those who spake them; to all others they would seem as gibberish.[11]

The third and last witness was called. He was Mr. David Ker, a deacon at Regent Square. Answering the questions of Messrs. Mann, McLean and the Moderator, he said that he had never used his authority to stop the manifestations. Once Irving had asked him to go and silence a person. The last manifestation in the church had been about the beginning of March. Irving had not said that they were to stop. He did not know why they had stopped during the Sunday services. He had not witnessed tongues before. He did not think there was any ruling in the Church of Scotland forbidding these things. He believed that people could be misguided and not speak the mind of God. He 'had heard a statement follow the tongue that our Lord's flesh was formed of corrupt humanity'. He also said that the utterances confirmed Irving's teaching on 'the coming of the Son of God in judgement, to establish righteousness, and to set up the kingdom of God' and that 'a poor sinner had liberty to attain to instant peace on his receiving the Word of God, without going through the various experiences which are given him by other preachers'. He agreed that these three doctrines were preached against in other churches.[12]

The complainers had finished their case which had taken eight hours. The court was adjourned until eleven o'clock the following day.[13]

18

Irving's Defence:
The Trustees' Reply

THE MODERATOR opened by saying that although the complainers had finished their case as far as the examination of witnesses was concerned, he would have no objection if other witnesses were called.[1] Mr. McLean agreed that more witnesses were necessary since those examined the day before 'were all of a particular character'. Mr. Cardale objected. He said that the Presbytery were not the judges of this question. They would make themselves parties in the matter if they interfered. It had been decided the day before that the complainants' case was concluded and that Irving should be called to give his defence. Irving said that it would be an infraction of justice to depart from what had been agreed on and covenanted between the court and the parties the day before. Further witnesses could be called after that if desired.[2] Dr. Crombie said he thought Irving was right and '– that if, after we have heard the other party, we wish it, we can call in further evidence'. Mr. McLean apologized for his procedural error. He would wait until the proper time came for calling further evidence. Dr. Crombie said his apology was accepted. Then Irving was called upon to give his defence.[3]

Irving's Defence
He began his speech with a brief outline of the Scriptural authority for believing in Jesus Christ as the baptizer with the Holy Spirit. It followed the first part of the tract *The Day of Pentecost* which has been already considered. He said that it was for the name and for the sake of He who baptizes with the Holy Spirit that he was on trial:

It is for the name of Christ, as 'baptizer with the Holy Ghost', that

157

I am this day called in question before this court; and it is for that name, which God deemed so sacred and important as to give it to the Baptist to proclaim – which the Son of God deemed so important as not to permit his disciples to go forth to preach until they had received the substance of it – it is for that name, even the name of 'Jesus, the baptizer with the Holy Ghost', that I stand here before you, Sir, and before this court, and before you all, called in question this day.[4]

God had been pleased to answer the importunate prayers of His people and had given to certain members of his church 'the baptism with the Holy Ghost, with its sign of speaking with tongues and with its substance of prophecy'. He did not believe that having asked God for bread, He had given them a stone. He believed God was faithful and having tested it in his conscience and amongst his people he had come to the conclusion that it was Scriptural and so had ordered it in the church according to the apostolic instructions. It was because he would not suppress this work of God that he was now on trial.[5]

He said that his speech would be in four parts. *First*, he would show the Scriptural basis for what he believed had come into their midst. *Secondly*, he would show how the thing they had received was that of which the Scriptures spoke. *Thirdly*, he would show how his ordering of it had been entirely in accordance with the word of God. *Fourthly*, he would conclude with the application of all this to the parties in the case.

He began by returning to his opening theme and continued with his exposition of Scripture after the manner of the opening pages of *The Day of Pentecost*.[6] He then began to tell the story of the development of his own thoughts on the matter of spiritual gifts from the time of his preaching his second sermon on baptism to the instituting of the early morning prayer meetings in May 1831.[7] He went on to recount the various steps he took to test and try the manifestations as they appeared, the details of which have already been used as the basis for the narrative in Part 3 of this study.[8] During this, the second part of his speech, he accused the trustees of driving Jesus out of his church. The Moderator called him to order, saying that he would not allow such allegations and that he was hearing Irving as a matter of courtesy: 'It is known from what was stated yesterday, that we hold this altogether to be an incompetent and irrelevant line of defence.' Nevertheless the court was listening out of 'tenderness and courtesy'. He asked Irving to show the same spirit.[9]

Having dealt with the first two parts, he moved on to speak of the way he had ordered the gifts in the church. He had dealt with this to some extent already. He would deal with the rest of it by defending himself against the specific charges of the trustees. The first charge was that he had allowed the Sunday services 'to be interrupted by persons not being either ministers or licentiates of the Church of Scotland'. He could say with Paul 'Men and brethren, I have committed nothing against the people or customs of our fathers.' He had only used his freedom under Christ, the head of the Church. He denied that it was necessary for a minister 'to have authority from the General Assembly to enable him to do anything which he discerneth to be his duty.'[10] The Moderator asked for these words to be taken down. Irving repeated his belief that serving Christ came before serving a denomination of the Church and the Word of God came before the Westminster Confession. To think otherwise was 'the very essence of antichrist' and 'popery in all its horrors'. To say that every difference must be taken up to the General Assembly was 'an easy method of appeasing a man's conscience'. It was 'Satan's trap to keep all things as they are, to prevent all things from returning to what they have been, and to prevent them from going forward to further things'. He never subscribed to the Westminster Confession in the belief that he should *only* preach what was in it.

Considering the terms of the trust-deed he said that these laid down that the administration of all the services in the church 'shall be left to the discretion of the minister'.[11] The complainers must prove that he had set up an ordinance for prophesying contrary to the constitution of the Church of Scotland. They must also prove that the Church of Scotland had forbidden prophesying in church by those who were moved by the Spirit. The evidence before the court was that they spoke by the Spirit of God. The court must decide on the fact and not their opinion of the fact:

> You are the judges of *the fact* instructed; yes, you are the judges of *the fact*. It is a complaint upon a point *of fact*; and the *fact* instructed is this, that they speak by the Spirit of God, by the evidence which the complainers themselves have adduced. It is not your opinion of a fact; it is *the fact* instructed by the complainers (as all men acquainted with courts of justice know well) that you have to bring to the consideration of the question. I charge the Presbytery before Him who is Judge of all, that they put aside their own opinions with respect to whether these

persons speak by the Spirit of God. They have not heard them, nor considered the matter; they have not proved them by the tests of Scripture. You are not in such circumstances competent to question it; and, as you value your precious immortal souls, (for that is what I am concerned about . . . *your souls*) as judges you must take the fact, and show me in the canons of the Church of Scotland that men are forbidden to speak with tongues, and prophesy in the church, and you will seek long before you find it.[12]

It was not true that he had allowed the worship services to be interrupted by lay people. It was by the Holy Spirit that the services had been interrupted. He had ordered it 'according to the Scripture canon, that if anything be revealed to him that sitteth by, the first shall hold his peace'.

The second charge, that he had allowed the services 'to be interrupted by persons not being either members, or seat-holders, of the said church', was also untrue:

I have not – by your own evidence I have not – by your own evidence I have permitted it only to be interrupted by the voice of the Holy Ghost, speaking in the members of Jesus.[13]

As regards them being neither members nor seat-holders he could only say that they were all members of the Church of Christ and that he wished there were no such unscriptural thing as 'seat-holders' at all.

The third charge was that he had allowed females to speak in church. He had not. He had allowed the Holy Ghost to speak in females and then only in accordance with the Scriptural rules. He also denied the fourth charge, that he had encouraged other members to 'interrupt and disturb' the services. The evidence from the complainers' witnesses showed that he had not.[14]

The fifth charge was that he had 'appointed times when a suspension of the usual worship in the said church takes place, for said persons to exercise the supposed gifts with which they profess to be endowed'. This needed some explanation. He had formulated his new order of service in order to cause the least upset to those who were unable to worship for fear of interruptions at any time. He had based his decision to have a pause for prophesying after the reading o Scripture and after the sermon, on his observation that these were the two moments when the utterances were most frequently given and on his reading of Mosheim's *History of the Church* which said that during the first three centuries it was at these times that the congregation rested and the prophets spoke.[15] He was not aware that the reformers had started *a new church*. In the First Book of Discipline there was an attempt to reconstitute the ordinance of *I Cor.* 14. There was also full authority for any one with a gift to speak in the Church:

> 'And, moreover, men in whom is supposed to be any gift which might edify the church, if they were well employed, must be charged by the ministers and elders to join themselves with the session, and company of interpreters, to the end that the kirk may judge whether they be able to serve to God's glory, and to the profit of the kirk in the vocation of ministers or not: and if any be found disobedient, and not willing to communicate the gifts and special graces of God with their brethren, after sufficient admonition, discipline must proceed against them, provided the civil magistrate concur with the judgement and election of the kirk. For no man may be permitted as best pleaseth him to live within the kirk of God, but every man must be constrained by fraternal admonition and correction to bestow his labours, when of the kirk he is required, to the edification of others.'[16]

The First Book of Discipline had never been abrogated. The Westminster Confession was adopted for the purpose of unity with English Presbyterians but not for supplanting the earlier standard. He had tried his people for the gift of prophesying and had found that they were able to serve the Church. If the Church had so ruled regarding ordinary gifts 'can any man believe that, if the gifts of the Spirit had been in the Church, they would not have ruled it in the *extraordinary* gifts?'[17] If there had been any canon of the Church that forbad these things, he would have broken it, but there was none. The Church recognized her fallibility when in the preface to the first confession it said:

> 'If any man do discover in these articles any thing which repudiateth God's word or right reason, we crave of him of his honour and of his kindness to inform us; and we promise that we will then give him satisfaction out of the word of God and sound reason, or admit that we are wrong.'[18]

He had found nothing wrong with the articles of his Church, so what was it then that he should bring before the General Assembly? Had there been anything to stop him ordering these gifts, he would have overruled it, but there was not. He had taken counsel with certain friends before presenting the matter to his Session. He might have brought the matter before Presbytery but he had already been condemned there as a heretic. He might have taken it to the General Assembly but that body had disclaimed authority South of the border. He was under no authority and so could not have done what was required of him. Even if he could have done these things constitutionally, he would not have allowed the authority of the Church to come between Christ and him and his people: 'I say it is only sound doctrine, that the minister of Christ and the power of the people stand directly responsible to Christ; all canons, creeds, and confessions, presbyteries, councils, and senates, notwithstanding.'[19]

He had now finished the third part of his defence, that is, his ordering of the gifts. He repeated his denial of all the charges of the complaint whose spirit was to prevent the voice of the Holy Spirit from being heard in the Church. The court objected to this. Mr. Mann repeated his earlier assertion that the spirit of the complaint was that the church should be kept for its original purpose and that doctrinal considerations did not come into it. Irving rephrased his allegation:

> The tendency and effect of the complaint is to destroy the name of Jesus as baptizer with the Holy Ghost . . . and to say that that name, in its full grace, and blessedness, and effects, belongeth not to him. It is the tendency and effect of this complaint to take away from every child of God in the bosom of the National Scotch Church, and, if the Presbytery sustain it, from the bosom of your own churches, the hopes and the desire of having the baptism with the Holy Ghost given to them for the edification of the church, according to the baptismal covenant.[20]

He said that the complaint exalted the trustees over the minister and in so doing elevated the secular and material over the spiritual and ecclesiastical.

He then said that the Presbytery had no jurisdiction over him. He was once a member but of his own free consent he had left and had subsequently been condemned as a heretic by them. His Session had acted with him and were not under Presbyterial authority either:

> I do not submit it to the Presbytery considering it as a Presbytery having superintendence over me; for though I was once a member of this Presbytery, by my own free consent I went out from the midst of you; and when I was gone forth from the midst of the Presbytery,

162

because I saw you not acting, as I judged, according to the ordinances of the Lord, you did, in my absence, judge me as a heretic on great points of faith. Then the session of my church, and myself sitting at the head of it, representing the rule and authority of the church, did withdraw our church from your jurisdiction by solemn act of the ruling elder; and, therefore, we are in no respect under your jurisdiction.[21]

He then returned to his earlier protest against the court's decision not to allow any appeal to the Scriptures. He said it was like the King's magistrates not allowing any appeal to the laws of the land.[22] He had brought before the court a most momentous cause, that had not been heard of in Christendom for centuries and which affected the very person of the Holy Spirit 'and you, when I come in with this cause, say, We will not practise by the Word of God'.[23] The court objected strongly to this accusation saying that they had not refused appeal to the Scriptures but that such appeal had to be through the standards of the Church.[24] Irving would not accept this:

> There is not a word concerning speaking with tongues and prophesying in the standards of the Church of Scotland; there is not a word within the whole compass of the Church to carry an appeal to; and I say it is a mere hood-winking of the whole question to say that it was not taken away when you prevented me appealing to the only book that is an authority. Find me in the standards of the church anything to appeal to.[25]

He repeated that the Presbytery must judge on the evidence of the witnesses. They had all testified that it was the work of the Holy Spirit. As ordinary men, quite apart from being Christians they could not possibly deny the evidence. If they did, he foretold the withering away of the Church:

> Ah, if you will turn aside and say, There is nothing in the Church of Scotland for it; there is no authority for it, and we will not consider whether the thing is in Scripture or not – I tell you, you shall be withered as a church – I tell you the waters in your cisterns shall be dried up – I tell you, you shall have no pasture for your flocks – I tell you, your flocks shall pine away and die.[26]

He said it was of little importance that he and his people should be cast out of their church because the Lord would look after them whatever happened. On the other hand, it was of great importance to the Church, the city and the land, if the Presbytery closed the doors

163

of the only church where the voice of the Holy Spirit was to be heard. He urged them to pause and consider before they acted rashly:

Ah, it will be a burdensome thing, not to this Presbytery alone, but to this city, if you shall shut the only church within it in which the voice of the Holy Ghost is heard – if you shall shut the only church in Britain in which the voice of the Holy Ghost is heard. Think you, oh, men, if it should be the voice of the Holy Ghost what are you doing? Consider the possibility of it, and be not rash; consider the possibility of your evidence being right; consider the possibility of our averments being right; and see what you are doing! . . . Pause! pause! pause! pause and reflect. You are going to set yourselves to the most terrible work to which a Presbytery ever set its hands. . . . Pause for the sake of this city. Pause for the sake of this land. Be wise men – come you and hear; come and hear for yourselves, when you will have an opportunity of judging. Come and hear for yourselves. The church is open every morning; the Lord is gracious almost every morning to speak to us by his Spirit. The church is open many times in the week; and the Lord graciously speaks to us. . . . Remember that this gift of tongues, this speaking with other tongues, is indeed for rest and refreshment; but it is also for the stumbling, and snaring, and taking of those who are not weaned from the breasts, and drawn from the milk. Aye, if you have in you the spirit of little children, you will beware; but if you have the spirit of strong men, believing that in the church there is enough, and in the traditions of the church there is enough, you will plunge headlong (I will say) into the wrath of God. I have no doubt in saying it, and I would be an unfaithful man pleading my cause – the cause of God, the cause of Christ, the cause of the Holy Ghost, in this Presbytery; for it is not man – no, man has no charge against me. I stand unimpeached, unblemished on their part: it is only this interruption – this new thing (not an interruption) that hath occurred, which is instructed in your evidence to be the voice of the Holy Ghost, and with tongues which I have declared to be the same, and which I solemnly set down, declaring before you all, declaring before God and the Lord Jesus Christ, upon the faith of a true Christian, that I believe to be the work of the Holy Ghost, for the defence of his church, for the warning of the world, and for the preventing of men from running headlong into the arms of antichrist, and for pointing out that condition of Babylonish confusion into which the churches have come. For we all lament with one accord that we are far departed from the condition of the church as it was in the beginning: and how shall the Lord show to us what he would have his church to be but by restoring to us the gift which was originally in his church? What can reconstitute

164

his church but that which constituted it at first? What can deliver the bondmen of Egypt but the same God who called Abraham out of his native land and preserved him in his wanderings? That God is now come in the person of the Holy Ghost to deliver his church out of the Egyptian bondage of the flesh in which she is, and to deliver the church of that present house of bondage in which she is held.[27]

Having expressed these sentiments on the future of the Church, Irving said that he separated himself and his congregation from 'that Babylonish confederacy'. The Lord was going to appear very soon and he wished those who had received the baptism with the Holy Spirit, to be ready for Him. He urged all those who loved the Scriptures to do the same. The Scriptures must be restored to their rightful pre-eminence:

> I solemnly beseech everyone of you to set up the Holy Scriptures as the only basis of all faith and practice; to look as ministers, and to look as people, to them, and them alone; and I know this, that if you do not look to them you will not look to much else that is good; you may talk about standards as you please, but I know that there will be little reading of standards, and there will be little reading of good books, if there be not much reading of the Scriptures. Therefore, I intreat you to put the standards on their own basis, and every moment to walk before the Lord in his commandments. Cry out, and repent of ungodliness: turn to the Lord, and call on him to lead you into the true faith, and baptize you with the Holy Ghost; and the Lord will soon teach you. And what I say to the Presbytery I say to every one here present. Do likewise, and fear not but that, in the day of his appearing, the Lord will hide you in the secret of his pavilion, and give you for ever reverently to inquire and to know him in his holy temple. Amen and Amen.[28]

Irving had finished his defence. He had spoken for four hours and five minutes. Mr. McLean asked if he could now call further witnesses. Mr. Cardale and Irving said it was unconstitutional for the court 'to take part in a cause and to call witnesses'. The matter was debated. In spite of the decision earlier in the day that further evidence could be called for if desired, the court ruled against Mr. McLean under pressure from the defendant and his counsel.[29] The Moderator then called on Mr. Mann to reply for the complainers.

Mr. Mann rejected most of Irving's speech as irrelevant and offensive. He would not reply in kind. The matter before the court was not doctrine, but discipline. He had a right to appeal to the standards of the Church of Scotland 'even though they are not to be found in the word of God'. – 'Because I do not go to the word of God to find that which may not be in the word of God, am I to be told I refuse an appeal to the word of God? Certainly not.'[30] The trust-deed was quite clear on the action which should be taken if there was a complaint against the minister. He was not convinced that these manifestations were of the Spirit. Mr. Taplin had admitted in evidence the day before that he had once been deceived. Might they not all be deceived?[31]

He denied Irving's charge that the trustees had absented themselves from the church and had not troubled to investigate the subject fully. He read out two letters, one of which was very long, which contained a detailed examination of the phenomena both biblically and experientially, in which he proved that Irving was unjustified in this charge. He had also proved to his satisfaction that these manifestations were 'delusions'.[32]

He also denied Irving's charge that the trustees had tried to restrict his preaching. They had never done so. They had only tried to stop unauthorized people from doing so.

The defendant had admitted that he had separated himself from the Church of Scotland in spirit. Why then did he not separate himself in fact? The Apostles left the Jewish Church. Luther left the Roman Church. The Nonconformists left the Church of England. Irving would be an honest man to leave the Church of Scotland.[33]

Mr. Mann repeated his introductory remarks by saying that it was not fair to the subscribers to the church, that it was now being used for purposes other than that stated in the original compact. 'Though the Church of Scotland and the Church of England are nearly similar, could we honestly permit the ritual of the latter to be read in that church? Most assuredly not.'[34] The old Presbyterian churches in Lancashire, Worcestershire and Somersetshire had all gone over to Arianism or Socinianism 'because the trustees of those churches have failed in their duty as honest men. Such shall never be the case with the National Scotch Church while breath proceeds from these lips or blood flows from this heart.' It was robbery to take the church from the use of the individuals who built it and give it to others. The trustees would not allow it. They were not judges of doctrine. It was not for them to say 'whether these practices are a new dispensation of the Spirit'. Their only concern was to maintain the order and discipline of the Church of Scotland.[35]

He reminded Irving that whatever he had said against the trust-deed, it had been drawn up under his superintendence and in full agreement with his wishes and desires. He then read out the relevant clauses. He said he had no choice but to put the whole matter before Presbytery. The trustees would abide by their decision either way with no ill feeling:

> If your decision shall be that it is in accordance with the doctrine and discipline of the Church of Scotland, as trustees, we say, Remain, and may the blessing of God remain with you and with the house: we do not, as has been done in that church, denounce all them that do not agree with us. If these individuals shall depart therefrom, our blessing shall rest on the house whether they go or stay. If the gentleman retires with his flock, our prayers follow him and we say, The blessing of God go with you; and if this which you profess to have is the power of the Holy Spirit, may you be endued therewith in a more copious abundance than ever has been the case. We have no sectarian feeling on this subject. That the day may come when the knowledge of the Lord shall cover the earth as the waters cover the sea – this is the subject of our ardent daily prayers. And whether the Holy Spirit be poured out on the Church of Scotland, or on the Church of England, or on the many Christian churches of the land, our thanksgivings shall ascend to God when and where we see it poured, and we will hail them all, and say, The peace and the blessing of God be with you, and rest upon you wherever you go, and wherever you dwell.[36]

Mr. Mann concluded his reply and the Presbytery adjourned until the following Wednesday, 2nd May.

19

Irving's Second Defence

THE MODERATOR opened by referring to the unusual position in which the Presbytery were legally placed. Normally the court would now hear the final reply of the complainers before the Presbytery decided the case. The defendant would then have the right of appeal to the General Assembly before whom he would speak in his own defence. But the London Presbytery were not under the General Assembly and so there was no higher court to which to appeal. Because of this, he proposed that Irving be allowed to reply to Mr. Mann and, as it were, make the speech which he would have been allowed, had his case gone before the Assembly.[1]

Mr. McKenzie said he had a memorial to present. The Moderator said he could not receive it since no new parties to the case could be admitted. Irving said it was not a new party. It was information from the congregation, who had only known that the court had decided to give judgement in this case at the last meeting. Dr. Crombie reminded Irving that when the court had asked for further evidence he had 'positively refused to allow us to receive it'. Since the Presbytery now felt that no more evidence was required, it would not be fair to the complainers to accept this memorial. The matter was debated.[2] The Moderator said that it would open up the case again. This would result in the proceedings dragging on and not being concluded that day as they had hoped. As for Irving maintaining that the congregation did not know that the court would judge in this matter until the last meeting, he said that it had been intimated in the press for weeks 'and that it was a matter which went far to involve the deposition of the rev. defender from the church he now occupies'. The document had come too late and could not be received. The court agreed.[3] Irving was asked to reply to Mr. Mann.

Irving began by denying Mr. Mann's allegations that his speech

168

had been largely irrelevant and offensive. This work of the Holy Spirit was not irrelevant and his denunciations were no more offensive than that he believed that God would come in judgement upon those who opposed His work:

> It was because I believe that the present question amounteth to this: whether the beginning of the latter day glory shall be quenched, or whether it shall be permitted to arise in the Church of Scotland, the Church of England, and the Church of Christ? It was because I clearly foresee that if you, as a Presbytery, shall decide on any ground earthly, that the voice of God, speaking in his church, shall be quenched, the end of it will be heavy judgements of the Lord, upon all concerned in the opposition to his work; yea, upon the church itself, if the church should take part in these proceedings, and not solemnly protest against them, and wash her hands of them altogether.[4]

Next he said that Mr. Mann's assertion that this was a matter of discipline, not doctrine was untrue. This was a question of doctrine:

> I aver this is a question of doctrine; for if these be the manifestations of the Holy Ghost, what court under heaven would dare to interpose and say, Let them not be? Is it possible this court would act upon the assertion that it is not a matter of doctrine to be sought into, when the evidence upon the table is unanimous to this effect, that it is of the Holy Ghost?[5]

The Moderator interposed to say that the court did not commit itself to Mr. Mann's declaration that this was only a question of discipline.

Irving then criticized Mr. Mann's rejection of the testimony of the witnesses when he had said that he could not accept their assumption that it was the voice of the Holy Spirit. 'Witnesses do not assume anything; they only answer the questions which are put to them. These men were put on their oaths, and you are bound to receive their testimony.'[6]

Mr. Mann had said that his doctrine regarding the minister's rule over the spirits was a form of Popery. He denied this. He said that he had Scriptural authority for rule in these matters but not for infallibility.

Commenting next on Mr. Mann's criticism of Mr. Taplin's confession of having been deceived, Irving said that he showed an ignorance of Scripture on this point. A prophet is still fallible, though he speaks the word of God. The only infallible man is the Lord Jesus Christ. Even Jeremiah thought God had deceived him (*Jer.* 20:7) and was a liar (15:15–18) so little did he understand the times and seasons when his prophecies would be fulfilled. He mentioned Mr. Baxter, who had been used in prophecy but who now had been 'taken in this very snare, of endeavouring to interpret, by means of a mind remarkably formal in its natural structure, the spiritual utterances which he was made to give forth; and perceiving a want of concurrence between the word and the fulfilment, he hastily said, "it is a lying spirit by which I have spoken" '.[7] The Scriptures explained Mr. Taplin's position very clearly. He went on to expand on the difficulties, temptations and weaknesses of the prophets from *Ezek*, 14:8–11; *I Kings* 22:15, 16, 17; *Deut.* 18:21, 22 and *Matt.* 7:15–21. In this he followed the teaching he had given in his articles on the gifts of the Spirit and his tract on *The Day of Pentecost.*[8]

He had tested all things in his church by the Scriptures and no one had found anything that he had done contrary to Scriptural authority. He spoke against those who had been led astray by 'evidence-writers' like Paley, Lardner and Macknight.[9] Supernatural signs and wonders were in themselves no proof of the authenticity of the prophet's word. Such supernatural phenomena could be evidence of the power of darkness. Such men had brought the Scriptural teaching on miracles into disrepute. He also spoke against the followers of Joanna Southcote who testified to signs and prophecies but not to the Lord Jesus Christ. They associated with familiar spirits. He had also had experience of some church members being deceived by Satan as an angel of light. They had been dazzled mentally and deceived in their conscience and been full of unrest and discontent. His experience had shown him that until the gift of discernment was given, the best way to distinguish between the work of the Holy Spirit and the work of Satan was by the fruit of the Spirit in individual lives.[10] These fruits he had found to be in those who had spoken by the Spirit in his church. He had also found the confessions 'that Jesus Christ is Lord' and that 'Christ is come in the flesh' very useful in detecting evil spirits. He said he could write a volume on the counterfeits which Satan had produced in this work and which God had allowed, not to snare them but that He might triumph over all evil:

> As in the days of our Lord, Satan's kingdom was manifested in demoniacal possessions, that Jesus might be proved not to have a devil, but the Holy Ghost, in casting them out; so amongst us hath Satan's power in utterances been permitted, in order that the work of the Holy

Ghost might be proved in detecting and exposing them, and putting them to silence. When they charged Jesus with casting out devils by Beelzebub the prince of devils, he answered, 'A kingdom is not divided against itself.' So can I, the minister of the church in which the Holy Ghost hath manifested himself, say to those who allege that it is a work of Satan, Satan would not cast Satan out, Satan would not silence Satan. In every form have I seen Satan seek to insinuate himself into this work and mar it; and as often have I seen him withstood by the supernatural power which speaketh amongst us in tongues and prophesying, whereby I know that it is the power of God, of Jesus the vanquisher of Satan, of the Holy Ghost in that very form in which he was manifested in the day of Pentecost.[11]

Next Irving denied that he had said that *all* the trustees had absented themselves from church and refused to examine the doctrine, as Mr. Mann had made out. 'I did not say that all had done so, but that a great portion of the trustees had done so; and if this is not true, let them now gainsay it. But you perceive they do not.'[12]

Mr. Mann had alleged that he had allowed unauthorized people to speak in church. This was not so. *He* had authorized them to speak on the authority of the Scriptures he had referred to earlier.[13]

Mr. Mann had said that if he were an honest man, he ought to leave the Church. He said that he had considered doing this but had felt bound by God to continue to be the responsible pastor of his people. The result had been that within the last six months, 200 new members had been added to the Church:

> Next Lord's day we sat down at the table of the Lord, and within six months the preaching of the word of the Lord, by my mouth, has added 200 members to the church; and I may say that not less than twenty of these were converted from the depths of infidelity and immorality, to become holy and God-fearing men. I thought on Monday, after having sat five hours and a half in the vestry of the church, examining candidates for communion, 'Ah, it is good that thou abidest here, and went not forth according to thine own heart.' The Lord hath given me hundreds of souls for my hire; I may not say thousands, but I can say upwards of a thousand, within my own knowledge, have been converted by the efficacy of my ministry.[14]

Replying to the charge that he had become a false witness to his earlier subscription to the Westminster Confession, he said he had subscribed to it honestly but not as absolute truth. 'I signed it not as

171

absolute truth, but as truth checked by Scripture; but I was not bound for one day from searching the Scriptures by that signature.' He instanced other fruits of his searchings which were not explicitly referred to in the Confession.[15]

He had finished his reply to Mr. Mann's speech. The Moderator corrected the mistake he believed Irving had made by alleging that the court had not allowed him to appeal to the Scriptures. He referred to the proceedings of the General Assembly the year before when a similar line of defence had been put forward by John McLeod Campbell:

> The General Assembly ruled that it was an incompetent line of defence, just as we have been called upon to rule, upon the present occasion, that it is an incompetent line of defence as to the matter in process before us. But we deny *in toto* having restricted his line of defence to the Holy Scriptures.[16]

He said that the Presbytery had listened to him quoting the Scriptures for four hours. Irving replied by referring to the first day of the trial when his question to the first witness regarding the Scriptures had been ruled out of order. The Moderator said he was not referring to that but to the defendant's speeches. Mr. McLean said that to seek Scripture proof 'would be in effect trying the question whether our Church were scriptural or not'. The ruling had been made in order to prevent such a development. Mr. Marshall wanted to know if Irving's case had been damaged by his not having been allowed to appeal to Scripture. Irving replied that the evidence that had been brought forward was as good as he could have produced. Mr. Cardale added that though this was true, the Presbytery was still guilty in refusing Irving's appeal to Scripture.[17]

Dr. Crombie moved the adjournment till 6 p.m. Irving said he could not be present as he had to preach at 7 p.m. The following day was suggested but this was Regent Square Church's fast day prior to communion. Irving said that the meeting should proceed that night without him. Mr. Cardale would act for him. This was agreed. Mr. Mann attempted to introduce further evidence against Irving by calling the court's attention to the fact that Miss Hall, one of the gifted, had recently, like Mr. Baxter, confessed that she had been acting under a delusion. This was ruled out of order. Irving spoke in defence of Miss Hall. He was greeted with great applause. The meeting was adjourned.[18]

172

20

The London Presbytery Decides

THE PARTIES had been heard and were now removed. The Moderator called for the judgement of the court. Dr. Crombie spoke first with great reluctance.[1] The case had only narrowly escaped the refusal of even a hearing before the Presbytery:

> You know well, Sir, how reluctant we all were to have anything to do with this case; and you know how narrowly it escaped the refusal of even a hearing in this court, where it now lies for your decision. I can therefore say, in the very strictest verity, that this arbitrament was unsought for by us, and was forced on us by the imperative nature of the trust-deed which so recently laid on our table.[2]

In this sad spirit he undertook his Presbyterial responsibilities. The court had been accused by the defendant of trying to quench the Spirit. But the prior question had to be asked, Was this the Spirit of God? Scripture said that the volume of revelation was closed and that there was a judgement on any who would add to it. It had also to be noted from the examples of Balaam and Judas that the hypocrite and profane could speak the words of God.

The Church standards defined prayer as 'an offering up of our desires to God'. Unintelligible tongues could not be such an offering. In the Confession, Article 21, sec. 3 it said that prayer must be offered 'in a known tongue'. The Directory for Public Worship strictly forbade any interruption of worship:

> 'The public worship being begun, the people are wholly to attend upon it, forbearing to read anything, except what the minister is then reading or citing; and abstaining much more from all private whisperings, conference, etc., and other indecent behaviour, which may disturb the minister or people, or hinder themselves or others in the service of God.'[3]

Irving had said that the occurrences in his church were not contrary to the standards of the Church which said nothing on the subject. Was this correct? The doctrine these people held he called 'miraculous illumination'. The First Book of Discipline, chapter 7 said that miracles had ceased:

> 'God having determined that his kirk here on earth shall be taught not by angels but by men, and seeing that men are born ignorant of God and of all godliness, and seeing, also, *that he ceases to illuminate miraculously*,' etc.[4]

By the act of uniformity of William and Mary's reign, every Church of Scotland minister had to subscribe to the following vow at licensing and ordination:

> 'I do hereby declare that I do sincerely own and believe the whole doctrine contained in the confession of faith, approved by the General Assembly of this National Church, in the year 1690, and confirmed by divers acts of parliament, to be the truth of God; and I do own the purity of worship, presently authorized and practised in this church,' etc.[5]

From these observations and others he could detail, Dr. Crombie had decided in favour of the complainers. He concluded his speech by reading out a proposed motion in which Irving was found guilty of all the charges against him and ordered to be removed from his church.

Mr. Miller then spoke. He observed that in the history of the Church it was usually 'pious and gifted' men who had introduced 'error and innovations'. He repeated Dr. Crombie's remarks about the closure of the canon of Scripture and quoted the *Confession of Faith*, chapter 1, section 6 in confirmation of this:

> 'The whole counsel of God, concerning all things necessary for his own glory, man's salvation, faith and life, is either expressly set down in Scripture, or by good and necessary consequence may be deduced from Scripture; unto which nothing, at any time, is to be added, whether by new revelations of the Spirit, or traditions of men. Nevertheless, we acknowledge the inward illumination of the Spirit of God to be necessary for the saving understanding of such things as are revealed in the word.'[6]

He gathered from Irving's defence that his doctrine of 'the supposed manifestations of the Spirit' originated in his doctrine of Baptism. He had read Irving's sermons on Baptism which he found acceptable except for the part in question. He quoted the Church's teaching on Baptism in which he could find no reference to that 'plenary patrimony' which had been claimed for it:

> 'Baptism is a sacrament of the New Testament, ordained by Jesus Christ, not only for the solemn admission of the party baptized into the visible church, but, also, to be unto him a sign and seal of the covenant of grace, of his ingrafting into Christ, of regeneration, of remission of sins, and of his giving up unto God, through Jesus Christ, to walk in newness of life.'[7]

Referring to the pauses which Irving had introduced into the worship, Mr. Miller said that from his questioning of one of the witnesses it had seemed to him that the utterances were echoes of the minister's Scripture reading and sermon. 'I am distinctly of an opinion, that there is nothing like proof before us that the individual had any criterion, by which to come to the judgement that he was speaking under any supernatural influence.'

He said that Irving spoke like a Congregationalist and not like a Presbyterian. Although he was in an isolated position, he still came under superior authority as a Presbyterian and especially as regards the terms of the trust-deed. According to the form of Church government 'the pastor is an ordinary and perpetual officer in the Church, and his character is thus explained: prophesying of the time of the Gospel'. The minister alone had the right to prophesy. He thought that the clause in the trust-deed which said that the minister should conduct services 'according to the doctrine, forms and discipline' of the Church of Scotland, restricted Irving to what was laid down in the Directory for Public Worship.

He concluded by reminding the court that Irving had said that he would submit to no authority which urged him to repress these alleged manifestations of the Spirit. What alternative had they then but to find him guilty.[8]

Mr. McLean was next to speak. For him the complaint involved breaches of discipline and doctrine:

> The breach of doctrine which is complained of is, that the utterances of certain persons are miraculous or supernatural gifts of the Holy Ghost, reviving the order of prophets which existed in apostolic times.

The breaches of discipline seem to me to be these: interruptions of the public worship of God by certain utterances called tongues; the institution of a new order of teachers in the church, neither sanctioned nor recognized in the Church of Scotland; and the destruction of uniformity of worship therein.[9]

What now had to be decided was, had these been proved? He was confident that they had. If Irving had wanted to change either the doctrine or the discipline of the Church he had only to overture one of the Scottish Presbyteries and carry the matter forward in the usual manner to the General Assembly. Irving had challenged them to produce anything out of the standards contrary to the doctrines he taught. Two passages had already been brought forward. He would produce a third from the first chapter of the Confession of Faith:

'Although the light of nature, and the works of creation and providence, do so far manifest the goodness, wisdom, and power of God, as to leave men inexcusable, yet they are not sufficient to give that knowledge of God, and of his will, which is necessary to salvation; therefore, it pleased the Lord, at sundry times, and in divers manners, to reveal himself, and to declare that his will unto his church; and afterwards, for the better preserving and propagating of the truth, and for the more sure establishment and comfort of the church against the corruption of the flesh, and the malice of Satan and the world, to commit the same wholly unto writing, which maketh the Holy Scripture to be most necessary; *those former ways of God's revealing his will to his people being now ceased.*'[10]

He then repeated Dr. Crombie's point from the Directory about prayer being 'in a known tongue'. He said that this had originally been put in to guard against the Latin and Greek used by the Roman Church. If the Directory objected to languages that at least some understood, how much more did it preclude languages which were wholly unknown.

What had the Directory of Public Worship to say about the officers of the Church? It said that some officers were extraordinary. These were apostles, evangelists and prophets. These had ceased. Others were ordinary. These were pastors, teachers, church governors and deacons. These were perpetual. The Second Book of Discipline said the same. He quoted from page 71:

'Some of these ecclesiastical functions are ordinary, and some extraordinary, or temporary. There be three extra-ordinary, or tem-

176

porary. There be three extraordinary functions – the office of the apostle, of the evangelist, and of the prophet; which are not perpetual, and now have ceased in the kirk of God; except when it pleased God extraordinarily for a time to stir some of them up again. There are four ordinary functions or offices in the kirk of God – the office of the pastor, minister, or bishop; the doctor; the presbyter, or elder; and the deacon. These offices are ordinary, and ought to continue perpetually in the kirk, as necessary for the government and policy thereof: and no more offices ought to be received or suffered in the true kirk of God, established according to his word.'[11]

The meaning of this passage, he said, was found on the following page:

'There are two sorts of calling: one extraordinary, by God immediately; as was that of the prophets and apostles, which, in kirks established, and already well reformed, hath no place. The other calling is ordinary, which besides the calling of God, and inward testimony of a good conscience, hath the lawful approbation and outward judgement of men, according to God's word, and order established in his kirk.'[12]

It was clear to Mr. McLean that the compilers of the standards were referring to Luther, Calvin and Zwingli who 'they called apostles, or prophets or evangelists – not in the strict sense, but as, in some measure, discharging the same duty at that period of apostasy, which the apostles, and prophets, and evangelists did in the Christian Church, when the Jewish Church had fallen into its apostasy'. They did not mean, as Irving had attempted to construe them, that God would continue to stir up the extraordinary functions from time to time. If they had meant that then the Second Book of Discipline would be contradictory to the Directory of Public Worship. Such were his grounds for believing that Irving was guilty and should be removed from his church.[13]

Mr. Macdonald was next to give his judgement. He said that his brother ministers had already mentioned all that he had been going to say. He reaffirmed what they had said and repeated the point made earlier by Mr. Mann, which had been considered a travesty of justice by Irving, that he could not accept the evidence of the witnesses that this was the work of the Holy Spirit. If 500 or even 5,000 should so testify, he would still not accept their testimony for 'number is no test of truth'. He believed that not only had the doctrine and discipline

177

of the Church been contravened but that 'the matter itself is a delusion'. He therefore considered Irving should be found guilty and unfit to remain as minister.[14]

The three elders of the court briefly stated their agreement with Dr. Crombie's proposed motion of condemnation. The Moderator then rose to sum up the case. He paid tribute to Irving's qualities as a man and as a minister. There was nothing personal in what he was about to say. He had followed the defendant's arguments from Scripture very closely and after much thought and consultation with others, he had come to the conclusion that he was 'under a strong and mornful delusion' which was dragging thousands into error. Would Irving come before his brethren who had laboured through University and studied God's word for years and tell them 'in a dogmatizing, bold, popish spirit, that what he says, because he does say it, is true'? God was unchanging. There was not one truth at the beginning of the Christian era and another in 1832. Irving had allowed people to speak in tongues without an interpreter. The Scripture said that that was not permitted and yet he had said that he based his doctrine on Scripture. Such a contradiction could only mean that it was a work of Satan:

> When we see such a contradiction to the Spirit of God, what conclusion can we come to but that it is a delusion of Satan; who, not for the first time, has transformed himself into an angel of light. It is a delusion, to say the very least of it, if it be not (not on the part of the rev. defender, for I believe that he is a simple-minded deceived man), I say it is a delusion, if not something worse on the part of others. Why, in its essential character it is altogether contrary to the very spirit of the Christian dispensation.[16]

The Christian dispensation was a spiritual one whereas the former dispensation was carnal. God proceeds from the carnal to the spiritual. Everyone at all versed in theology knew that the inward and not the outward things were what mattered. Irving had reversed this order and was leading them from the spiritual to the carnal, from faith to sight:

> Is it not a fact, known and recognized by the simplest tyro in theological knowledge, that in proportion as we have abstracted ourselves from outward things, or in other words, in proportion as we can walk by faith and not by sight, we reach to the highest and holiest attain-

ments of the Christian character? And now are we to be told that the essential order of this dispensation is to be reversed? that we are to come back from what is declared to be spiritual, to what is carnal? – that we are not to walk by faith, but by sight? – that the Spirit of God, instead of leaving us to the exercise of holy humble faith in him, looking to him alone for guidance – to him, and to him alone, for the blessing; that now he is to set up visible and audible agency, sounds and sights addressed to my ears and to my eyes? I hold it to be altogether contrary to the very spirit of the Christian dispensation.[17]

Turning to consider the trust-deed, he said that the church had most definitely not been built for Irving. It was not true that the trustees were only responsible for the building. They were the legal guardians according to all the terms of the deed. They represented the subscribers. They had come before the court according to the provisions of their deed of trust.

He agreed with all the speeches already made by the members of the court. Irving had not denied that he had been acting unconstitutionally when he maintained that this was all new. He had said that he had propounded 'this baptism of the Holy Ghost' as he called it, only five years before.[18] He had been preaching it, then praying for it and rousing his followers' excitement so that the surprising thing was not that these manifestations had occurred, but that they had not appeared sooner.

He repeated Mr. Mann's opinion that if Irving refused to proceed with his new doctrine according to the rules laid down by the Church for dealing with any novelty or change, he would have been more honest to leave the Church. He had so refused. He had also repudiated the Church standards when he had said 'Show me a passage in the New Testament that calls on us to carry a matter from the Presbytery to the Synod, and from the Synod to the General Assembly.' He had said that he never would have signed the Confession if he had known that such obstacles would be placed in his path. He had 'placed himself in a dilemma, on one of the horns of which he must be tossed'.[19] He had acted with a high hand. If he refused to be bound by the acts of the Church, he should have left.[20]

He rejected Irving's interpretation of the passage in chapter twelve of the First Book of Discipline in which other than ordained ministers or licentiates were authorized to lead worship. He said that this did not refer to prophets, or tongues. It referred to the time when there were not enough ministers to fill the pulpits of the land. At that time, men with Bible knowledge were asked to read and expound the Scriptures and 'to serve the kirk as necessity may require'. They were not for all time but only for when they could not get ministers. The hearing of them by ministers and elders, was not, as Irving had made out, to test the spirits of the prophets with the gift of discernment, but to see whether they possessed that 'knowledge of the Bible, that discretion of judgement, and gravity of deportment, that might qualify them in the peculiar circumstances of the Church to supply the want of a regularly educated and regularly ordained clergy'.[21]

The defendant was a 'holy and amiable man' but he was none the less a 'deceived and deluded man'. All the great heresies, for example Arianism and Socinianism, had been started by holy and amiable men. That did not mean that they should shrink 'from branding this foul heresy in the manner it deserves'. Irving was a powerfully minded man who had gone grievously astray. He urged those who might still feel that their minister was right, not to be blown about by his 'winds of doctrine'. On Friday last he had spoken as if with infallibility while earlier that day he had not only said that prophets were fallible but that they could even be deceived by God. This was 'monstrous'! This was the 'wind of doctrine'.[22]

The court had given its opinion and it was now his painful duty to read the finding that they had 'determined to come to'. Before he did so he asked Dr. Crombie to lead in prayer. This done, he read the preamble and judgement. This is here given in full. It deals in the preamble with the fact that Irving had already been condemned by the Presbytery for his views on the human nature of Jesus Christ:

Whereas the trustees of the National Scotch Church, Regent Square, having on the 22nd of March last delivered to the moderator of this Presbytery a memorial and act, charging the Rev. E. Irving with certain deviations from the doctrine and discipline of the Church of Scotland, and praying that this Presbytery would forthwith take the same into consideration, so as to determine the question whether by such breaches of doctrine and discipline, the said Rev. E. Irving hath not rendered himself unfit to remain the minister of the said church, and ought not to be removed therefrom pursuant to the conditions of the trust-deed of the said church. And whereas the said Rev. E. Irving hath been delated and convicted before this Presbytery on the ground of heresy concerning the human nature of our Lord Jesus Christ, has

180

been declared to be no longer a member thereof, yet in respect that the trust-deed, legally drawn with the consent of the Rev. E. Irving, and the parties thereto, provides not only that this Presbytery shall act and adjudicate in all cases of complaint brought in against the minister for the time being by such persons, but that the said award shall be final and conclusive; and further, in respect that the trustees of the said church being the parties competent to complain as aforesaid, have laid before this Presbytery, in manner provided by the trust-deed, the memorial, as aforesaid, against the Rev. E. Irving, charging him with deviations from the doctrine and discipline of the Church of Scotland, in as far as he has permitted and publicly encouraged the exercise of certain supposed supernatural gifts, by persons neither ministers nor licentiates of the Church of Scotland, in contravention as well of his ordination vows as the true intent and meaning of the trust-deed, which in the governing clause provides that the 'said church shall at all times be used, occupied, and enjoyed, as a place for the worship of God, according to the doctrine, forms of worship, and order of discipline, of the Established Church of Scotland'; on account of which deviations and innovations the said trustees have petitioned this Presbytery to discern in the premises, according to the provisions in the said trust-deed; and further, in respect that the said complainers have in all respect proceeded on the 26th and 27th of April, and on the 2nd of May, on the part of the trustees, and they and the Rev. E. Irving having severally compeered before this Presbytery, and probation having been taken by the examination of certain witnesses and by certain documentary evidence, and parties having been heard and removed; therefore the Presbytery having seriously and deliberately considered this complaint and the evidence adduced, together with the statement of the Rev. E. Irving, and acting under a deep and solemn sense of their responsibility to the Lord Jesus Christ, the great Head of his Church, DO FIND that the charges in said complaint are fully proved; and therefore, while deeply deploring the painful necessity thus imposed upon them, they did, and hereby do discern that the said Rev. E. Irving has rendered himself unfit to remain the minister of the National Scotch Church aforesaid, and ought to be removed therefrom in pursuance of the conditions of the trust-deed of the said church.[23]

It was ordered that extracts of the minutes of the proceedings should be issued to all parties including Irving. The Moderator then closed the meeting with prayer.[24]

The Congregation Leaves with Irving

THE NEXT morning Thursday 3rd May, the press celebrated the victory of the trustees with unanimous congratulations. Irving was everywhere dismissed with contempt. *The Times* devoted a leading article to the subject:

> The blasphemous absurdities which have for some months past been enacted in the Caledonian Church, Regent Square, are now, we trust, brought to an effectual conclusion. The Scotch Presbytery in London, who are, by the trust-deed of the chapel, appointed to decide on any alleged departure of its minister from the standards of the Kirk of Scotland, to which, by the same deed, he is sworn to adhere, last night, after a laborious investigation, declared that the fooleries which he had encouraged or permitted were inconsistent with the doctrine and dis-cipline of the Scotch National Establishment. It would, indeed, have been a subject of wonder had they come to a different conclusion, though they had had the benefit of a concert upon the 'tongues' from the whole male and female band of Mr. Irving's select performers. So long as the rev. gentleman occupied the stage himself, he was heard with patience – perhaps, sometimes with pity; . . . but when he entered into partnership with knaves and impostors, to display their concerted 'manifestations' – when he profaned the sanctuary of God, by intro-ducing hideous interludes of 'the unknown tongues', it was impossible any longer to tolerate the nuisance.[1]

That day was the National Scotch kirk's fast day prior to com-munion. Irving spent it quietly in devotions and preparation.[2] In the evening the trustees met to minute and endorse the findings of the Presbytery of the day before. They sent a letter to Irving expressing their deep sorrow at what had come about, their sincere appreciation of his ministry in the church, and the admiration, affection and Christian love in which they still all held him. They included this with an extract of their endorsement of the Presbytery's decision.[3] The next morning, those who gathered for the early morning prayer meeting found the church doors locked against them.[4] Shortly before the trial Mr. Hamilton, who, throughout the whole proceedings had been allowed to hold a neutral position, because he was Irving's brother-in-law as well as an elder and trustee, gave the following assessment of the congregation's attitude to the manifestations:

> I believe that a large proportion of the present congregation agree with Edward in the belief of the reality of those manifestations, and that they will follow him where ever he may remove to; and I must say that they are in general very pious people, zealous for God, and most exemplary in the discharge of their religious duties.[5]

It was this 'large proportion' of the congregation who had tried to present a memorial of their opinions through Mr. McKenzie to the Presbytery at the opening of the third day of the trial. This had not been received by the Presbytery since further evidence by that stage was not in order. It was signed by Elders, Deacons, Members and Seat-holders, many of whom were subscribers to the church. They bore testimony that the forms and practices of the Church of Scotland had been adhered to; that although some of them did not agree with the manifestations, they would like to have left it to God to decide; that although strangers had caused disturbances to begin with, these had soon passed away; that those who were undecided would have liked to keep an open mind about these things; that they did not recognize the trustees' power in this matter; that 'not one in twenty' would have agreed with the trustees' action had they been told about it and that for all these reasons the court should not decide hastily nor give in to the wishes of the few who had instituted these proceedings of which they, the vast majority, strongly disapproved:

> THAT your memorialists can bear the fullest testimony, that his ministry has been eminently blessed; and that the forms and practices of the Church of Scotland have been most minutely and strictly adhered to. And your memorialists are not aware, that there is any canon, or statute of the church, condemning the matter which is now before your reverend court.
> THAT notwithstanding some of us do not agree with our faithful

183

and beloved pastor in his views concerning the manifestations of the Holy Spirit, yet we would leave it to the Most High to work his own will, believing that whatever is the work of God, cannot be put down by any effort of man, or by all the power of the enemy of souls; nor that anything not of God can long be permitted to prosper.

THAT although, at first, there were unseemly disturbances in the church, arising, not from the people of the flock, but from strangers, it soon, by the divine blessing, passed away, and the worship of God has, for many months past, continued to proceed with the utmost regularity and order.

THAT such of your memorialists as have not yet been able to come to the same mind with their revered pastor, have, in common with the rest of their brethren, witnessed so much of holy love, zeal, and integrity in him, that they are willing, according to the rule of the apostle, to follow his faith for a season – considering the end of his conversation; and to wait to see if the Lord shall bring them to be of one mind.

THAT your memorialists do not recognize in the trustees, as trustees, even were they unanimous, a power to call our minister to account in this matter; their power, as originally intended, being only to take care that no other than an ordained minister of the Church of Scotland should be the minister of our church. And your memorialists believe, that not one in twenty of the members of the church in Regent Square, would give any countenance to the proceedings of the trustees; but they are directly opposed to them, as would have been shown, had the trustees made their proceedings known to the congregation.

Your memorialists, therefore, earnestly implore your reverend court not to decide hastily in so solemn a matter; nor yield to the wishes of a few, themselves not thoroughly acquainted with the statutes, forms, and usages, of the Church of Scotland (some of them, we believe, consider that they are not even members of that church); and that this memorial and declaration may be taken into your very grave, deliberate and godly consideration; and that you will be pleased to pause before you give a decision which may lead to expensive and tedious litigation – to ill-will and hatred among Christian brethren; and, for a time, to leave an attached congregation of thousands destitute of divine ordinances, and separate them for ever from the Church of Scotland.[6]

The signatories of this comprehensive statement of faith, claimed to speak for more than ninety-five per cent of the congregation. By communion Sunday 6th May, two days after Irving had been locked out of Regent Square Church, a hall had been hired nearby in Gray's Inn Road in which all those who agreed with him, including the two hundred new communicants, were invited to keep the feast. The very high percentage for whom the memorialists had claimed to speak put their faith into action for 'almost the entire church, about eight hundred communicants' came to celebrate the sacrament in the new premises.[7] There were no services that day in the National Scotch Church. The next Sunday 13th May, the church was reopened with the supply preacher Rev. James Marshall of the Tolbooth Church, Edinburgh taking the services.[8] The scene was a sad one:

> With the office-bearers reduced in number, the congregation but a handful, the great body of the people having gone with Mr. Irving, we may conceive the feeling of desolation which pervaded the meagre gathering in the deserted sanctuary.[9]

PART SIX

22

The Apostate Church

SINCE THE General Assembly had ruled against John McLeod Campbell, Hugh Maclean, Alexander Scott and himself the previous May, Irving had been planning to write an article in defence of the four alleged heretics.[1] He had finally done this and published it in the March issue of *The Morning Watch*. It was called 'A Judgement – As to what course the ministers and the people of the Church of Scotland should take in consequence of the decisions of the last General Assembly.'[2] He began by stating the four allegedly heretical doctrines:

The General Assembly, in May last, did depose the Rev. John Campbell, Minister of Row, from the office of the holy ministry; and deprive the Rev. Hugh Baillie Maclean, presentee to the parish of Dreghorn, of his licence to preach the Gospel. The former was declared unfit to be a minister of the Church of Christ, because he held that God loves all men, and out of this love gave his Son to die for all men, whereby all the sins of every man are freely pardoned; and that the faith of this truth doth beget assurance in the soul of God's forgiveness and favour. The mouth of the other was shut from preaching, because he maintained that the Son of God took our nature in its fallen, and not in its unfallen state; and that its holiness was not necessary and essential, and inherent in his creature part, but derived from his union to it; and the unction of it by the Holy Ghost. There was also a decision depriving Mr. Alexander Scott of his office as a preacher of the Gospel, because he disagreed with the Westminster Confession of Faith in three points – namely, (1) its view of redemption, which he interpreted as limiting Christ's atonement to the elect only; (2) of the Sabbath, which he interpreted as confounding the Christian institution of the Lord's-day with the Jewish ordinance of the Sabbath; and (3) of the powers given into the hands of church officers, which he thought larger than God had given into man's hands; and which, in point of

189

fact, he argued that no Presbytery did believe they did by ordination confer. On these points he asked a trial of his opinions by the Holy Scriptures, which was refused to him, and his licence to preach was taken from him upon the simple ground that he could not renew his subscription to the said Westminster Confession of Faith. And, finally, there was a decision, finding my book, entitled *The Orthodox and Catholic Doctrine of our Lord's Humanity* chargeable with Bourignionism, upon the mere report of a committee, without any propositions exhibited or argued, or any hearing of the author, delay, or dealing of any kind whatsoever and branding me the author of that book, as a broacher of heresies; and warning all the ministers of the church against me accordingly.[3]

He then examined the four cases and came to the conclusion that the Church itself was guilty of total apostasy:

If these two cases of the Rev. John Campbell and the Rev. Hugh Baillie Maclean have dragged into light such fearful heresies in the doctrine of the church, as to amount to the entire apostasy of denying the Father and the Son, (for what is the Father when his love is denied, and what the Son when his flesh is denied?) then the two remaining cases adjudged by that Assembly, of Mr. Alexander Scott, preacher of the Gospel, and myself, do shew the utter ignorance of the church of her own constitution, and her departure from every sound principle of ecclesiastical polity and righteous judgement.[4]

This being so, what course should the ministers and people of the Church of Scotland take? If the apostate Church did not repent, they should separate themselves and come out from under its false administrations:

The whole of this judgement I rest upon the fact, that these ministers have declared themselves apostate from the faith in what they did in the last General Assembly; whereof if they repent not, nor give public confession of the same, they are to be concluded apostate; and therefore must be separated from upon the same principle that the Reformers separated from the Roman-Catholic system, when by the Council of Trent it had so constituted itself apostate. All sound-minded men would agree with me in thinking, that if the Church of Scotland, considered as a whole, were to substitute the Creed of Pope Pius IV for the Westminster Confession, it would be the duty of every true man to come out of her. In thinking thus, the principle is allowed. But then the Church is considered to be national, constituted in a human

190

document, which is man's view of the matter, whereas God's view of a church, is a body of believers in some one town or neighbourhood, gathered together and constituted under their angel. The apostasy of that angel is the apostasy of that church, and the signal for removing his candlestick out of its place, except he repent; and being so, each man according to the principle of apostasy ought to come out from under his administration.[5]

Within two months of advocating this separation from the Church of Scotland, he had been forced to set an example of practising what he had preached by his eviction from his church. After the pronouncement of the London Presbytery against him, these his censures on the Church, were further justified in the eyes of his supporters. In the conclusion of his article he had said that the Church was on the brink of catastrophe: 'The Church of Scotland is shooting fast ahead; already the rapids have a hold of her, and she is not far from the fatal plunge: the precipice and the yawning gulf are hard at hand.'[6] His eviction from the National Scotch Church seemed further indication of this headlong rush to spiritual disaster. This article was read in Scotland, causing new hostility, so much so that at the Commission of Assembly in October it was decided that the Presbytery of Annan, who had ordained Irving, should be instructed to proceed to his trial as soon as possible.[7] Annan Presbytery accordingly wrote to him and asked if he was the author of *The Orthodox and Catholic Doctrine of our Lord's Human Nature*; *The Day of Pentecost*; and the recent article 'A Judgement' – . Technically he had no need to reply since the Assembly and Presbytery had no jurisdiction South of the border but he did so with promptness and animation. He admitted that he was the author of those works. He also said that he could no longer have any relationship with the General Assembly 'but that of open and avowed enmity'. He accused that court again of the total rejection of God in the threefold character of His revelation – the love of the Father, the humanity of the Son and the gifts of the Spirit:

> Men and Brethren, – I avow myself to be the author of the three tracts, whose titles are recounted in the General Assembly's instructions to you, and in your letter to me, whereof the first-named was written to set forth the foundation of the Christian verity, – viz., Christ's evenness with us in the flesh. The second, the glorious head-stone of the same. It is our evenness with him in the Spirit. And the last to denounce the General Assembly of the Church of Scotland as one of

191

the most wicked of all God's enemies on the face of the earth, for having denied and fought against all the foundations of the truth as it is in Jesus, and cast out his servants for preaching the same. With that wicked Assembly, now three times tried of God, and three times found wanting, and with all who in any way adhere to it, or do its evil deeds, I can make no relationship, but that of open and avowed enmity. 'Do I not hate them, O Lord, that hate thee; and am I not grieved with all those that rise up against thee? I hate them with a perfect hatred; I count them mine enemies.'

I am grieved in my heart that you should yield obedience to the decrees of that synagogue of Satan, and thereby make yourselves partakers of her evil deeds; and I beseech as many of you as are the Lord's people to come out of that Babylon which she ruleth over, that ye be not partakers with her of her plagues, which are ready to come upon her.[8]

Further letters were exchanged. Irving agreed to travel North to stand trial. The date was fixed for Wednesday 13th March, 1833. He arrived in Annan that day by the London mail coach and was greeted by a large crowd. The trial was due to start at noon in the parish church and by that time it was estimated that 2,000 people had crammed themselves into the building.[9]

23

Irving's Trial, his Deposition and Death

THE MODERATOR constituted the meeting with prayer. There were present the Revs. Roddick, Gretna, Moderator; Sloan, Dornock; Nevison, Middlebie; Dr. Duncan, Ruthwell; Gillespie, Hodham and Monilaws, Annan.[1]

Dr. Duncan, Presbytery clerk, read out the libel which was to the following effect:

> He was indicted for maintaining the sinfulness of the Saviour in his human nature: 1st in a pamphlet entitled, *The Catholic and Orthodox Doctrine of our Lord's Human Nature, in four parts.* 2nd. In a pamphlet called *The Day of Pentecost; or the Baptism of the Holy Ghost.* 3rd. In No. 13 of *The Morning Watch,* or *Quarterly Journal on Prophecy.*[2]

Then followed a long list of quotations similar to those already examined in part 1 of this study and more from 'A Judgement' in which he had indicted the Assembly of apostasy and urged all true Christians to leave the Church. His letter to Annan Presbytery of 10th October 1832, quoted above, was also read out as further evidence of his 'calumnious attacks'. The accusation in the libel was of his 'printing, publishing, and disseminating heresies and heretical doctrines, particularly the doctrine of the fallen state and sinfulness of our Lord's human nature'. These were declared to be 'contrary to the Holy Scriptures, and to what is taught in the standards of the Church of Scotland'. Because of this it was concluded that he ought to be 'deposed from the office of the holy ministry, and deprived of his licence as a minister of the said Church'.

Irving was then asked if he accepted the truth of the libel that he taught 'the fallen state and sinfulness of Christ's nature'.[4] He replied that he did not know whether the libel was true or not, but he certainly knew that he had never written anything which denied the perfect holiness of Christ. He was then asked if he admitted the correctness of the extracts from his writings contained in the libel. He replied that he would not ensnare himself in catch questions. He admitted the extracts were true but said they had been misrepresented by being taken out of their context. This admission was considered enough to sustain the libel.[5] The court then moved on to the proof. The Moderator asked for the members of the Presbytery to give their views. They each did so, agreeing with the libel. The Moderator summed up the court's views 'that the words, "*liable to, yea, inclined to sin, fallen, sinful, rebellious*", as applied to any department of our Saviour's person, are altogether unwarrantable'.[6] The words *peccability of our Lord's human nature*, were added to the libel. When Irving was asked if he objected to the addition he said 'That is your matter, not mine; I answer not a word.' This was greeted by loud applause from the galleries. The Moderator restored order, cautioned the audience, and said that Irving's silence implied consent. This provoked great remonstrance from the galleries and ominous crackings were heard as many rose to their feet. The Moderator once more restored order.[7] It was then proposed to consult with Irving privately. The court was adjourned for half an hour while the Presbytery retired with the accused to the Session House. Nothing was achieved by this. Irving wrote next day his account of the unfruitful interlude:

> They then proposed to have a private conference with me in the Session-house, apart from all the people, where God gave me grace to refuse to every one of them the right hand of fellowship, yea, and not to eat bread with them, and drink wine with them; and to tell them that they had lifted up the standard of rebellion against the Lord Jesus Christ, and that I would hold no conference of friendship with them, but be at open and avowed enmity until they had ceased from persecuting his faithful members. So I sat in the midst of them in silence and sorrow, very much burdened and afflicted in soul, that I should be thus called upon to separate myself from them, of whom many were members of the church before me, and some of them had laid their hands on me.[8]

On resuming, the court asked Irving to speak to his defence. He used the opportunity to proclaim the doctrine for which he had already been condemned by the London Presbytery. He wrote to his congregation afterwards:

> I was strengthened by your prayers to speak with great boldness for the name of Jesus, and to justify his truth and to vindicate myself as a member of Christ; also to reprove and rebuke them all, both elders, and people, of their sins, and to proclaim in their hearing the coming of the Blessed One, and the mercy and truth which are now going before him to prepare his way, and set us in his steps. Oh! it was a gracious and sweet opportunity which he gave me of certifying to his great name and his perfect work of mercy and judgement.[9]

While he was expounding his doctrine Dr. Duncan interposed to say that he was preaching his doctrines to the people and not speaking to the Presbytery in his defence. The Moderator added that he thought he must be imagining he was in London preaching to his congregation. He denied this. He said he was simply expounding the truth: 'Ye ministers, elders, and presbytery! This is no question of scholastic theology. I speak for the sanctification of men. I wish my flock to be holy – and unless the Lord Jesus has contended with sin, as they are commanded to do, how can they be holy when they follow him?'[10] He went on to recapitulate many of the doctrinal points he had made in his writings on the humanity of Christ touching once again on the relationship between holiness and power, the fruits of our union with Christ:

> Moderator, ministers, elders, and people of Israel (for there is but one church – one body), if ye but believe in the Word which was made flesh, and walk in his footsteps, ye shall be temples of the Holy Ghost. Doth not the Holy Apostle say 'Covet earnestly the best gifts, but rather that ye may prophesy?' Why should there be any difference among Christians? Are we not servants of the same master? I come here with no new banner.[11]

He then turned to his article and pamphlet 'A Judgement'. He was convinced that the Assembly had denied God in its decisions against Campbell, Maclean and Scott, but especially in its denial of God's love in the rejection of Campbell. He said he did not know what sinners could trust in if they did not know that God loved them all. Campbell was a man of God, as great or greater than Knox. He had to take his part:

The very reason which keeps people from God is, that they think that God will not accept of them until they do something to deserve his favour. God loves even the prodigal, and sends his messengers on earth to seek sinners and bring them back to the fold. Jesus – he came to tell us that God is light, and that in him is no darkness at all. The gates of heaven are open even to the blackest sinner. This is the doctrine which was cast out. The greatest gift ever bestowed on the people of Scotland since the days of Knox – yea, a greater than he – I mean John Campbell – has been cast out. He was a *spotless* man of God. In him was *no fault* – albiet no fault that man could lay to his charge. He was a godly man. But him ye have cast out with scorn; and shall I not take his part – shall I not receive him to my bosom? – because in receiving him I receive Christ. Shall I be terrified by the name of the General Assembly? God's name is a greater name than the name of the General Assembly. What are they but a company of miserable sinners? When God's name is in question shall I not hate the name of the General Assembly?[12]

He concluded his defence by saying that he had come before them of his own free will. If they valued the future spiritual prosperity of their land they would repent of their sin in having implemented the orders of 'that wicked Assembly'.[13]

The Moderator then asked each member of the court to give his opinion. Mr. Sloan spoke first saying that all the accused's arguments were ineffective attempts to explain his heretical doctrines. He considered Irving guilty.

Dr. Duncan spoke next.[14] He had been a friend and admirer of Irving for many years, but had now with sorrow realized that his mind had become alienated from the truth. He believed him to be guilty but he prayed that 'he might be delivered from the strong delusion under which he laboured, as another individual had lately been, who was well known to have been one of the most influential of the party with which Mr. Irving is connected.'[15] He then told the story of Robert Baxter, pointing out that the first thing that led to that deluded man being delivered from 'the powers of darkness' had been his realization that Irving's doctrine of Christ's humanity was erroneous:

The first thing which shook the faith of the gentleman alluded to (Mr. Baxter), in the supernatural gifts with which he had conscientiously believed himself to be endowed, was the very doctrine regard-

196

ing our Lord's humanity, which was the subject of the libel. He discovered that Mr. Irving and some of his followers taught that in Christ's flesh there is 'a proclivity to the world and to Satan', and that Christ received 'such a measure of the Holy Ghost as sufficed to resist this proclivity', which he could not help considering a fearfully erroneous doctrine. Mr. Baxter corresponded with Mr. Irving on the subject, and received from him an explicit avowal of this dreadful doctrine. This led him seriously to examine the whole matter, and a light broke in on his mind, which ended in his perceiving how fatally he had been led astray. And now this worthy person, had not hesitated to make an open recantation, and to publish a pamphlet explaining the whole delusion, and making a most extraordinary and edifying exposure of the snares in which he had been entangled.[16]

He echoed the sentiments expressed by the London Presbytery the previous April when he said that the accused was wrong to set the Church standards against the Scriptures. The Church had not adopted the standards for any other reason than 'that they believed them to contain a true exposition of the truths contained in the Bible'. Anything contrary to the *Confession of Faith* was contrary to the word of God. It was clear to him that Irving's doctrine was contrary to both.[17]

He quoted passages from the *Confession of Faith* which proved that the humanity of Christ was always excepted from the terms 'fallen' and 'sinful nature'. These terms only applied to those descended from Adam *'by ordinary generation'*. Jesus was *miraculously* conceived. In chapter 8 it said 'The Son of God did, when the fulness of time was come, take upon him man's nature, with all the essential properties and common infirmities thereof, *yet without sin*'. Sin was not an essential property of man's nature as he said Irving had tried to make out, but was 'an *accident* which did not belong to man in his perfect state in Paradise'. He said that the next clause in the Confession confirmed this where, after saying that Christ was 'without sin, being conceived by the power of the Holy Ghost in the womb of the Virgin Mary', it said 'So that two whole, perfect, and distinct natures – the Godhead and the Manhood, were inseparably joined together in one person, without conversion, composition, or confusion.' It was clear to Dr. Duncan that 'the word "perfect" as applied to the humanity, being evidently introduced here to intimate that, as a man, he was not fallen and sinful'.[18]

He said that both Scripture and the Church standards taught that

Christ was free from original sin. Had this been otherwise He could not have been the Redeemer. Following the pattern of earlier criticism of Irving's position, he spoke of these things as they related to the atonement:

> In opposition to Mr. Irving's position, that Christ was not in his human nature 'separate from sinners' till his resurrection, it was further urged that it is said of him, in describing his character while on earth, that 'he was holy; harmless, undefiled, and separate from sinners', that 'he knew no sin, neither was guile found in his mouth', that 'he was in all points tempted like as we are, *yet without sin*', etc. etc., and that the whole doctrine of the atonement which Christ made, and the sacrifice which he offered up for sin must fall to the ground, if he, in his own nature as a man, inherited the sinfulness and the curse of the fall.[19]

Dr. Duncan continued his denunciations of Irving's doctrine. Christ was 'not first sinful and then sinless' as he said the accused maintained. It was not true that Christ continued to have fallen manhood until His resurrection. Irving had said even worse things than that:

> But Mr. Irving still further maintained that Christ's *will* as well as his flesh was in a fallen state – that it was 'in bondage to the devil, the world, and the flesh' – that his human nature, 'though a servant in all things, was yet an unwilling servant', and that 'he was conscious of the motions of the flesh, and of the fleshly mind, in so far as any regenerate man, when under the operation of the Holy Spirit, is conscious of them'. Nor was this all; for Mr. Irving further held that Christ possessed the feelings, and performed the actions, of a fallen man – that, while on earth, 'he carried himself with the sorrow, and *penitence*, and *confession* of the fallen creature.'[20]

These were the doctrines which Dr. Duncan said that Irving believed. His great eloquence might delude some for a while but the people of Scotland would never accept them as the faith of their fathers. These new doctrines were abhorrent to the Scottish tradition. Irving should not be allowed to remain a minister of the Church of Scotland any longer.

Messrs. Nevison, Monilaws and Gillespie then spoke and condemned Irving's doctrines as heretical in similar vein. The Moderator then asked the accused if he had any objection to raise as to why the Presbytery should not now pass the sentence of deposition against him. Irving rose at once and said vehemently that he had every objection. He said that if they did so they would call down on their own heads the righteous wrath of God. 'I object for the Church's sake, who are led blindfold to ruin.' He repeated that he had never taught 'the sinfulness of the human nature of Christ'. He objected strongly to Dr. Duncan's speech, especially to the extracts, all of which had been taken out of their context and misconstrued. If the Presbytery valued the salvation of their souls, they would not pass sentence against him.[21]

The Moderator was about to pass sentence and had asked Mr. Sloan, the senior minister, to lead in prayer before he did so, when he was interrupted by Mr. Dow, recently minister of Irongray and friend of Irving, speaking out loudly in the Spirit: 'Arise, depart! – Arise, depart! flee ye out; flee ye out of here. Ye cannot pray. How can ye pray? How can ye pray to Christ, whom ye deny? Ye cannot pray. Depart, – depart, – flee, – flee!' It was now almost 7 p. m. and quite dark in the church except for one candle. There was a commotion in the gallery as the voice rang out. In the darkness one of the ministers lifted the candle and started to peer about to see who had spoken. He discovered that it was Mr. Dow and immediately moved that he be removed from the court for breach of order. Confusion was growing. Mr. Dow rose to leave. Irving rose to follow. The crowd was so dense in the church that their passage was obstructed. Irving shouted 'Stand forth! Stand forth! What! Will ye not obey the voice of the Holy Ghost! As many as will obey the Holy Ghost, let them depart!' The crowd parted. He strode to the door. Just before he reached it he exclaimed 'Prayer, indeed! Oh!' He was followed out by several friends.[22]

The confusion was now great. Mr. Sloan offered a brief prayer. Irving was called three times. There was no answer. 'The Moderator formally pronounced the sentence of deposition of the Rev. Edward Irving from the ministry of the Church of Scotland.'[23] The crowd began to disperse. The proceedings had taken seven hours. As they left it was announced that Irving would preach the next day in a field near the town.

At 11 a.m. the next day Irving preached from a tent in a field nearly opposite the church to a congregation of 1,700. His text was *Zech.* 9:9 'Rejoice greatly, O daughter of Zion.' After prayer and praise he read out a letter which he sent later that day to his congregation in

London. In it he gave his own account of the trial, the first part of which has already been given above. He urged his flock to abide steadfast in Christ and 'to pray always for the outpouring of the Holy Spirit in the abundance, the superabundance of the latter rain, which prepareth for the coming of the Harvest-man'.[24] He gave thanks, and urged them to give thanks to God for his deliverance from the bondage of the courts of the Church:

> I sang in my heart, 'Blessed be the Lord, who hath not given us as a prey to their teeth; our soul is escaped as a bird out of the snare of the fowler.' The snare is broken, and we are escaped; our help is in the name of the Lord who made heaven and earth. Now give thanks my dearly beloved, for the Lord himself hath broken my bonds.[25]

The word of the Lord, spoken through Mr. Dow, had snatched him away out of the Presbytery.

He had been so moved by 'the gross darkness of these poor ministers, and the error with which they have filled the breasts and minds of the people in all these parts' that he had decided that he ought to stay on for a few days 'and preach the Gospel to the benighted people around', particularly as he did not think he would be visiting Scotland again. He then concluded by commending his faithful people to the Lord:

> I do propose by the grace of God to tarry in these parts certain days, and to publish, in the towns of the coast, the great name of the Lord . . . I commend you to the Lord and to the riches of his grace, which is able to build you up and to give you an inheritance among all those which are sanctified. – Your faithful and loving pastor and angel over Christ's flock in London.[26]

(Signed) EDWARD IRVING

Annan, 14th March, 1833.

Irving conducted his open air preaching tour along the coast of Dumfriesshire, greeted everywhere by vast crowds. He then returned to London. Mr. Cardale had been called as the first Apostle of the new Church on 7th November, 1832.[27] On 5th April, 1833, he ordained Irving, who had now no ministerial status, Angel or Pastor of their congregation.[28] Over the next two years the people who had left Regent Square Church with their minister, by direction of the Holy Spirit, were transformed into the emergent Catholic Apostolic Church.[29] The outworking of the doctrines that have here been looked at, in that body, would require another study.[30] It does not directly concern the examination of the writings of Edward Irving. From the day when he ceased to be a minister of the Church of Scotland, although he continued to preach and to have his sermons recorded, he published nothing further under his own hand. He was now under the authority of the Apostles and Prophets of the new Church. Having never been sealed with the sign of tongues nor spoken in prophecy, 'the least in the kingdom was greater than' he. It also soon became apparent that his health was failing.[31] He had always been an unusually strong man. Now he complained of fatigue. In the summer of 1834 many of his friends became anxious about him.[32] In September he left London for Glasgow alone on horseback. He caught a chill on the way which further weakened him. He was able to found a congregation in Glasgow before he took to his bed late in November. It was diagnosed that he had consumption. He was visited by John McLeod Campbell among other friends before he died on 7th December. *The Scottish Guardian* wrote: 'Every other consideration was forgotten, in the universal and profound sympathy with which the information was received.'[33] He was buried in the crypt of Glasgow Cathedral. Among the crowds attending were many who had disagreed with his doctrines. The sermon was preached on *II Sam.* 3:38, 'Know ye not that there is a prince and a great man fallen this day in Israel?'

ABBREVIATIONS

H: John Hair, *Regent Square, Eighty Years of a London Congregation*, Revised Edition, 1899.

O: Mrs. M. O. W. Oliphant, *The Life of Edward Irving*, 1862, Fifth Edition.

P: Edward Irving, 'Preface' to *Christ's Holiness in Flesh*, 1831.

I: Edward Irving, *The Doctrine of the Incarnation Opened in Six Sermons*, 1828.

M.W: *The Morning Watch or Quarterly Journal on Prophecy and Theological Review.* 7 Vols. 1829–1833.

H.N.: Edward Irving, *The Orthodox and Catholic Doctrine of Our Lord's Human Nature*, 1830.

C.H: Edward Irving, *Christ's Holiness in Flesh, The Form, Fountain Head, and Assurance to us of Holiness in Flesh*, 1831.

B: Edward Irving, 'The Sealing Virtue of Baptism', Homily II. 'Homilies on Baptism', *Collected Writings*, Vol. II.

F: Edward Irving, 'Facts Connected with Recent Manifestations of Spiritual Gifts', *Frasers Magazine*, January 1832.

N: Robert Norton, M.D. *Memoirs of James and George Macdonald of Port-Glasgow*, 1840.

D: A. L. Drummond, *Edward Irving and His Circle*, 1936.

C: Edward Irving, 'The Church, With Her Endowment of Holiness and Power', *Morning Watch*, Vol. II and *Collected Writings*, Vol. V.

T: *The Trial of the Rev. Edward Irving, M.A. Before the London Presbytery*, 1832.

G.H.G: Edward Irving, 'On the Gifts of the Holy Ghost, Commonly Called Supernatural', *Morning Watch*, Vols. II and III, and *Collected Writings*, Vol. V.

N2:   Robert Norton, M.D. *The Restoration of Apostles and Prophets, In the Catholic Apostolic Church*, 1861.

D.P: Edward Irving, *The Day of Pentecost, or The Baptism With the Holy Ghost*, 1831.

T2:   *The Trial of the Rev. Edward Irving, M.A., Before the Presbytery of Annan*, 1833.

C.W.:   *The Collected Writings of Edward Irving in Five Volumes.* ed. Rev. G. Carlyle, 1864.

P.E.D.: Paul Ewing Davies, *An Examination of the Views of Edward Irving concerning the Person and Work of Jesus Christ*, 1928. Unpublished Ph.D. Thesis. New College, Edinburgh.

J.:   Edward Irving, 'A Judgment – As to what course the ministers and the people of the Church of Scotland should take in consequence of the decisions of the last General Assembly', *Morning Watch*, Vol. V.

NOTES

INTRODUCTION

1. Rowland A. Davenport, *Albury Apostles*, United Writers 1970, pp. 92 and 100.
2. H., pp. 45–123.
3. 'Perhaps the most striking thing about the claim to speak with tongues is its infrequency. . . . What does not appear is that it was ever claimed, at least on a large scale, as a symptom of divine inspiration, until the end of the seventeenth century. Then you find it cropping up in two separate movements, among the Huguenots of the Cevennes and among the appellant (but still nominally Catholic) Jansenists. A nine days wonder in either case, it goes underground again for the next hundred years. In 1830, quite without warning, it begins to be practised by a handful of simple people in the neighbourhood of Port Glasgow.' Ronald Knox, *Enthusiasm, A Chapter in the History of Religion*, Oxford, 1950, p. 551. Cf. Watson E. Mills, *Understanding Speaking in Tongues*, Eerdmans, 1972, p. 15.
4. 'And it's in its theological self-consciousness that Irvingism is significant, more so than in the warning it offers of the way Pentecostal revival can cool off. Irvingism is an important case where biblical examination created expectations about possible experiences of the Spirit – in other words, and contrary to what the opponents of Pentecostal movements maintain is more usual, theology had precedence over experience: experience didn't generate the theology, rather the reverse. And the theological awareness makes Irvingism quite distinct from any isolated but perhaps ill-understood, occurrences of tongues among earlier revivalists; perhaps for the first time since Tertullian the participants knew precisely what was afoot.' Valentine Cunningham, 'Texts and their Stories – 14', *Redemption Tidings*, 1st October, 1970, p. 3.
5. B., pp. 276–80.
6. F., p. 755.
7. F., p. 760.
8. T., p. 3.
9. 'Substance of the Trust Deed of the New National Scotch Church.' pp. 1, 5, 6.
10. T., pp. 19f.
11. T., p. 89.

12. E.g., '. . . the exhibitions of the Spirit . . . disgraceful breaches of decorum'
S. T. Coleridge, 1831, cited in D., p. 221. '. . . insane jargonings of hysterical
women, and crack-brained enthusiasts.' T. Carlyle, 1831. J. A. Froude,
Thomas Carlyle, A History of the First Forty Years of his Life, 1901, Vol. II,
p. 219. '. . . blasphemous absurdities . . .', *The Times,* 3rd May, 1832. 'decep-
tions' William Jones, *Biographical Sketch of the Rev. Edward Irving, A.M.*
1835, p. 361. '. . . melancholy errors and extravagances . . .' William Anderson
The Scottish Nation, 1865, Vol. 2, p. 540. 'the so-called manifestations'
The Weekly Review, 20th April, 1878. '. . . gigantic wickedness . . . orgies of
vice' Jabez Marrat, *Northern Lights,* 1885, p. 134. '. . . delusion . . .', John
Tulloch, *Movements of Religious Thought in Britain During the Nineteenth
Century,* 1885, p. 160. '. . . the "utterances" of excitable men and women', A.
Saunders Dyer, *Sketches of English Nonconformity,* 1904, p. 99. '. . . wild,
hysterical . . .' P.E.D., 1928, p. 208. '. . . scandal . . .' J. H. S. Burleigh, *A
Church History of Scotland,* Oxford, 1960, p. 330. This attitude has been
carried over into the Pentecostal tradition by those who might have been
expected to be sympathetic. E.g., 'A great deal of attention has been given to
the movement associated with Edward Irving and its unfortunate accom-
paniments. The wildest fanaticism spoiled what could have been a movement
of rich blessing to the churches'. Michael Harper, *As At the Beginning,*
Hodder, 1965, p. 21.
13. C., pp. 449–506. G.H.G., C.W., Vol. V, pp. 509–61.
14. H., p. 124.
15. In addition to those already cited, the following examples of psychological/
psychiatric opinions of Irving are given: '. . . in the midst of his fame, delusion
like a summer cloud, overcame him.' Rev. James Monilaws, 'Parish of
Annan', *Statistical Account of Scotland,* 1845, Vol. IV, p. 524. '. . . incipient
disease of the brain.' J. W. Taylor, *United Presbyterian Magazine,* August,
1862, p. 403. '. . . diseased imagination.' William Anderson, *loc. cit.,* His
death is likened to the death of mad King Lear, 'Vex not his ghost . . . etc.'
H. R. Story, *St. Giles Lectures,* 1883, Lecture VII, p. 272. 'Without moral
restraint . . .' Jabez Marrat, *loc. cit.,* 'Irving, with his mind enfeebled . . .'
John Tulloch, *loc. cit.,* '. . . less than sane'. J. H. Leckie, *Fergus Ferguson,* 1923,
p. 31. 'His wild prophesyings were the result of an over-wrought brain . . . a
disappointment in love led to Irving taking to religious excitement as grosser
natures take to drink.' A. L. Drummond, *The Times,* 7th December, 1934,
p. 16. 'abnormal psychology', D. S. Cairns, review of D. in undated newspaper article in archives of the Presbyterian Historical Society of England.
'. . . not without madness.' Albert J. LaValley, *Carlyle and the Idea of the
Modern Yale,* 1968, p. 332. '. . . lacked mental ballast . . .' Bernard M. G.
Reardon, *From Coleridge to Gore, A Century of Religious Thought in Britain,*
Longman, 1971, p. 410. '. . . his strange pathetic story is a cautionary tale
about the waywardness of even the noblest of human spirits.' R. Buick
Knox, 'Edward Irving', *Outlook,* September 1971, p. 18.
16. E.g., 'To me, it seems that never was Edward Irving's genius more vigorous –
never his giant faculties more under his command – than when he wrote the

statement of Facts for "Fraser", or stood at the bar of Annan Presbytery'. Washington Wilks, *Edward Irving: An Ecclesiastical and Literary Biography*, 1854, p. 271. 'Are the days of Pentecost gone never to return? Have miracles ceased from amongst men? Cannot signs and wonders still be wrought by men filled with the Holy Ghost?' J. E. Ritchie, *The London Pulpit*, 1854, p. 218. 'Men and women were claiming there to have received a revival of the ancient gifts of the Church; they spake it was asserted, as they were moved by the Holy Ghost. It is impossible, it ought to be impossible to speak lightly on such a subject.' *Blackwoods Magazine*, June 1862, cited by Roland A. Davenport. *Op. cit.*, p. 65. Of Irving's patient attempts to persuade Presbytery to allow him to cite Scripture in his defence or to accept the testimony of the witnesses. 'Such a singular and obstinate evasion of the real point at issue . . . might well chafe the spirit of the meekest of men; yet he returns again and again with indignant patience to the question which his judges refused to consider.' O., 1862, p. 360. 'I know that a cold-blooded logic can sit down and . . . demonstrate that miraculous endowments are not to be expected in the present age . . . Irving, however, thought . . . and not without some show of reason, that they were still needed . . .' William Landels, *Edward Irving*, 1864, p. 42. 'tongues, prophets, apostles, all followed in a natural order, and the word was once more confirmed by signs following. This may seem at first sight absurd, but surely from the orthodox stand-point there should be a very strong case for all of these.' C. Kegan Paul, *Biographical Sketches*, 1883, p. 27. '. . . these unexpected experiences were . . . glorious . . . by Christly standards.' Jean Christie Root, *Edward Irving, Man, Preacher, Prophet*, 1912, p. 77. 'Irving's theoretical position regarding these outward manifestations of the Spirit is not easily assailable.' P.E.D., 1928, p. 208. '. . . prophecy, healing and speaking with tongues . . . were part of the endowment of the Church which Irving had looked for.' Henry C. Whitley, *Blinded Eagle, An Introduction to the Life and Teaching of Edward Irving*, S.C.M., 1955, p. 83.

17. John Macquarrie, *Principles of Christian Theology*, London, 1966. 'Miracles', p. 227. The reference is to Ernst Troeltsch and historical method.

18. W. Hall; *Edward Irving as John the Baptist*, engraving 1823, with text 'The voice of one crying in the Wilderness, Prepare the way of the Lord.'

19. 'Edward Irving . . . has more of the head and heart, the life, the unction, and the genial power of Martin Luther than any man now alive; yea, than any man of this and the last century.' S. T. Coleridge, *Church and State*, 1830, p. 154.

20. David Wilkie, John Knox preaching before the Lords of the Congregation; the figure of John Knox is drawn from Irving.

21. D.P., p. 28.

22. C., G.H.G., F., T., etc.

23. *For Judgment to Come*, 1823; *Babylon and Infidelity Foredoomed of God*, 1826; *Sermons, Lectures and Occasional Discourses*, Vol. III, 1828; *Introduction to Ben Ezra*, 1827; *The Last Days*, 1828; *The Church and State*, 1829; *Lectures on Revelation*, 1831.

24. 'But the movement associated with Irving ebbed considerably, and its existence was probably not known to the Pentecostals until in retrospect its similarities were discovered.' Frederick Dale Bruner, *A Theology of the Holy Spirit*, Eerdmans, 1970, p. 40.
25. Michael Harper, *op. cit.*, p. 26. Vinson Synan, *The Holiness-Pentecostal Movement in the United States*, Eerdmans, 1971, p. 101. F. D. Bruner, *op. cit.*, p. 119, etc.
26. Donald Gee, *Wind and Flame, The Pentecostal Movement*, Assemblies of God, 1967, p. 16. James D. G. Dunn, *Baptism in the Holy Spirit*, S.C.M., 1970, p. 2.
27. Donald Gee, *Wind and Flame, The Pentecostal Movement*, Chapters 8, 9 and 10.
28. 'There are some rather striking similarities between the Irvingites and the Pentecostals who flourished seventy years later. First, it is believed that the Irvingites thought that the occurrence of *glossolalia* among them was of the same nature as that which took place on the Day of Pentecost. To them, speaking in tongues was an evidence of Spirit baptism. Second, the Irvingites seem to have regarded such an experience as a prerequisite for obtaining one of the nine gifts of the Spirit. Third, the Irvingites insisted that the *charismata*, as manifested at Pentecost and in the Apostolic Church, were a permanent possession of the Church, withheld because of the unfaithfulness of the Christian believers. Fourth, Edward Irving and his charismatic followers were expelled from the Presbyterian Church and were forced to establish a new denomination, the Catholic Apostolic Church.' J. T. Nichol, *Pentecostalism*, Logos, 1971, p. 24. 'The parallels between Irvingism and 20th Century Pentecost are clear. Both are rooted in strong expectations of the second advent. . . . Both movements involved men who were rather Arminian than Calvinist: Irving supported Campbell of Row, whose doctrine 'that God loves every man, and that Christ died to redeem all mankind' caused his expulsion from his Presbytery. Irving also, interestingly, had a fully developed doctrine of tongues as the sign of the Baptism in the Spirit.' Valentine Cunningham, *loc. cit.*
29. John Sherrill, *They Speak With Other Tongues*, Hodder, 1967, p. 50.
30. 'In recent discussions of the Catholic-Protestant issue, and of the deadlock in which these discussions seem to have become immobilized, it is often suggested that the way forward may be found in a new understanding of the doctrine of the Holy Spirit. But of course the illumination which is needed will never come as a result of purely academic theological study. May it not be that the great Churches of the Catholic and Protestant traditions will have to be humble enough to receive it in fellowship with their brethren in the various groups of the Pentecostal type with whom at present they have scarcely any Christian fellowship at all? The gulf which at present divides these groups from the ecumenical movement is the symptom of a real defect on both sides, and perhaps a resolute effort to bridge it is the next condition for further advance.' Lesslie Newbigin, *The Household of God*, S.C.M. 1953. 'The Community of the Holy Spirit', pp. 109–10.
31. Henry Pitney van Dusen, *Life Magazine*, 6th June, 1958.

32. Even his last unpublished letter, dated Glasgow, 21st November, 1834, and addressed to his father-in-law, shows a clear and unimpaired mind. In the archives of the Presbyterian Historical Society of England.

33. 'According to the best sources, although Edward Irving 'was not called to be an Apostle, nor were prophetic gifts given to him or recognized in him', (Shaw, *Catholic Apostolic*, p. 58; cf. 'Irving and the Catholic Apostolic Church' in James Hastings (ed.), *Encyclopedia of Religion and Ethics* (New York: Charles Scribner's Sons, 1928), VII, 422f.) he did function as a sort of John the Baptist, introducing a new era in which spiritual gifts would flourish. Shaw is doubtless right in claiming that Irving's immense prestige 'gave recognition to the "tongues" and "prophesyings" and made both of them respectable as far as that was possible'. J. T. Nichol, *op. cit.*, p. 23.

34. W. W. Andrews, *Martin Luther and Edward Irving: Their Work and Testimony Compared*, 1883. This now appears as a prophetic article, as does William Landels, *op. cit.*, p. 50.

35. Without any obvious Pentecostal reference this has been looked for from time to time, e.g., Jean Christie Root, *op. cit.*, p. 3; also: 'In time to come the condemnation will surely be withdrawn, for the vindication of Irving. . . .' P. E. Shaw, *The Catholic Apostolic Church*, Kings Crown, 1946, p. 242; and: 'It remains the task of this generation to clarify the issues which he raised, and to make vivid and strong the doctrines which he drew out of the shades of unbelief and obscurity. . . . It is possible that Irving's claim to a place among Scotland's great theologians may yet be upheld when these comparatively unknown works are tested and more clearly understood.' Henry C. Whitley, *op. cit.*, pp. 104, 106. Now that the neo-Pentecostal or charismatic has penetrated the kirk, Irving's spiritual and theological exile may be drawing to a close. 'There are now about a hundred ministers of the Church of Scotland who have either received, or are expecting, some recognizably Pentecostal experience or gift of the Spirit.' C. G. Strachan, 'A Second Chance', *Life and Work*, May 1972, p. 27.

36. 'All earlier theology, up to and including the Reformers and their successors, exercised at this point a very understandable reserve, calculated to dilute the offence, but also to weaken the high positive meaning of passages like *II Cor.* 5:21, *Gal.* 3:13. In virtue of its distinctive moralism, modern theology as a whole is obviously unable to change this. But we have to admit that at the very heart of it, certain sorties have actually been made in this direction. Above all, mention must be made of Gottfried Menken . . . and . . . the Scottish theologian Edward Irving. . . .' *Church Dogmatics*, T. and T. Clark, 1956, Vol. I: 2, pp. 153–4.

37. There is no reference to speaking with tongues in 'Baptism with the Holy Spirit', *Church Dogmatics*, Vol. IV: 4, pp. 3–40. He speaks of 'the central significance' of tongues in *Acts* 2 but does not elaborate on it in *Church Dogmatics*, Vol. I: 1, p. 521.

38. He speaks favourably of speaking with tongues and prophecy in the context of *I Cor.* 13 but does not go into detail concerning other manifestations of the Spirit in *Church Dogmatics*, Vol. IV: 2, pp. 828–31.

39. D. Gee, *op. cit.*, pp. 9–10. J. T. Nichol, *op. cit.*, pp. 22–4. W. E. Mills, *loc. cit.*, V. Synan, *op. cit.*, p. 98 etc.
40. 'The "doctrine of the two natures" (Christ is true man and true God) is simply repeated without comment in Pentecostal confessions of faith. Its function is unknown to Pentecostal writers.' Walter J. Hollenweger, *The Pentecostals*, S.C.M., 1972, p. 312. Also Nils Bloch-Hoell, *The Pentecostal Movement*, Allan and Unwin, 1964. 'Ideas about God, Christology and demonology', pp. 109–113.
41. Paul Ewing Davies, in his doctoral thesis on this subject in 1928, *An Examination of the Views of Edward Irving concerning the Person and Work of Jesus Christ* (cited as P.E.D.), does see the inter-relatedness of the humanity and the Spirit in Irving's Christology (Chapter VI 'Christ and the Holy Spirit.') He is the only one who does. However, he fails to follow through the implications of this, giving only slight attention to Irving's later writings and speeches.
42. C.H., p. 92.

CHAPTER ONE

1. *The Last Days*, p. viii
2. H., p. 36.
3. *The Last Days*, p. viii.
4. *Ibid.*, p. ix.
5. H., p. 46.
6. O., p. 220
7. *Fraser's Magazine*, January 1835, p. 5.
8. 'De Quincey said of Irving . . . that he was "unquestionably, by many, many degrees, the greatest orator of our times".' A. J. A. Symons, *Essays and Biographies*. ed. J. Symons, Cassell, 1969, 'Irving and the Irvingites', pp. 53–73. 'An orator of the pulpit, peerless in his generation, spoken of as "the greatest preacher the world has seen since Apostolic times".' *Fasti Ecclesiae Scoticanae*, rev. ed. 1928, Vol. 7, p. 493. '. . . bestrides the world like a colossus.' W. Hazlitt, *The Spirit of the Age*, 1825, edn. 1969, p. 70. '. . . . an "orator for the human race".' G. Gilfinnan. *Literary Portraits*, cited in D., p. 52.
9. *The Last Days*, p. x.
10. O., p. 219.
11. P., p. v.
12. P., p. v.
13. I.e. six months before Mr. Cole visited Regent Square Church.
14. W. Jones, *Biographical Sketch of the Rev. Edward Irving, A.M.*, 1835, pp. 228–9.
15. Rev. Henry Cole, *A Letter to the Rev. Edward Irving, Minister of the Caledonian Chapel, Compton Street, in Refutation of the Awful Doctrines (held by him) of the Sinfulness, Mortality, and Corruptibility of the Body of Jesus Christ*, 1827, p. 6.

16. *Ibid.*, pp. 7–9.
17. *Ibid.*, p. 14.
18. *Ibid.*, p. 98.
19. 'To say that Christ assumed our fallen human nature may, indeed, mean only that He was subject to pain and death as other men are in this 'fallen' state, but might also be taken to mean that He inherited original sin as other men do, though He was never guilty of committing actual sin. The latter meaning seems to have been definitely intended by the Adoptionists, and also by Menken, though not by Irving, who was astonished and greatly distressed by the accusation of heresy which ultimately resulted in his deposition from the ministry of the Church of Scotland.' Donald Baillie, *God Was in Christ*, Faber, 1948, pp. 16–17.
20. P., p. vi.
21. I., p. iv.
22. I., pp. iv–v.
23. O., p. 244, 246–7.
24. O., p. 247.
25. I., pp. 140–(140) CXCV.
26. I., p. v–vi. 'In the same sermon in which Irving enunciated the doctrine of the sinful humanity of Christ, there was explicit reference to the sanctifying work of the Holy Spirit in the body of that Christ. It is no hasty inference that the unusual stress laid on the work of the Holy Spirit in the Incarnation paved the way for, if it did not in some measure cause, the 'sinful flesh' idea. Certainly the large place attributed to the Spirit made Irving safe in giving such a dark character to the human nature. (The risk is not so great, if we are sure of the effectiveness of the antidote.) P.E.D., p. 187.
27. I., p. vi.
28. I., p. vii.
29. I., p. vii.
30. I., p. vii.
31. 'The late Mr. Irving, bred in the straitest school of Presbyterianism, and retaining, I believe to the last, a vehement admiration for Knox and his principles, was yet led to adopt the conviction, that the doctrine of the Incarnation had been strangely kept out of sight in all Protestant systems; that it is the centre of all divinity; the deeper mystery of the Trinity being at once the foundation upon which it rests, and the truth, to the full knowledge and fruition of which it is to lead us. In the attempt to reassert this doctrine, he was betrayed, it is well known, into the use of strange and perilous language, which was vehemently attacked and often greatly misrepresented – language which a man will, I believe, inevitably adopt who has not quite divested himself of the notion that the Fall is the law of the universe, and is trying to reconcile that Calvinistical theory with the Catholic faith.' F. D. Maurice, *The Kingdom of Christ*, 1883, Vol, I., p. 167.
32. I., p. (140) lxxv.
33. P., p. viii.
34. I., p. (140) lxxvi.

35. I., p. (140) lxv.
36. P., p. ix.
37. I., p. (140) lxvi.
38. 'A cry arose that he was preaching heresy as to our Lord's human nature.
The truth was, as is now universally admitted, that in this matter Irving had
really reverted to an older and more catholic type of doctrine. It had not
been customary in Scotland to dwell on the Incarnation in connection with
the sufferings and atonement of Christ. Irving saw, as Dr. Campbell afterwards (*Nature of the Atonement*, 1856) so powerfully developed, their
organic connection. . . . That he ever meant to inculcate the actual sinfulness
of Christ's human nature, no candid mind can maintain. But he was at fault
here, as often, from the rhetorical extravagance of his language. He used
unguardedly such expressions as that "Christ's human nature was in all
respects as ours!" "fallen and sinful" – he meant in the *potency*, not in the
fact of sin. But the subject was not one easily understood, while it was easily
misrepresented.' J. Tulloch, *op. cit.*, pp. 158–9. This interpretation is strongly
opposed by a hundred years of main-stream Church of Scotland thinking,
e.g.: 'Indeed, we cannot see how the Scriptural language in regard to the
incarnation can be explained on Irving's theory.' J. W. Taylor, *United
Presbyterian Magazine*, August, 1862, pp. 401–2. 'It is true, indeed, that
Irving speaks of the manner of Christ's conception as having the effect of
taking away original sin. (*Incarnation*, p. 159) But this is simply a quibble;
for he explains his meaning by remarking that Christ was not a human
person, never had personal subsistance as a mere man. Beyond a doubt, the
theory requires that original sin should be ascribed to Christ; for original sin
is a vice of fallen human *nature*; and the doctrine that our Lord's human
nature was fallen, means, if it means anything, that it was tainted with
original sin.' A. B. Bruce, *The Humiliation of Christ*, 1881, p. 254. This
opinion is repeated by H. R. Mackintosh, *The Doctrine of the Person of Jesus
Christ*, 1912, 2nd edn., p. 278. He finds Irving's views '. . . eccentric though
touching . . .'

CHAPTER TWO

1. O., p. 269. H. Drummond, *Candid Examination of the Controversy between
Messrs. Irving, A. Thomson, and J. Haldane, respecting the Human Nature
of the Lord Jesus Christ*, 1829.
2. *Dialogues on Prophecy*, Vol. I, 1829, Preface.
3. M.W., Vol. I, pp. 75–99. He refers to *Barker's Bible*, 1608; *The Scots Confession of Faith*; *Calvin's Catechism*; *The Palatine Catechism*; *The Helvetic
Confession*, 1566; *The Belgic Confession*; *Hooker's Ecclesiastical Polity*, p. 290;
The Nicene, Constantinople, Ephesus and Chalcedon Councils; *Sermons
on the Incarnation*, by John Tillotson, 1679; Jewell, *Apology*, 1562; *The
Gallican Confession*, 1561–66; *Confessio Ecclesiarum Gallicarum*, 1562; *Calvin
against Menno*; Gelasius; *Tertullian de Carne Christi*, p. 555; Cyprian;
Athanasius contra Arrian; Chrysostom in I Tim. Hom. VI; Ambrose on

Heb. ii. 14; Jerome on *Rom.* viii; Augustine; Hilary; Justin Martyr; Lombard, *Magister Sententiarum*; Leo Primus; Daniel Heinsius; Basilius Seleuciae Episcopus; Beza; Vatablus; Clarius; Zeger; Castalio.

4. P., p. xi.
5. 'Far from being unorthodox Irving went back to the older, sounder orthodoxy, that of the Fathers and the Councils, and one from which later thinking had departed.' P. E. Shaw. *op. cit.*, p. 23. H. C. Whitley. *Edward Irving. An Interpretation of his Life and Theological Teaching*, 1953, Ph.D. thesis. New College, Edinburgh, p. 156.
6. H.N., p. vii.
7. H.N., pp. vii–viii.
8. H.N., p. ix.
9. H.N., p. x.
10. H.N., p. x. 'What precisely was Irving's teaching? It was not that there was sinfulness in Christ, though in the heated controversy that ensued his applying the term 'sinful flesh' to Christ led his opponents to interpret it in that sense. But a careful study of his writings and of the purpose he had in mind would not justify these criticisms.' P. E. Shaw, *op. cit.*, p. 23.
11. H. N., p. xi. 'In other words, Christ was the prototype of the Holy Spirit's power over sinful flesh, the model of the Spirit's working in subduing, restraining, conquering the evil propensities of the fallen manhood. The result of this process, holiness or sinlessness, was always so certain in the mind of Irving that he could not understand why his opponents objected to his application of the adjective 'sinful' to Christ's humanity. Did not the Spirit always preserve Christ sinless in that flesh? And was not this the only method of attaining to that perfect state under the conditions of the fall – by the power of the Holy Spirit?' P.E.D., p. 193.
12. He refers to Cyril of Jerusalem, Athanasius, Augustine, Calvin etc., refutes Irving's interpretation of these authors and finds him guilty of the heresies of Cerinthus, Nestorius, Socinius and Bourignon. Marcus Dods, 'Review of Publications on Christ's Human Nature', *The Edinburgh Christian Instructor*, January 1830, pp. 1–96.
13. I., p. vi.
14. *Op. cit.*, pp. 84–5.
15. *Op. cit.*, February, 1830, pp. 118–63; March, 1830, pp. 187–221.
16. P., p. xv.
17. P., p. xiv.
18. I., p. vi.
19. P., p. xv.

CHAPTER THREE
1. O., pp. 283ff.
2. H., p. 93.
3. P., p. xv.
4. P., p. xvi.

5. O., p. 292.

6. *The Opinions Circulating Concerning Our Lord's Human Nature*, etc., pp. 3–4.
'Irving then was right! His expression was imperfect, but he was feeling
after the true idea. He meant by 'fallen flesh' the organic cravings of the body,
those involuntary impulses from beneath a man's consciousness which cry
out for satisfaction. These natural instincts were branded by original sin as
sinful or even criminal. Irving as a child of his time could not divorce himself
from the old phraseology, and so the nearest approach he made to the true
statement of the case was his description of Christ's flesh as 'instinct with
every form of sin'. But when we define between sin and the material of sin,
the case becomes plain: Christ as a man did have these physical cravings
from his bodily nature. This truth Irving was ready to assert in the face of a
doctrine of original sin which declared that they were evil. If Christ did not
feel this conflict between flesh and spirit, his moral experience lacked the
first essential of human likeness.' P.E.D., p. 122.

7. H., p. 93.

8. H., p. 93.

9. H., p. 93.

10. P., p. xvii.

11. H., p. 94.

12. P., p. xviii.

13. P., p. xix.

14. P., pp. xviii–xix.

15. H., p. 94.

16. P., p. xxi.

17. P., p. xxxii.

18. P., p. xxxiv.

19. P., p. xxxviii.

20. H., p. 94.

21. H., p. 95.

22. P., p. xxi.

23. P., pp. xxi–xxxix.

24. H., pp. 95–6. 'With the misguided cries of heresy – based on a mistaken
belief that by claiming Christ as truly man, Irving was denying that He was
truly God – the congregation would have nothing to do.' G. T. Bellhouse,
Regent Square Magazine, December, 1934, p. 9.

CHAPTER FOUR

1. 'Irving defended his position, and in examining his defence we shall see his
adherence to orthodoxy. The main charge levelled against him was that he
had relinquished his belief in the sinlessness of Christ. No charge could have
been more groundless, for he was always at great pains to show that he
firmly held this concept.... His book *Christ's Holiness in Flesh*, in its entirety,
is a defence of the sinlessness of Christ. . . . In this book, in which he is
primarily concerned to maintain the sinlessness and holiness of Christ, he still

affirms the doctrine that Christ assumed "fallen human nature", but he holds these two positions in harmony; to him they were not a discord . . . Irving states that he would prefer to have shunned the word "sinful", but had to use it if his meaning was to be clear. He is continually at pains to show, however, that the term only applies to the nature as assumed, and not to the life of Christ.' H. Johnson, *The Humanity of The Saviour,* Epworth 1962, pp. 153–4.

2. I., p. vii.
3. H.N., p. xi.
4. C.H., p. 49.
5. C.H., pp. 49–50.
6. C.H., pp. 50–1.
7. C.H., p. 18.
8. H.N., p. viii.
9. C.H., pp. 18–19.
10. C.H., p. 63.
11. C.H., p. 91.
12. C.H., pp. 91–2.
13. C.H., pp. 24–6.
14. 'When we examine his writings, however, and when we allow for his rather extravagant style, we find a clarity of thought, a depth of understanding, and often powerful exposition and persuasive argument. Many of his points of exposition must carry our assent.' H. Johnson, *op. cit.,* p. 155.
15. H.N., p. 121.
16. H.N., pp. 121–2.

CHAPTER FIVE

1. H., p. 51.
2. H., p. 71.
3. T., p. 22.
4. B., C.W., Vol, II. pp. 270–88.
5. B., p. 276.
6. B., p. 276. 'But a man of Irving's temper could not remain content with this sane and purely spiritual view. He who argued before thousands a return to apostolic methods of missionary enterprise, soon came to champion a return to the supernatural manifestations which accompanied that work. There is no gulf, he declared, between the times of Christ and the Apostles, and our days. The same Spirit worked in Christ as works in us, and the evidences must be the same.' P.E.D., p. 206.
7. B., p. 277.
8. B., p. 277.
9. B., p. 278.
10. B., p. 279.
11. B., p. 279.
12. B., p. 280.
13. B., p. 280.

14. F., p. 754.
15. T., p. 32.
16. Reviewing the publication of *The Collected Writings of Edward Irving* in 1864–5, Professor Lorimer said of his sermons: 'If it also be considered, that each of those progressive and systematic courses of instruction in Christian faith and hope, ceremony and duty, has an equally admirable filling up, and that every discourse is an elaborate treatment of the theme which naturally turns up, it will be seen how thoroughly the common estimate of Irving's genius, as irregular, desultory, or fragmentary, is disproved by the remains of his ministry. Few men, placed in the unprecedentedly brilliant, stimulating and distracting circumstances of his London career, would have had such an organic and methodical ministry. That he should *there* study to such a purpose is a notable tribute to the completeness of his genius, and to its orderly operations.' P. Lorimer, *The United Presbyterian Magazine*, October 1865, p. 443.
17. 'Next (after the Trinity) the doctrine of the Gentile Apostasy, as exhibited in the Papal superstition, and in Protestant liberalism, was made instrumental, under God, to deliver the Church from the false hope of converting a world which standeth ripe and ready for judgment; and did set us free from the spirit of expediency, that spirit which now worketh in the religious world.' *Last Days*, p. x. On this theme: *For Judgment to Come*, 1823; *Babylon and Infidelity Foredoomed of God: A Discourse on the Prophecies of Daniel and the Apocalypse, which relate to these Latter Times, and until the Second Advent*, 1826; *Sermons, Lectures and Occasional Discourses*. Vol. III. *On Subjects National and Prophetical*. 1828.
18. B., pp. 277–8.
19. On this theme: *The Coming of Messiah in Glory and Majesty*, by Juan Josafat Ben-Ezra, translated, E.I. with Introduction, 1827. *The Last Days: A Discourse on the Evil Character of These Our Times: Proving them to be the 'Perilous Times' of the 'Last Days,'* 1828. *The Church and State Responsible to Christ and to one another. A Series of Discourses on Daniel's Vision of the Four Beasts*, 1829.
20. F., p. 755.
21. F., p. 755.
22. F., p. 755.

CHAPTER SIX
1. O., p. 234.
2. H., p. 85.
3. H., p. 86.
4. H., p. 86.
5. F., p. 756.
6. N., p. 51.
7. N., p. 55.
8. N., pp. 59–60.

9. R. A. Davenport, *op. cit.*, p. 40. Also, F., p. 756; and T. Carlyle (advocate) 'Whilst the wicked were stirred up to wrath by this preaching of living facts, and not empty doctrines, thousands were converted, and such a confidence in God awakened in them as they had never before experienced. By this means God was enabled to pour out His Holy Spirit. For where no filial feeling towards God exists, how can the spirit of adoption be given.' C. W. Boase, *Supplement to the Elijah Ministry*, p. 753. Other writers dispute the link between Campbell's preaching and later manifestations notably, N. pp. 58–9; also J. H. Leckie, *op. cit.*, p. 27.

10. N., pp. 64–75.

11. N., p. 77.

12. F., p. 757.

13. F., p. 757.

14. Robert Story, *Peace in Believing: A Memoir of Isabella Campbell of Fernicarry, Roseneath, Dunbartonshire, 1829*. This account of the life and death (1st Nov, 1827) 'of the holy and blessed Isabella' by her parish minister, quickly became a minor devotional classic.

15. F., p. 756.

16. F., p. 756.

17. F., p. 757.

18. F., p. 757.

19. F., pp. 757–8.

20. F., p. 758.

21. F., pp. 759–60. 'The origins of the Pentecostal movement go back to a revival amongst the negroes of North America at the beginning of the present century.' Walter J. Hollenweger, *op. cit.*, p. xviii. Defining Pentecostalism in his terms as 'the view that the baptism of the Spirit is to be recognized by the "initial sign" of speaking with tongues', the evidence above proves him to be inaccurate. Also J. D. G. Dunn, *op. cit.*, pp. 1–2., makes no mention of these events in his summary of the history of the origins of Pentecostalism.

22. N., pp. 107–9.

23. N., pp. 109–10.

24. N., p. 110.

25. N., p. 111. From the reference on p. 104, it would appear that 'Mr. C.' was John McLeod Campbell.

26. F., p. 755.

27. F., p. 755.

28. F., p. 755.

29. F., p. 755.

30. F., p. 755.

31. F., pp. 755–6.

CHAPTER SEVEN

1. F., pp. 755–6.

2. W. Hanna, ed. *Letters of Thomas Erskine, of Linlathan* 2nd ed, 1878, p. 132.
3. N., p. 125.
4. Rev. A. Robertson, *A Vindication of the Religion of the Land*, p. 311.
5. O., p. 290.
6. R. H. Story, *Memoir of the Life of the Rev. Robert Story*, pp. 209–11.
7. F., p. 756.
8. D., p. 142. 'The number of those who made up the party appears to have been six, though some accounts say eight; what would seem to be a reliable list gives them as John Bate Cardale, a young London lawyer, his wife and his sister Emily. Edward Oliver Taplin, Robert Norton, and Dr. J. Campbell. R. A. Davenport, *op. cit.*, p. 47.
9. O., pp. 299–303.
10. O., p. 304.
11. M.W., Vol II., December 1830. John B. Cardale, 'On the Extraordinary Manifestations in Port Glasgow,' pp. 869–73.
12. W. Hanna, *op. cit.*, p. 133. 'Mr. Erskine is here at present. He went up to Port Glasgow yesterday, or the day previous, and held a prayer meeting. The meeting was peculiarly solemn, and sweetly overpowering were the emotions of those in prayer, and they seemed filled with the Holy Ghost. Young James Macdonald started suddenly up and spoke the unknown tongue. While speaking his countenance all at once assumed a new expression, and he exclaimed – 'The shout of a king is among us! God is in this place. He has taught me the interpretation!' Straightway he proceeded to interpret what he had said! Mr. Erskine was in floods of tears today in speaking of it at my bedside.' Alan Ker, 29th April, 1830 in C. W. Boase, *op. cit.*, p. 764.
13. Alan Ker, 29th April, 1830 in C. W. Boase, *op. cit.*, p. 138.
14. Thomas Erskine, *The Brazen Serpent*, p. 203.
15. F., p. 755.
16. F., p. 756.
17. F., p. 755. 'The same logical requirement of Christ's example made necessary a sinful flesh in Christ as in us, upon which the Holy Spirit could work. If the sinfulness of Christ's humanity be denied, then, reasoned Irving, I have no assurance of the Holy Ghost's willingness to wrestle with wicked flesh in me, nor of his ability to overcome it in his own person. The Spirit must find the same force of opposition in Christ and in us, or the action is not on the same moral level in both cases. There is nothing shocking, said Irving, in the Spirit's abiding and working in Christ's sinful flesh, for he comes into a similar relation with our flesh. Only thus could Christ's work be morally effective for us.' P.E.D., pp. 192–3.

CHAPTER EIGHT
1. O., p. 386.
2. O., p. 293.
3. M.W., Vol. II. pp. 630–60. C.W., Vol V. pp. 449–506. 'The section of his

Collected Works (Vol. 5) which deals with the Church and her Endowment, gives us a first clue to his preoccupation with "tongues" as a necessary mark of the Church's returning vitality.' H. C. Whitley, *Ph.D. thesis, op. cit.*, p. 204. In spite of Irving's supposed 'preoccupation with "tongues",' Whitley makes no further statement or assessment of his teaching on this or any other gift of the Spirit.

4. C., pp. 449–59.
5. C., p. 459.
6. C., p. 464.
7. C., p. 449.
8. C., p. 470.
9. C., pp. 467–71.
10. C., p. 471.
11. C., p. 472.
12. C., p. 475.
13. C., p. 476.
14. C., p. 479.
15. C., p. 479.
16. C., p. 480.
17. C., p. 480.
18. C., p. 482.
19. C., p. 486.
20. C., p. 486.
21. C., p. 491.
22. C., p. 492.
23. C., p. 492.
24. C., p. 493.
25. C., p. 494.
26. C., p. 495.
27. C., pp. 496–7.
28. C., p. 498.
29. C., pp. 498–9.
30. C., p. 455.
31. C., p. 455.
32. C., pp. 499–500.
33. C., pp. 500–1.
34. C., p. 501.
35. C., p. 503. 'The Church is about to receive a fresh baptism of the Holy Spirit. You cannot doubt Irving's sincerity nor his real concern to see a revived Church. He begins to go wrong with his over-preoccupation with tongues and prophecy.' H. C. Whitley, *Ph.D. thesis, op. cit.*, p. 205. Irving gives explicit teaching on *all* the gifts of the Spirit. Like Paul in *I Cor.* 14, he speaks most about tongues and prophecy because they were the gifts which were particularly in evidence and most needed to be understood and controlled.

CHAPTER NINE

1. D., p. 152.
2. M.W., Vol II. pp. 850–69. C.W., Vol V. pp. 509–33.
3. G.H.C., p. 509.
4. G.H.G., p. 510.
5. G.H.G., p. 511.
6. G.H.G., p. 512.
7. G.H.G., p. 514.
8. G.H.G., p. 518.
9. G.H.G., p. 518.
10. G.H.G., p. 519.
11. G.H.G., p. 520.
12. G.H.G., p. 522.
13. F., p. 755.
14. G.H.G., p. 522.
15. G.H.G., p. 523–4.
16. F., p. 757.
17. F., p. 757.
18. G.H.G., p. 524.
19. G.H.G., pp. 524–5.
20. G.H.G., p. 525.
21. G.H.G., p. 527.
22. G.H.G., p. 528.
23. G.H.G., p. 531.
24. G.H.G., p. 531.
25. G.H.G., p. 532.
26. G.H.G., p. 532.
27. B., p. 278.
28. G.H.G., pp. 532–3. 'The existence of such a divine humanity was not a prospect, but a reality. . . . But such a Church, he contended, does not exist; it has been, but it has ceased, or is on the point of ceasing to be; it must be restored; it can only be restored by a divine intervention. There must be a fact embodying the principle of a union of God with man which is the Church; this is the incarnation, there must be an organized body built upon that fact; there must be the manifestation of a spiritual power to attest its existence, and to enable its respective members to perform their functions. The religious public of England might safely indulge their humour, if these be ever safe occasions for jesting, with the evidence which the disciples of this system produced to show that they had been constituted the Church of God in the world. But I maintain that this public cannot set at naught the principles which led men to desire such evidence, and to accept almost anything as if it were the answer to their wishes.' F. D. Maurice, *op. cit.*, Vol. I, p. 168.

CHAPTER TEN

1. C.H., pp. 24–5.

2. H.N., p. xi.
3. C.H., pp. 102–6.
4. C.H., p. 107.
5. C.H., pp. 108–9.
6. C.H., pp. 109–10.
7. C.H., pp. 111–12. 'There is much sound doctrine in Irving's conception of the Holy Spirit in Christ. Certainly he followed in the wake of the reformed theologians in declaring that the union between the Son of God and man was mediated by the Holy Spirit. One of the results of this mediation, namely, a real humanity, was also quite in accord with reformed Christology. Moreover the idea of progress or development in the possession of the Holy Spirit, although it was rather mechanically conceived, is worthy of consideration. Irving's opponent, Marcus Dods, maintained that such development was inconceivable, that Christ was our Prophet, Priest and King from the beginning, independent of the successive baptisms of the Spirit. On the contrary, we in these last days are finding it absolutely essential that Christ's development in person, strength and effective power be a true development.' P.E.D., pp. 183–94.

CHAPTER ELEVEN
1. H., p. 104. Davies, who has followed Irving with perception, at this point renounces theology for psychology and with it his objectivity. Although he has interesting comments to make, they are not based on an examination of the evidence of events or Irving's later writings: 'We cannot here go into detail concerning the outbreak of this gift in the National Scotch Church. It seems that for several months previous to the first appearance in the fall of 1831 Irving had held early morning prayer meetings to pray for the Church and the gifts of the Spirit. When in 1830 the gift of tongues appeared in Scotland, he sent a delegation to make enquiries. We cannot then wonder that under the influence of this expectation and constant suggestion a number of "tongues" finally did speak in Irving's own church. . . . What they said was usually a wild, hysterical repetition of the words of the speaker of the hour.' P.E.D. pp. 207–8.
2. T., p. 24.
3. J. H. Leckie, *op. cit.,* p. 18.
4. O., p. 315.
5. P., p. xix.
6. O., p. 314.
7. W. Hanna, ed., *op. cit.,* p. 523.
8. *Loc. cit.*
9. *Op. cit.,* p. 524.
10. M.W., Vol. III., pp. 473–96. C.W., Vol. V., pp. 533–61.
11. G.H.G., p. 533.
12. I., pp. 67–139.
13. O., p. 247.

14. I., pp. 5–6.
15. I., p. 2.
16. I., p. 1.
17. I., p. 91–2.
18. I., p. 80.
19. I., p. 81.
20. I., p. 82.
21. I., p. 83.
22. I., p. 105.
23. I., p. 106.
24. I., p. 138.
25. I., pp. 138–9.
26. G.H.G., pp. 533–56.
27. G.H.G., p. 557.
28. G.H.G., p. 557.
29. G.H.G., p. 557.
30. G.H.G., p. 557.
31. G.H.G., p. 558.
32. G.H.G., p. 558.
33. G.H.G., p. 559.
34. G.H.G., p. 559.
35. G.H.G., p. 560. . . .'we can criticize Irving's over-abundant emphasis on these phenomena,' P.E.D., p. 208. 'The gibberish of a "tongue" might well be taken as a symbol of Irving's idea of Spirit possession: man's best faculties are set at naught, overwhelmed by the power of the Spirit.' p. 210. Davies offers no Scriptural or theological reasons for this criticism. It is a travesty of Irving's exposition and doctrine.
36. G.H.G., p. 560.

CHAPTER TWELVE
 1. T., p. 25.
 2. T., p. 27.
 3. T., pp. 27–8.
 4. T., p. 28.
 5. T., p. 28.
 6. T., p. 31.
 7. T., p. 31.
 8. T., pp. 31–2.
 9. T., p. 32.
10. H., p. 108.
11. H., pp. 108–9.
12. T., p. 32.
13. O., H., D., and N2 differ in the chronology of these weeks.
14. O., pp. 323–4.
15. N2., p. 48.

16. T., p. 32.
17. N2., p. 49.
18. O., p. 326.
19. O., p. 326.
20. O., p. 326.
21. O., p. 326.
22. O., p. 325.
23. O., p. 325.
24. N2., p. 50.
25. O., p. 324–5. The evidence is against V. Synan when he says 'As more people began to manifest the tongues phenomenon in his services, Irving attempted to calm the worshippers and to maintain order, but his efforts largely failed.' *op. cit.*, p. 98.
26. N2., p. 51.
27. H., p. 112.
28. O., p. 333.
29. H., p. 112.
30. O., p. 333.
31. O., p. 331.
32. O., p. 333.
33. O., pp. 333–4.
34. O., p. 320.
35. O., p. 333.
36. T., pp. 3–4.
37. H., p. 113.
38. N2., p. 51.
39. H., p. 114.
40. T., p. 5.
41. T., p. 5.
42. F., p. 754.
43. T., p. 4.
44. D.P., p. 29.
45. D.P., p. 29.

CHAPTER THIRTEEN
1. D.P., p. 1. J. D. G. Dunn, *op. cit.*, makes no reference to this work (nor to Irving at all). Apart from the few references in P.E.D. it seems to have been completely overlooked by Protestant and Pentecostal writers.
2. D.P., p. 2. 'It is not difficult to see how this emphasis on the Holy Spirit fitted into the rest of his doctrine of the person and work of Christ. We have noted in the last chapter Irving's interpretation of Christ as an "ensample" *for* all men and a sample *of* all men. For the support of these functions of the Christ in their application to men, Irving had recourse to the power of the Holy Spirit. As the Spirit was in Christ, so the Spirit will be in us. Here is to be found the true link between Christ's example and our imitation, between Christ's work of redemption and its saving power over us.' P.E.D., p. 190.

3. D.P., p. 3.
4. D.P., p. 3.
5. D.P., p. 4.
6. D.P., p. 5.
7. D.P., p. 7.
8. D.P., p. 8.
9. D.P. p. 9.
10. D.P., p. 10.
11. D.P., p. 11.
12. D.P., pp. 13–4.
13. D.P., p. 15.
14. D.P., p. 16. 'Irving's whole doctrine of the Headship of Christ was built upon the power of the Holy Spirit common to Christ and to us. In the Gospels he found support for this idea of a common Spirit, and Christian experience itself would reason back from the power of God in men's lives to the same power in Christ. The difference between Christ and men, then, lies only in the fullness of possession of the Holy Spirit, and Christ is truly our Head because we share with him in some degree the power of the Spirit.' P.E.D., p. 191.
15. D.P., pp. 16–18.
16. D.P., p. 19.
17. D.P., p. 20.
18. D.P., pp. 21–2.
19. D.P., p. 25.
20. D.P., p. 26.
21. D.P., p. 27.
22. D.P., pp. 28–9.

CHAPTER FOURTEEN
1. D.P., p. 30.
2. D.P., p. 30.
3. D.P., pp. 31–2.
4. D.P., p. 33.
5. D.P., p. 34.
6. D.P., pp. 36–7.
7. D.P., pp. 37–8.
8. D.P., pp. 39. 'Irving would read the whole active ministry from the temptation in the wilderness to the offering on the cross, in terms of the Holy Spirit's power.' P.E.D., p. 189.
9. D.P., p. 40.
10. D.P., p. 41.
11. D.P., p. 42.
12. D.P., p. 42.
13. D.P., p. 42.
14. D.P., pp. 43–4.
15. D.P., pp. 45–7.

16. D.P., pp. 49–50.
17. D.P., p. 55.

CHAPTER FIFTEEN
1. D.P., pp. 56–8.
2. D.P., pp. 58–62.
3. D.P., pp. 62–5.
4. D.P., pp. 65–8.
5. D.P., pp. 68–72.
6. D.P., pp. 72–6.
7. D.P., p. 76.
8. D.P., p. 77.
9. D.P., p. 77.
10. D.P., p. 78–9.
11. D.P., p. 81.
12. D.P., pp. 81–2.
13. D.P., p. 83.
14. D.P., p. 84.
15. D.P., p. 85. 'The passive voice expresses well the part of the Son and men generally in relation to the Spirit. The Holy Spirit is the active agent in all good works. The Son of God was therefore quiescent and passive as far as his divinity was concerned.' P.E.D., p. 191.
16. D.P., pp. 86–7.
17. D.P., pp. 87–8.
18. D.P., pp. 88–90.
19. D.P., pp. 90–2.
20. D.P., p. 92.
21. D.P., pp. 92–5.
22. D.P., pp. 95–6. 'If the Holy Spirit were not active to mediate and to sanctify, there would result that impossible condition of a confusion of natures! But by the work of the Holy Spirit over the passive Son, the manhood was preserved distinct and entire, and Christ was truly our example and representative because he was truly a man.' P.E.D., p. 192.
23. D.P., pp. 97–101.
24. D.P., p. 102.
25. D.P., p. 103.
26. D.P., p. 104.
27. D.P., p. 105.
28. D.P., p. 106.
29. D.P., p. 108.
30. D.P., p. 109.
31. D.P., pp. 109–11.
32. D.P., p. 112.
33. D.P., p. 113.
34. D.P., p. 114.

35. D.P., pp. 114–15.
36. D.P., p. 116.
37. D.P., pp. 9–10.

CHAPTER SIXTEEN
  1. F., p. 754.
  2. T., p. 5.
  3. H., p. 116.
  4. T., p. 5.
  5. O., p. 348.
  6. T., p. 6.
  7. T., p. 6.
  8. H., p. 117.
  9. H., p. 119.
 10. T., p. 90.
 11. T., p. 91.
 12. H., p. 119.
 13. T., pp. 1–3.

CHAPTER SEVENTEEN
  1. Davies is wrong to say 'The trial before the Presbytery of London had no direct bearing upon Irving's doctrine of the person and work of Jesus Christ. . . . The accusation and the defence were on different issues, and the trial brought out no new features of either.' P.E.D., p. 246. This is only true if theory is divorced from practice and doctrine from discipline; a position which was denied by both parties in the case. This trial is of supreme importance because it is the most explicit record of the debate between the Reformed and Pentecostal doctrines as they are expressed in the practice and procedure of Church worship services. This trial is a definitive statement on all the issues which make Irving an important Pentecostal-Presbyterian today. His case is by no means closed. It is presented here in detail for scrutiny on every point of theology and ecclesiology.
  2. T., p. 6.
  3. T., p. 8. 'It was very much of a technical question which was actually submitted to the court, but no one doubted the right of the trustees to complain, or the right of the Presbytery to judge of the complaint; and every one understood that the real point in debate was whether Mr. Irving, having recognized the standing in his congregation of certain persons, whom he believed to be inspired, could consistently continue any longer the minister of a church, which was not prepared to recognize the advent of a new and miraculous era.' N. L. Walker, *The British and Foreign Evangelical Review*, April 1869. p. 347.
  4. T., p. 10.
  5. T., p. 11. 'It is impossible to give any report of this trial in the limited space

permitted here. It was as irrelevant, confused, and partial as an examination conducted by untrained and biased judges must always be.' O., p. 357.

6. T., p. 12.
7. T., p. 13.
8. T., p. 14.
9. T., p. 15.
10. T., pp. 15–16.
11. T., p. 16.
12. T., p. 17.
13. 'The three witnesses examined upon oath proved, as far as a man's solemn asseveration can, not that unlawful and riotous interruptions had taken place in the Regent Square Church, but that the Holy Ghost had there spoken with demonstration and power. This was the real evidence elicited by the day's examination. Nobody attempted to impeach the men, or declare them unworthy of ordinary credit; and this was the point which, according to the common principles of evidence, they united to establish. I cannot tell what might be the motive of the complainants for keeping back all who held their own view of the question, and resting their case solely upon the testimony of believers in the gifts; but the fact is apparent enough, and one of the most strange features of the transaction, that the witnesses, upon whom no imputation of falsehood was cast, consistently and solemnly agreed in proving an hypothesis which the court that received their testimony, and professed to be guided by their evidence, not only negatived summarily, but even refused to take into consideration.' O., p. 358.

CHAPTER EIGHTEEN

1. T., p. 17.
2. T., p. 18.
3. T., p. 19.
4. T., p. 19.
5. T., p. 20.
6. T., p. 21.
7. T., pp. 22–4.
8. T., pp. 25–34.
9. T., p. 30.
10. T., p. 35.
11. T., p. 36.
12. T., pp. 36–7.
13. T., p. 37.
14. T., p. 37.
15. T., p. 38.
16. T., pp. 38–9.
17. T., p. 39.
18. T., p. 40.
19. T., p. 41.

20. T., p. 42.
21. T., p. 43.
22. T., p. 44.
23. T., p. 45.
24. T., p. 46.
25. T., p. 47.
26. T., p. 48.
27. T., pp. 49–50.
28. T., p. 50.
29. T., pp. 51–2.
30. T., p. 53.
31. T., p. 54.
32. T., pp. 54–7.
33. T., p. 58.
34. T., p. 58.
35. T., p. 59.
36. T., p. 60.

CHAPTER NINETEEN

1. T., p. 61.
2. T., pp. 62–3.
3. T., p. 64.
4. T., p. 65.
5. T., p. 65.
6. T., p. 66.
7. *A Word of Testimony; or, corrected account of the Evidence Adduced by the Trustees of the National Scotch Church, in support of their Charges Against the Rev. Edward Irving, and his Defence*, p. 59. A full account of the part Baxter played in the development of the manifestations was given in his own confession the following year, Robert Baxter, *Narrative of Facts, Characterizing the Supernatural Manifestations in Members of Mr. Irving's Congregation, and other Individuals and Formerly in the Writer Himself*, 1833.
8. *Ibid.*, pp. 60–5.
9. *Op. cit.*, p. 66.
10. *Op. cit.*, p. 67.
11. *Op. cit.*, p. 68.
12. *Loc. cit.*
13. T., p. 67.
14. T., p. 68.
15. T., p. 68.
16. T., p. 69.
17. T., p. 70.
18. T., p. 71.

CHAPTER TWENTY

1. T., p. 71.
2. T., p. 72.
3. T., p. 73.
4. T., p. 73.
5. T., p. 73.
6. T., p. 74.
7. T., p. 75.
8. T., p. 76.
9. T., p. 76.
10. T., p. 77
11. T., p. 78.
12. T., p. 78.
13. T., p. 79.
14. T., p. 80.
15. T., p. 81.
16. T., p. 82.
17. T., p. 82. This sentiment is also expressed by Coleridge in the application of his distinction between the ideal reason and the sensual understanding, to Irving's thought: 'I look forward with confident hope to a time when his soul shall have perfected her victory over the dead letter of the senses and its apparitions in the sensuous understanding; when the halcyon ideas shall have alit on the surging sea of his conceptions,

>"Which then shall quite forget to rave,
>While birds of calm sit brooding on the charmed wave."

S. T. Coleridge., *op. cit.*, p. 154. Also by Davies: 'However, we can criticize Irving's over-abundant emphasis on these phenomena. It illustrates that tendency in his thinking to de-spiritualize religion. We lose sight of the primary blessings of God in us; the spiritual elements of power are obscured by these miracles in the natural sphere.' P.E.D., p. 208.
18. T., p. 83.
19. T., p. 84.
20. T., p. 85.
21. T., p. 86.
22. T., p. 87.
23. T., pp. 87–8.
24. 'I have no desire to represent these men as judging unfairly, or as acting in this new matter upon their own well known prior conclusions. But the fact is remarkable, in a country so familiar as ours with all the caution and minute research of law, that the judgment of this Presbytery, involving, as it did, not only the highest privileges of Christian freedom, but practical matters of property and income, uttered itself in a shape of so many opinions as loose, slight, and irregular as might be the oracles of a fireside conclave. To people who are accustomed to see the columns of newspapers filled day after day with close, lengthened, and it may be tedious arguments concerning the true meaning of the articles of the Church, it will be almost inconceivable that

any decision bearing weight in law, could be come to upon grounds so trivial. . . . Had the matter been argued before a civil court, it might indeed have been decided that the proceedings complained of were contrary to the *usage* of the Church of Scotland, no doubt an important point – but it must have been satisfactorily established that no ecclesiastical law forbade them, and that no direct ordinance of the Church had been in any way transgressed. (That this is the case, and that no such rigid adherence to the proprieties of custom binds the Church when she chooses to be tolerant, might be proved by the many irregularities permitted in connection with the late 'revivals'.)' O., pp. 364–5.

CHAPTER TWENTY-ONE

1. O., p. 367. There is no basis for the assertion that 'It is only in this century that the gift of tongues has come dramatically into the limelight.' Simon Tugwell, *Did You Receive The Spirit?* Darton, Longman and Todd, 1972, p. 66.
2. O., p. 368.
3. T., p. 92.
4. O., p. 369.
5. O., p. 352.
6. T., p. 89. J. H. S. Burleigh, is inaccurate when he says 'Then came the scandal of his allowing persons claiming 'the gift of tongues' to exercise it in his London church, which alienated his congregation and led to his ejection from the Church by the presbytery of London.' *op. cit.*, p. 330. This memorial and the subsequent exodus, indicates that, apart from the trustees, very few were alienated.
7. O., p. 369.
8. H., p. 124.
9. H., p. 124.

CHAPTER TWENTY-TWO

1. 'Now no one at all acquainted with the religious condition of the Church of Scotland in 1828–1834, can possibly be unaware of the fact that heresy was in the air. New views were abroad on the subject of Christ's person; new views about the nature, extent, and application of the atonement; new views about the work of the Holy Ghost; new views in regard to the constitution and organization of the Church. The special charge brought against Campbell was one thing, the special charge brought against Irving was another; and we admit that the justice or injustice of the sentences passed upon them must be judged of in connection with the particular offences of which they were accused; but in settling with ourselves the question of whether they should have been prosecuted at all, we ought not to forget this, that not only were the men as individuals engaged with all their hearts in a work of propagandism which aimed at the overthrow of the commonly received faith, but that Campbell, and Irving, and Scott and Maclean, and Tait, formed substantially

one party, and that this party had heresies among them sufficient to have sunk in time any orthodox church in Christendom.' Norman L. Walker, *op. cit.*, pp. 336–7.

2. M.W., Vol. V, pp. 84–115.
3. J., pp. 84–5. Antoinette Bourignon (1616–1680) was a Flemish enthusiast and adventurist. F. L. Cross, *The Oxford Dictionary of the Christian Church*, Oxford, 1958, p. 189. Her influence was felt mainly in Scotland where candidates for ordination had to disavow her views between 1711 and 1889. R. A. Knox, *Enthusiasm*, Oxford, 1950, pp. 352–5. Also, A. MacEwan, *Antoinette Bourignon. Quietist*, London, 1909. The General Assembly of the Church of Scotland of 1701 condemned her heterodoxy on eight counts, two of which concerned Christ's humanity. 1. That His humanity was pre-existent, which was condemned as Marcionite. 2. 'The assertion of the sinful corruption of Christ's human nature and a rebellion in Christ's natural will to the will of God,' which was condemned as Nestorian. Irving examines her beliefs in detail and points out the differences between her views and his. H.N., pp. 54–80.
4. J., p. 103.
5. J., p. 103.
6. J., p. 115.
7. O., pp. 384–5.
8. T2., p. 6.
9. T2., p. 3.

CHAPTER TWENTY-THREE
1. 'A poor aggregate of Reverend Sticks in black gown, sitting in Presbytery, to pass formal condemnation on a man and a cause which might have been tried in Patmos under presidency of St. John without the right truth of it being got at! I knew the 'Moderator' (one Roddick, since gone mad), for one of the stupidest and barrenest of living mortals; also the little phantasm of a creature – Sloan his name – who went niddynoddying with his head, and was infinitely conceited and phantasmal.' T. Carlyle, *Reminiscences*, 1881, Vol. I, p. 324.
2. T2., p. 4.
3. T2., p. 6.
4. T2., p. 8.
5. T2., p. 9.
6. T2., p. 10. 'The question which the Annandale Presbytery had to decide, was not so much the truth or falsehood of certain views about the humanity of Christ, as simply whether or no Mr. Irving held them. Some of the members might choose to go into the merits of the subject, and give their own reasons for the belief which was in them, but the General Assembly had already condemned the doctrines which he was charged with, and had actually pointed himself out by name as a heretic, against whom action was in certain circumstances to be taken.' N. L. Walker, *op. cit.*, p. 348.

7. T2., p. 11.
8. T2., p. 28.
9. T2., p. 28.
10. T2., p. 15.
11. T2., p. 17.
12. T2., p. 18.
13. T2., p. 20.
14. 'Never surely was a small country presbytery confronted with a more awesome task. . . . It must have taken courage in such circumstances to condemn Annan's most illustrious son, but all the ministers in turn pronounced the libel proven. Among them was one minister of real distinction, Henry Duncan of Ruthwell, founder of savings banks, restorer of the famous Ruthwell Cross, a man of extensive culture and a noted evangelical, who confessed that conscience alone drove him to the most painful judgment of his life.' J. H. S. Burleigh, *op. cit.*, p. 330.
15. T2., p. 21. Robert Baxter. *op. cit.*, pp. 100f.
16. T2., pp. 21–2.
17. T2., p. 22.
18. T2., p. 23.
19. T2., pp. 23–4.
20. T2., p. 24.
21. T2., p. 25.
22. T2., p. 26.
23. '. . . to excommunicate him on account of his language about Christ's body was very foolish; his apparent meaning, such as it is, is orthodox.' S. T. Coleridge, cited in D., p. 221. 'He was deposed – as one, who knew his teaching well, has said – on the ground of statements never made, and of inferences from them solemnly abjured.' R. H. Story, *op. cit.*, p. 268. 'In spite of Irving's words, in spite of the fact that the terms in which both the old Scottish and the Westminster Confessions state the doctrine of our Lord's humanity agree with Irving's, the little men won. . . . They did what they were determined to do – rid themselves of this disturbing John the Baptist. The certified soundness of dull men had triumphed.' H. C. Whitley. *op. cit.*, p. 93.
24. T2., p. 27.
25. T2., p. 29.
26. T2., p. 30.
27. R. Davenport, *op. cit.*, 1970, p. 92.
28. *Ibid.*, p. 100.
29. P. E. Shaw, *op. cit.*, pp. 63–140.
30. *Ibid.*, pp. 155–217.
31. O., pp. 404–28.
32. T. Carlyle, *op. cit.*, pp. 329–34.
33. O., p. 427.

BIBLIOGRAPHY

WORKS REFERRED TO

BY IRVING: BOOKS

For the Oracles of God, four Orations, and For Judgment to Come, an Argument in nine parts, London: T. Hamilton, 1823.

The Coming of Messiah in Glory and Majesty, by Juan Josafat Ben-Ezra a converted Jew: Translated from the Spanish, with a Preliminary Discourse by E.I. London: L. B. Seeley and Son, 1827.

Homilies on The Sacraments, Vol. 1. On Baptism, Ten Homilies. With an Introductory Statement of the Doctrine from Hooker's Ecclesiastical Polity, and Confirmations from the Fathers and the Protestant Churches, London: Andrew Panton, 1828. Reprinted without the Introduction in *The Collected Writings of Edward Irving in Five Volumes*, Ed. Rev. G. Carlyle, Vol. II. London, Alexander Strahan, 1864.

Sermons, Lectures and Occasional Discourses, Vol. I, The Doctrine of the Incarnation Opened in Six Sermons, London: R. B. Seeley and W. Burnside, 1828.

Sermons, Lectures, and Occasional Discourses, Vol. II, On the Parable of the Sower, Six Lectures, London: R. B. Seeley and W. Burnside, 1828.

Sermons, Lectures and Occasional Discourses, Vol. III, On Subjects National and Prophetical, Seven Discourses, London: R. B. Seeley and W. Burnside, 1828.

The Last Days: A Discourse on the Evil Character of these our Times: Proving them to be the 'Perilous Times' of the 'Last Days', London: R. B. Seeley and W. Burnside, 1828.

Babylon and Infidelity Foredoomed of God: A Discourse on the Prophecies of Daniel and the Apocalypse which relate to these Latter Times, and until the Second Advent, 2nd edn., Glasgow: William Collins, 1828.

The Church and State Responsible to Christ, and to One Another. A Series of Discourses on Daniel's Vision of the Four Beasts, London: James Nisbet, 1829.

The Orthodox and Catholic Doctrine of Our Lord's Human Nature, London: Baldwin and Cradock, 1830.

The Opinions Circulating Concerning Our Lord's Human Nature, Tried by the Westminster Confession of Faith, Edinburgh: John Lindsay, 1830.

Christ's Holiness in Flesh, The Form, Fountain Head, and Assurance to us of Holiness in Flesh, Edinburgh: John Lindsay, 1831.

The Day of Pentecost or The Baptism with the Holy Ghost, Edinburgh: John Lindsay, 1831.

Exposition of the Book of Revelation, in a series of Lectures, in 4 Volumes, London: Baldwin and Cradock, 1831.

The Confessions of Faith and the Books of Discipline of the Church of Scotland, of date Anterior to the Westminster Confession, London: Baldwin and Cradock, 1831.

BY IRVING: ARTICLES

'The Church, with Her Endowment of Holiness and Power', *The Morning Watch,* Vol. II. 1830. Reprinted in *The Collected Writings of Edward Irving in Five Volumes,* 1864, Vol. V.

'On the Gifts of the Holy Ghost, Commonly Called Supernatural', *The Morning Watch,* Vol. II. 1830 and Vol. III, 1831. Reprinted in *The Collected Writings of Edward Irving in Five Volumes,* 1864, Vol. V.

'Facts Connected with Recent Manifestations of Spiritual Gifts', *Fraser's Magazine,* January, March, April, 1832.

'A Judgment, as to what course the Ministers and the People of the Church of Scotland should take in Consequence of the Decisions of the Last General Assembly', *The Morning Watch,* Vol. V. 1832. Also printed as a pamphlet at Greenock: R. B. Lusk, 1832.

PAMPHLETS CONNECTED WITH EDWARD IRVING (3 Volumes).

Volume 1

The Rev. Henry Cole, *A Letter to the Rev. Edward Irving, Minister of the Caledonian Chapel, Compton Street, in Refutation of The Awful Doctrines (held by him) of the Sinfulness, Mortality, and Corruptibility of the Body of Jesus Christ.* London: J. Eedes, 1827.

Henry Drummond, *Candid Examination of the Controversy between Messrs. Irving, A. Thomson, and J. Haldane, respecting the Human Nature of The Lord Jesus Christ.* London: James Nisbet, 1829.

Volume 2

William Harding, *The Trial of the Rev. Edward Irving, M.A. Before The London Presbytery; containing The Whole of the Evidence; Exact Copies* of the Documents; Verbatim Report of the Speeches and Opinions of the Presbyters, etc. London: W. Harding, 1832.

William Harding, *A Word of Testimony; or, A Corrected Account of the Evidence Adduced by the Trustees of the National Scotch Church, in support of their Charges Against the Rev. Edward Irving, and his Defence.* London: Adam Douglas, 1832.

The Trial of the Rev. Edward Irving, A.M. before the Presbytery of Annan, On Wednesday, March 13, 1833. London: W. Harding, 1833.

The Rev. Marcus Dods, 'Review of Publications on Christ's Human Nature', *The Edinburgh Christian Instructor*, January, February, March, 1830.

BIOGRAPHY

William Watson Andrews, *Edward Irving*, reprinted from *The New Englander*, 1863; Edinburgh, 1864.

Thomas Carlyle, 'Edward Irving', *Reminiscences*, Vol. I. ed. J. A. Froude, Longmans, 1881.

Andrew Landale Drummond, *Edward Irving and his Circle*, J. Clarke, 1936.

William Jones, *Biographical Sketch of the Rev. Edward Irving, A.M.* London: John Bennett, 1835.

Charles Kegan Paul, 'Edward Irving', *Biographical Sketches*, London, 1883.

William Landels, *Edward Irving*, London, 1864.

Jabez Marrat, 'Edward Irving', *Northern Lights*, London, 1885.

Mrs. M. O. W. Oliphant, *The Life of Edward Irving*, London, 1862.

Jean Christie Root, *Edward Irving; Man, Preacher, Prophet*, Boston, 1912.

Henry C. Whitley, *Blinded Eagle, An Introduction to the Life and Teaching of Edward Irving*, S.C.M. 1955.

Washington Wilks, *Edward Irving, An Ecclesiastical and Literary Biography*, London, 1854.

PH.D. THESES

Andrew Landale Drummond, *Edward Irving and the Gift of Tongues: An Historical and Psychological Study*, Edinburgh, New College, 1930.

Paul Ewing Davies, *An Examination of the Views of Edward Irving Concerning the Person and Work of Jesus Christ*, Edinburgh, New College, 1928.

Henry C. Whitley, *Edward Irving, An Interpretation of his Life and Theological Teaching*, Edinburgh, New College, 1953.

HISTORICAL AND THEOLOGICAL: BOOKS

William Anderson, *The Scottish Nation*, Vol. II, Fullarton, 1865.

Donald M. Baillie, *God Was In Christ*, Faber, 1948.

Karl Barth, *Church Dogmatics,* Vols. 1:1; 1:2; 4:2; 4:4. T. and T. Clark, 1956–69.

Robert Baxter, *Narrative of Facts, Characterising the Supernatural Manifestations, in Members of Mr. Irving's Congregation, and other Individuals, in England and Scotland, and in the Writer Himself.* London, 1833.

Alexander B. Bruce, *The Humiliation of Christ,* T. and T. Clark, 1881.

John H. S. Burleigh, *A Church History of Scotland,* Oxford, 1960.

Samuel T. Coleridge, *On the Constitution of Church and State,* London, 1830.

Rowland A. Davenport, *Albury Apostles,* United Writers, 1970.

Henry Drummond, *Dialogues on Prophecy,* London, Vol. I, 1827; Vol. II, 1828; Vol. III, 1829.

Thomas Erskine, *The Brazen Serpent, or Life Coming Through Death,* Edinburgh, 1831.

Thomas Erskine, *On the Gifts of the Holy Spirit,* Greenock, 1830.

Thomas Erskine, *Letters,* ed. W. Hanna, Edinburgh, 1878.

Fasti Ecclesiae Scoticanae, Vol. 7. Oliver and Boyd, 1928.

James A. Froude, *Thomas Carlyle, A History of the First Forty Years of his Life.* Vol. II. Longmans, 1901.

John Hair, *Regent Square, Eighty Years of a London Congregation,* J. Nisbet, 1899.

William Hazlitt, *The Spirit of the Age,* 1827, Collins edn. 1969.

Harry Johnson, *The Humanity of the Saviour,* Epworth, 1962.

Ronald A. Knox, Enthusiasm, *A Chapter in the History of Religion,* Oxford, 1950.

Albert J. LaValley, *Carlyle and the Idea of the Modern,* Yale, 1968.

Joseph H. Leckie, *Fergus Ferguson, His Theology and Heresy Trial,* T. and T. Clark, 1923.

Hugh R. Mackintosh, *The Doctrine of the Person of Jesus Christ,* T. and T. Clark, 1912.

Frederick D. Maurice, *The Kingdom of Christ,* 2 Vols., Macmillan, 1883.

Frederick D. Maurice, *The Doctrine of Sacrifice,* Macmillan, 1893.

James Monilaws, *Statistical Account of Scotland,* Vol. 4, 1845.

Edward Miller, *The History and Doctrine of Irvingism,* 2 Vols., Kegan Paul, 1878.

Robert Norton, *Memoirs of James and George Macdonald of Port-Glasgow,* London, 1840.

Robert Norton, *The Restoration of the Apostles and Prophets in the Catholic Apostolic Church,* London, 1861.

Bernard M. G. Reardon, *From Coleridge to Gore, A Century of Religious Thought in Britain,* Longman, 1971.

J. E. Ritchie, *The London Pulpit,* London, 1854.

P. E. Shaw, *The Catholic Apostolic Church, Sometimes Called Irvingite*, King's Crown, N.Y. 1946.

Robert Story, *Peace in Believing: A Memoir of Isabella Campbell of Fernicarry, Rosneath, Dunbartonshire*, Greenock, 1829.

Robert Story, *Memoir of the Life of the Rev. Robert Story*, Cambridge, 1862.

Robert H. Story, *St. Giles Lectures, Third Series, Scottish Divines*, Lecture VII, Edinburgh, 1883.

Arthur J. A. Symons, *Essays and Biographies*, ed. J. Symons; Cassell, 1969.

John Tulloch, *Movements of Religious Thought in Britain During the Nineteenth Century*, Longmans, 1885.

HISTORICAL AND THEOLOGICAL: ARTICLES

William Watson Andrews, 'Martin Luther and Edward Irving: Their Work and Testimony Compared', *The Hartford (U.S.) Daily Times*, December 29th, 1883.

G. T. Bellhouse, 'Edward Irving' *The Regent Square Magazine*, December, 1934.

J. C. S. Brough, 'Regent Square and Edward Irving', *The Centenary of Edward Irving*, London, 1927.

J. C. S. Brough, 'Edward Irving, One Hundred Years After', *The Presbyterian Messenger*, December, 1934.

David S. Cairns, 'Edward Irving', Review of A. L. Drummond in undated newspaper article in possession of the Presbyterian Historical Society of England.

John Bate Cardale 'On the Extraordinary Manifestations in Port-Glasgow', *The Morning Watch*, December, 1830.

Andrew L. Drummond, 'Edward Irving, Rise and Fall of a Prophet, Martyrdom by Mistake', *The Times*, 7th December, 1934.

A. Saunders Dyer, 'The Irvingites, or the Catholic Apostolic Church', *Sketches of English Nonconformity*, Mowbray, 1904.

William Graham, 'Edward Irving and James Hamilton', *United Presbyterian Magazine*, October, 1879.

R. Buick Knox, 'Edward Irving', *Outlook*, September 1971.

P. Lorimer, 'Edward Irving, A Review of *The Collected Writings of Edward Irving*, *The United Presbyterian Magazine*, October, 1865.

J. W. Taylor, 'Edward Irving', Review of Mrs. Oliphant's *Life*, *The United Presbyterian Magazine*, August, 1962.

Norman L. Walker, 'The Trials of Irving and Campbell of Row', *The British and Foreign Evangelical Review*, April, 1867.

PENTECOSTAL: BOOKS

Nils Bloch-Hoell, *The Pentecostal Movement, Its Origin, Development and Distinctive Character*, Allan and Unwin, 1964.

Frederick Dale Bruner, *A Theology of the Holy Spirit, The Pentecostal Experience and the New Testament Witness*, Eerdmans, 1970.

James D. G. Dunn, *Baptism in the Holy Spirit, A Re-examination of the New Testament Teaching on the Gift of the Spirit in relation to Pentecostalism today*. S.C.M. 1970.

Donald Gee, *Wind and Flame, The Pentecostal Movement*, Assemblies of God, 1967.

Micheal Harper, *As At The Beginning, The Twentieth Century Pentecostal Revival*, Hodder, 1965.

Walter J. Hollenweger, *The Pentecostals*, S.C.M. 1972.

Watson J. Mills, *Understanding Speaking in Tongues*, Eerdmans, 1972.

Lesslie Newbigin, *The Household of God*, S.C.M., 1953.

John Thomas Nichol, *The Pentecostals*, Logos, 1971.

John L. Sherrill, *They Seek With Other Tongues*, Hodder, 1965.

Vinson Synan, *The Holiness-Pentecostal Movement*, Eerdmans, 1971.

Simon Tugwell, *Did You Receive the Spirit?* Darton Longman and Todd, 1972.

PENTECOSTAL: ARTICLES

Valentine Cunningham, 'Texts and Their Stories – 14, Acts, 2:38', *Redemption Tidings*, 1st October, 1970.

Henry Pitney Van Dusen, *Life Magazine*, 6th June, 1958.

C. Gordon Strachan, 'A Second Chance' *Life and Work*, May, 1972.

SELECT BIBLIOGRAPHY

WORKS NOT REFERRED TO BUT FOUND USEFUL IN PREPARATION

HISTORY, CULTURE AND THEOLOGY

Hendrikus Berkhof, *The Doctrine of the Holy Spirit*, Epworth, 1965.

Henry Bettenson, *The Early Christian Fathers*, Oxford, 1969.

Thomas Boys, *The Suppressed Evidence: Or Proofs of the Miraculous Faith and Experience of the Church of Christ in all Ages. from Authentic Records of the Fathers, Waldenses, Hussites, Reformers, United Brethren, etc. An Historical Sketch Suggested by the Hon. and Rev. B. W. Noel's 'Remarks on the Revival of Miraculous Powers in the Church'*, London, 1832.

Thomas Carlyle, *Sartor Resartus*, (1836) Everyman's 1967.

Thomas Carlyle, *On Heroes and Hero Worship*, (1841) Everyman's, 1967.

Norman Cohn, *The Pursuit of the Millennium, Revolutionary millenarians and mystical anarchists of the Middle Ages*, (1957) Paladin, 1970.

Arnold B. Come, *Human Spirit and Holy Spirit*, Westminster Press, Philadelphia, 1959.

Henry Drummond, *Narrative of the Circumstances which led to the setting up of the Church at Albury*, Albury, 1834.

Henry Drummond, *A Narrative of Events Affecting the Position and Prospects of the Whole Christian Church*, 2nd. edn. London, 1885.

W. H. C. Friend, *The Early Church*, Hodder, 1965.

George S. Hendry, *The Holy Spirit in Christian Theology*, Westminster Press, Philadelphia, 1956.

George S. Hendry, *The Westminster Confession for Today*, S.C.M. 1960.

John McIntyre, *Prophet of Penitence: Our Contemporary Ancestor*, St. Andrew Press, 1972.

John McIntyre, *The Shape of Christology*, S.C.M. 1966.

J. Cameron Peddie, *The Forgotten Talent, God's Ministry of Healing*, Oldbourne, 1961.

G. L. Prestige, *Fathers and Heretics*, S.P.C.K., 1968.

G. L. Prestige, *God in Patristic Thought*, S.P.C.K., 1964.

Robert Norton, *Neglected and Controverted Scripture Truths, with an Historical Review of Miraculous Manifestations in the Church of Christ*, London, 1839.

Murray Roston, *Prophet and Poet, The Bible and the Growth of Romanticism*, Faber, 1965.

Albert Schweitzer, *The Quest of the Historical Jesus* (1906) A. and C. Black, London, 3rd edn. 1956.

Paul M. Van Buren, *The Secular Meaning of the Gospel*, S.C.M. 1963.

Maurice Wiles, *The Christian Fathers*, Hodder, 1966.

Basil Willey, *Samuel Taylor Coleridge*, Chatto and Windus, 1972.

Basil Willey, *The Eighteenth Century Background*, Chatto and Windus, 1940.

Basil Willey, *Nineteenth Century Studies*, Chatto and Windus, 1949.

Maria Winowska, *The True Face of Padre Pio, A Portrait of Italy's 'miracle' priest*, Souvenir Press, London, 1955.

PENTECOSTAL AND NEO-PENTECOSTAL

Dennis J. Bennett, *Nine O'Clock in the Morning*, Coverdale, 1971.

Larry Christenson, *Speaking in Tongues, A Gift for the Body of Christ*, Fountain Trust, London, 1963.

Ian Cockburn, *The Baptism in the Spirit: Its Biblical Foundations*, Fountain Trust, London, 1971.

Leslie Davison, *Pathway to Power, The Charismatic Movement in Historical Perspective*, Fountain Trust, London, 1971.

Stanley Howard Frodsham, *Smith Wigglesworth, Apostle of Faith*, Elim, 1949.

Donald Gee, *The Ministry Gifts of Christ*, Gospel Pub. Ho. Springfield, Mo. 1930.

Micheal Harper, *Prophecy, A Gift for the Body of Christ*, Fountain Trust, London, 1964.

Micheal Harper, *Life in the Holy Spirit, Some Questions Answered*, Fountain Trust, London, 1966.

Gordon Lindsay and William Branham, *A Man Sent from God*, Jeffersonville, Ind., 1950.

Kilian McDonnell, *Catholic Pentecostalism: Problems in Evaluation*, Dove, N. Mexico, 1970.

David J. du Plessis, *The Spirit Bade Me Go*, Logos, 1970.

Presbyterian Church of the United States, *The Person and Work of the Holy Spirit, with Special Reference to 'The Baptism of the Holy Spirit'*, 1971.

Kevin and Dorothy Ranaghan, *Catholic Pentecostals*, Paulist, N.Y., 1969.
United Presbyterian Church in the U.S.A. *Report of the Special Committee on the Work of the Holy Spirit*, Gen. Ass. off. Philadelphia, 1970.
Smith Wigglesworth, *Ever Increasing Faith*, Gospel Pub. Ho. Springfield Mo. 1924.
J. Rodman Williams, *The Era of the Spirit*, Logos, 1971.